THE HISTORY OF FINNISH ECONOMIC THOUGHT 1809–1917

The History of Learning and Science in Finland
1828–1918

17 a

EDITORIAL NOTE

The history of learning in Finland could be said to begin with the foundation in 1640 of the Academia Aboensis at Turku (Åbo). Finland was at that time a part of the kingdom of Sweden. As a consequence of the Napoleonic wars the country became an autonomous Grand Duchy under Russia. In 1828, after Turku had been devastated by fire, the university was moved to the country's new capital, Helsinki (Helsingfors), and its name was changed to the Imperial Alexander University of Finland. It became Helsinki University in 1918, when Finland emerged as an independent republic from the turmoil of World War I.

The history of learning in Finland in the period 1640–1828 has been recorded in the ten volumes of the series Åbo Universitets Lärdomshistoria (The History of Learning in the University of Turku). The series was published round the turn of the century 1800–1900 by the Swedish Society of Literature in Finland. It remains the standard work on the early history of scholarship and science in this country.

The idea of treating the history of learning in Finland during the time of the Imperial Alexander University in a series of monographs was first suggested by the late Chancellor of Helsinki University, Edwin Linkomies. The idea was followed up by the Finnish Society of Sciences, which announced its realization in connection with the Society's 125th anniversary in 1963.

During the whole of its existence, the Imperial Alexander University was the only university in Finland. Practically all research and scholarship during the period 1828–1918 was therefore intimately connected with this one institution of learning and higher education. This, in combination with the facts of political history, gives to the material presented in the projected volumes a historical unity which has been thought to justify their planning and publication as a series.

According to the editors' plans, the series will comprise 20 volumes, some of which will be divided into two or more self-contained parts. The authors are distinguished representatives of the various fields of scholarship or science, with the history of which their contributions deal. In practically all cases the ground covered has not been treated in a monograph before. The works are thus the fruit of original research on the part of their authors in the history of ideas and learning.

THE HISTORY OF FINNISH ECONOMIC THOUGHT 1809–1917

by
Sakari Heikkinen, Visa Heinonen,
Antti Kuusterä and Jukka Pekkarinen

Tammisaari – Ekenäs 2000

ISBN 951-653-303-5

Printed in Finland by
Ekenäs Tryckeri Aktiebolag
Ekenäs 2000

CONTENTS

Sources of illustrations

Illustrations on pages 38 and 64, Helsinki University Library. All the other pictures, The National Museum of Finland.

PREFACE

This book has had a long period of gestation. The proposal for us to write a volume on the history of economic ideas for the *Societas Scientarium Fennica* Series on 19th-century doctrinal history in Finland was put forward by Professor Georg Henrik von Wright, a Member of the Academy of Finland, as early as in the mid 1980s. A study group, which originally consisted of Dr. Jukka Pekkarinen, Dr. Ilkka Patoluoto, Dr. Uskali Mäki and Dr. Visa Heinonen, started to discuss ideas for the book in 1986. Dr. Sakari Heikkinen and Dr. Antti Kuusterä joined the research group later. The untimely death of Ilkka Patoluoto, whose deep knowledge as well as originality of thinking in the area of the history of ideas left an unforgettable impression on all of us, was a serious drawback to our work in the early stages. Later on, the move of Uskali Mäki to a chair in economic methodology at the Erasmus University of Rotterdam necessitated a further change to the original plan for the study. The influence of both Ilkka and Uskali, we believe, is strongly reflected in this final version of the work, and we are deeply grateful to them.

Given these losses of human resources and the many demands of the main jobs of each of us, our work has been further delayed by the fact that we have had to cover partly unconquered ground, especially as far as the interplay between economic ideas and policies, as well as between economic and other areas of social thought, are concerned. It should be mentioned from the outset, however, that we have immensely benefited from the pioneering, systematic study by the late Professor Heimer Björkqvist on the history of economic thought in Finland during the Russian rule.

In the course of the study, we have received most helpful comments and encouragement, above all from Professor von Wright. It is fair to say that without his help and understanding this work would not have been finalised. At the final stage of the study, the kind comments of Professor Matti Klinge and the late Professor

Kauko Pirinen were also useful. Our warmest thanks are also due to Ms. Joan Nordlund for professionally checking and improving our English and to Ms. Elina Pekkarinen for editorial help.

The book represents a collective piece of work. Its outline, ideas and emphasis, as reflected in the introduction and concluding chapter, are the result of our combined effort. Although we have all contributed to most parts of the book and share responsibility for it, we divided among ourselves the bulk of the responsibility for collecting the material and writing the other sections. Chapter 2 was mainly compiled by Sakari Heikkinen. Jukka Pekkarinen drew together Chapter 3, partly relying on material provided by Visa Heinonen. Sections 1 and 2 of Chapter 4 again resulted from Sakari's pen. Together with Antti Kuusterä, he also wrote the paragraph "Two Practical Liberalists" in section 4.4. Otherwise, Chapter 4 is a result of the work of Visa Heinonen. Earlier versions of his work in the area of 19th-century economic thought which are utilised in this book have been published elsewhere (Heinonen 1996a and 1996b). Chapter 5 was written by Antti Kuusterä and Jukka Pekkarinen, except for section 5.5. on tariffs which was contributed by Sakari Heikkinen and Visa Heinonen.

In order to emphasise the variety of traditions that have shaped economic thought, as well as the many changes in substance of the subject in Finland over time, we have reserved the modern phrase *economics* mainly to refer to the body of theories which is nowadays called neo-classical economics and which was brought into being in the late 19th century. Elsewhere, more diffuse terms such as "economic thought" or "economic discipline" are used, their specific contents and doctrinal references being clear from the context. English translations of the citations from Swedish and Finnish texts are ours.

We are grateful to the Yrjö Jahnsson Foundation and *Societas Scientiarum Fennica* for grants for our work, and to the latter for including this book in its publication series.

Helsinki, December 1999

Sakari Heikkinen, Visa Heinonen,
Antti Kuusterä and Jukka Pekkarinen

1. INTRODUCTION

Writing a history of a scientific discipline is often conceived of as a tracing of the discoveries and insights which have contributed to the gradual, cumulative growth of knowledge in its present-day form. The vantage point for such a conventional doctrinal history is the present pattern of the discipline, which is taken as the outcome of a linear progress of knowledge. Account can, of course, be taken of some approaches which have played an important role in the past but which no longer feature on the present agenda of the discipline. Yet, their relevance is also assessed from to-day's perspective: attention is mainly paid to the past approaches which have somehow influenced the paths through which the present discipline has evolved, either as side-paths or as criticism. Such a "teleological" view of doctrinal history tends to neglect past approaches, which lived independently of the present mainstream but which disappeared later on, no matter how dominant they might have been in their hey-day.

There are several reasons why such a linear view does not fit in well with the history of economic thought in 19th-century Finland. Firstly, Finnish economics has not produced any major discoveries to contribute to the growth of present-day economics in any significant way. Its relative backwardness was particularly appalling at the turn of the century, when Finland still largely lacked both the institutional and intellectual infrastructure of economics in the modern sense of the term. If limited to genuine scientific contributions, our story would be very short indeed.

The second reason is that the economic discipline in Finland at the end of the 19th century attached itself to the German historical school, i.e. to an approach which turned out later on to be a decaying school of thought. Since Finnish scholars were not at the frontier of this school of thought either, but rather remained passive followers, the economic discipline in Finland seems to have been subject to a dual disadvantage in its early stage of development in the late 19th century: it remained on the periphery of an approach which itself turned out to be left on the sidelines in the progress of economics.

Consequently, our object of study does not submit itself to the conventional, unilateral view of scientific progress. What this implies, however, is not that the economic discourse in 19th- century Finland is without interest even from the present perspective; it is rather that it has to be approached from a different angle. What we aim to do in this study is to look at the Finnish case as an instance of the gradual process by which economics rose to become a self-reliant academic discipline.[1]

This process has consisted of the gradual emergence of the economic discipline from more diffuse philosophical, legal, social and political discourse (Klami 1981; Allardt 1997). This has been conditioned by specific historical, political, socio-economic, intellectual and institutional circumstances, which differ from one country to another and whose role can be illuminated by comparing different country cases.

What we will emphasise as being pivotal for the development of economic thought in 19th-century Finland is the close interconnection between nation formation, the state and the economy. The use of economic arguments was unquestionably tied to the struggle to enhance Finnish nationhood, in which strengthening the economic base of the country was in turn considered to be of pivotal importance.

This close overlapping between state and nation formation and economic thought was, in fact, shared by many other countries where nationalism was a driving force in the 19th century. Germany is a prime example. The German historical school can be considered a reflection of this overlapping in economic thought. It is also clear that the economic discourse in other countries, where the nation-building process played a central role, turned to the German historical school as a source of inspiration in the late 19th century. Finland is a good example of this, but there are many others, such as Japan and the United States.

Apart from an emphasis on the historical school, as well as on the neighbouring disciplines of economics, the above kind of

[1] Our approach is related to the perspective of Michel Foucault (1966; 1969). Foucault emphasises discontinuities, discursive practices, power relations and interaction in the simultaneous transformation of three discourses: political economy, biology and psychology.

wider socio-economic perspective on the emergence of economics has certain further implications for the nature of our study. Instead of searching for symptoms of progress at the frontier of a scientific discourse, we will place our emphasis on the use of economic arguments in the wider social and political debate. These arguments are well known as such, and in the Finnish case they were almost without exception borrowed from abroad; what interests us is their context and internal prioritisation, as well as the gradual process by which they began to be built upon as a wider body of self-contained economic discourse.

As far as the agents of the discourse are concerned, our subject matter makes it natural to consider a wider community than that of professional economists, which in fact was almost non-existent in Finland until the 20th century. Apart from looking at lawyers and moral as well as political philosophers, we will pay attention to politicians, businessmen, journalists and other prominent intellectuals who made use of economic arguments while arguing their own case. What is particularly noteworthy in the case of Finland is the significant role of a few prominent civil servants dealing with economic affairs. Some of these people served for several decades in the civil service, and had great influence on the economic policy of the country. It seems that many of them were also well versed in the trends of the economic-policy thinking of their times. Their work is still largely unexplored in Finland. We will attempt to rectify this by drawing attention to the thinking of these individuals.

We should also consider a wider forum for debate than professional journals or books, which were very few in 19th-century Finland. The broad economic discourse which interests us was, to a large extent, distributed in a wide range of books addressed to a general audience, as well as in newspapers, committee reports and archive material.

To sum up, our task consists of reporting the evolution of economics in a country which lies on the periphery of the discipline. According to Uskali Mäki, a country ”constitutes an intellectual periphery if and only if it has a high propensity to import ideas” (Mäki 1996, 309). Rather than looking for genuine scientific inventions, we will pay attention to the ways in which well-known economic arguments have been used in socio-political debate and decision making, as well as to the process by which economics was gradually formed as a self-contained academic discipline. Where did Finnish authors pick up their arguments? In what aspects of the work of foreign scholars were they interested? What use did they make of the political, administrative and intellectual discourse? Finally, what determined the changes in the sources of influence? We will consider the general political and ideological, historical as well as institutional and organisational factors shaping this pattern of foreign contacts.

This wide scope is also reflected in the structure of our study. Chapter 2 provides a short general introduction of the economic and political as well as the general intellectual landscape of 19th-century Finland. The institutional and organisational prerequisites of economic studies are described in Chapter 3. Chapter 4 sets out the main stages in the development of economic thinking in the country from the end of Swedish rule until the beginning of the 20th century, i.e. the period of independence. The discussion proceeds through six stages: the heritage of the Swedish era; the dominance of the cameralist approach in the first half of the 19th century; reflections of Listian ideas of economic nationalism in the writings of Johan Vilhelm Snellman, an outstanding philosopher in Finland in the middle of the 19th century; the dialogue between nationalist ideas and economic liberalism; and finally, the impact of the dominant currents of late 19th-century economic thought, i.e. the German historical and the marginalist school, are discussed separately.

The use of economic arguments in economic policy debate is discussed separately in Chapter 5 in the context of successive monetary reforms, taxation, tariff policy and the formation of an infrastructure. Chapter 6 draws together the main conclusions of the study.

2. THE MAKING OF FINLAND

2.1 Economy and Society

In the war of 1808–1809 Russia took Finland from Sweden. Finland became part of the Russian Empire, a Grand Duchy, and stayed as such until the end of 1917, when it gained independence. Although the formal status of Finland from the point of view of international law remained the same from 1809 to 1917, its internal life changed profoundly. This was the period during which the Finnish nation and state were built; becoming an independent state in 1917 was only the formal end of a long process. The Russian period of Finnish history is habitually also called "the period of autonomy", emphasising the "semi-independent" status of Finland. It should, however, be remembered, that the autonomy of Finland was a result of long nation-building and state-making processes; "autonomy" was not something constant during the more than a century-long period as a Grand Duchy. Finland was not raised to the status of state in 1809, but on the other hand, it was not fused totally into Russia. This manner of conquest, which was quite common in the history of Russian expansion, laid the basis for the development of Finland as a state on its own (Jussila 1987). It also had an effect on the course that Finnish economy and society took, as well as on the intellectual climate of the country.

Finland was an almost totally agrarian society at the beginning of the nineteenth century, and still fairly agrarian at the beginning of the twentieth. In 1910, two thirds of the population was still counted among the agricultural population, although a century earlier that ratio would have been near nine tenths. The proportion of urban population, i.e. those living within official city limits, was 15 per cent in 1915, but if the people living in suburban areas, or in new industrial centres without city status are also counted, this figure rises to 25 per cent (Haapala 1992 26). It should also be remembered that the Finnish population grew rapidly during the "Russian century": from one million inhabitants in the 1810s to three million in the 1910s, an annual average of one per cent. Therefore, the slow decline in the percentage of agricultural population, and the tardy growth in that of urban population paint a little too undynamic picture of the 19th-century Finnish economy. A look at the structure of production shows that Finland was not as agricultural as the population figures indicate: the proportion of primary production in the gross domestic product was 44 per cent in 1909–1913, a figure which includes the 15-per-cent share of forestry, the growth of which was largely caused by the expansion of the forest industry. Thus, in the 1910s, the secondary and tertiary sectors of the Finnish economy with their 56-per-cent share (1909–1913) were already larger than the primary sector. In short, the effects of industrialisation and urbanisation significantly altered the structure of the Finnish economy in the 19th century (Hjerppe 1989).

The structural change sketched above occurred not in a static, but rather in a growing economy. The rate of growth, however, was not steady during the 19th and early 20th centuries. From the perspective of the dynamics of economic change, the century of Grand-Duchy Finland falls into four main periods. During the first period, from 1810 to the 1830s, the economy grew at a slow rate, the old economic structure dominated by agriculture was maintained, and the role of foreign trade remained minor. During the second period, from around 1840 to 1870, the rate of economic growth (gross domestic product per capita) accelerated, but still remained under one per cent annually. Another notable change was the growing importance of foreign trade. The ratio of exports to gross domestic product grew from 5 to 14 per cent. The sectoral structure of the economy, however, did not change profoundly during these decades. During the third period, from 1870 to 1890, economic growth averaged one per cent annually, and at the same time the structure of the economy started to change because of the hastened industrialization. Foreign trade, relatively speaking, reached its record level with the proportion of exports of the gross domestic product at around 20 per cent. During the fourth period, from 1890 onwards, economic growth accelerated still more, with an annual per capita growth rate of 1.9 per cent between 1890 and 1913. The growth in manufacturing and services changed the sectoral structure of the economy, and the agricultural sector was transformed fundamentally with dairy farming becoming its most important branch.

The development of the Finnish economy was in many ways connected to its position in the world economy. To put it more simply, there were three major links: to Sweden, to Russia, and to Western Europe. Economic ties to the old Swedish motherland were maintained during the first decades of the Russian period: Swedish money was valid in Finland, and trade between Finland and Sweden was at first free, and then became burdened with lower duties than trade with other countries. It was only in the 1840s that Sweden was like any other country to Finland, at least in terms of economic relations. Russia, again, was never a "foreign country". Trade between Finland and Russia was regulated by special decrees, and it remained free to a great extent. It was the Russian market that gave impetus to the growth of the Finnish iron, cotton and paper industries, especially until the 1880s, when Russia started to restrict imports from Finland by imposing duties on several Finnish manufactured products. Yet, the Russian market continued to be the most important market for the Finnish paper industry. The third link to the world economy connected Finland to the Western European core. The export of forest products, first tar and then sawn timber, to Western Europe, and especially to England, was one important factor accentuating Finnish economic growth since the 1860s. Later on, pulp, cardboard and butter were also exported to Western Europe. As far as imports were concerned, Germany was the first among Finland's trading partners in Western Europe.

Along with its economy, the social structure of Finland also underwent a transformation, which might be characterized as the transition from a society of estates to a class society. As mentioned above, until the parliamentary reform of 1906, Finland was officially an estate society whose population was divided between the huge majority with no voting rights and the four estates which were represented in the Diet. However, the social structure of the Finnish estate society started to break down much earlier than its political system.

At the beginning of the 19th century, the upper class in Finland consisted of the nobility, the clergy, estate owners and wealthy merchants and manufacturers. The structure and role of the nobility changed in many ways after the annexation of Finland by Russia in 1809. One of the changes was caused by the disbanding of the Finnish units of the Swedish army. Although it was now possible to embark on a military career in the Russian army, such a military career did not have the same significance for the domestic aristocracy. However, new career prospects opened up in the rapidly expanding civil administration of the Grand Duchy. As a consequence, the nobility became an urbanized estate paying keen attention to the education of its offspring. A further change in the structure of the nobility was its growing activity in business life. Thus, we might speak of the bureaucratization and embourgeoisement of the aristocracy (Peltonen 1989).

As far as the clergy was concerned, there was no great upheaval caused by the joining of Finland to Russia, because the status of the Finnish Evangelical-Lutheran church was guaranteed by Emperor Alexander I and his successors. The position of the clergy as such thus remained stable, but it was, relatively speaking, affected by the strengthening of the other groups in the intellectual field. Professors, teachers, civil servants, writers and journalists were some of the representatives of the "educated class" gaining new momentum during the 19th century.

Apart from that in the hands of the estate owners, much of the economic power in the early decades of the 19th century was held by the merchant houses with their wide variety of business activities: foreign and domestic trade, banking, shipping and manufacturing. They were the crucial link between Finnish tar and timber producers, for instance, and Western-European buyers; and they also had an important role in establishing the modern manufacturing industry. Along with the industrialization and the freedom of trade, new entrepreneurs, coming from various social backgrounds, rose to become the economic elite of Finnish society. A new class of businessmen had been formed (Schybergson 1974).

Among the agricultural population, it was the estate owners who were traditionally counted among the upper class, the gentry. Under them in the rural social hierarchy were the landowning peasants, followed by crofters and agricultural labourers. Landowning peasants were represented in the Diet, crofters and labourers were not. This structure of the agricultural population changed in the 19th century in at least two respects. First, the line between the gentry farmers and the top layer of peasant farmers became blurred with the economic and cultural rise of the latter. Second, the landless population grew more quickly than the landowner population. Some of landless were absorbed by industrialization and emigration, some remained in the countryside as labourers employed in agriculture, forestry or manufacturing, or in all three.

Because of the agrarian dominance in the Finnish economy, there was no large urban population at the beginning of the 19th century, and no strong middle class either. With creeping urbanization, the situation changed, relatively slowly, but in absolute numbers the middle class in some towns, especially the capital Helsinki, was already considerable at the turn of the 20th century. A still more significant phenomenon was the birth of the modern wage-worker class brought up under industrialization. The rural landless population and the new urban working class were two central themes of contemporary socio-political discussion, and of economic science too.

2.2 State and Nation

From 1809 to 1917, Finland was a Grand Duchy and the Russian Emperor was its Grand-Duke. The highest power in matters concerning Finland was in his hands. However, when Finland was incorporated into the Russian empire, Emperor Alexander I gave his assurance that the old laws would be kept in force. The same assurance was also given by subsequent Emperors and Grand Dukes of Finland. Thus, the Swedish judicial tradition was maintained, although the Russian administration tried to contest the judicial autonomy of Finland, especially after the 1880s. The separate legislation, although dependent on the Emperor, was one of the constituents of Finnish semi-independence and then independence.

Another important element in the making of the Finnish state was its state administration. The Grand Duchy of Finland had a central administration of its own. Its highest organ was the Senate, which was not a government in the modern sense of the word, in other words an administrative body holding political power and being responsible to parliament. The Senate had only as much power as the autocratic Emperor granted it. Therefore the Finnish Senate was mostly a bureaucratic organization dealing with the practical administration and judicial matters of the Grand Duchy. All the major decisions, and many of the minor ones too, had to be approved by the Emperor. Otherwise, the central administration consisted of boards dealing with different sectors. Many of them were established in the 1810s. The essential condition of Finland's administrative autonomy was its own state finances. All the taxes and other income collected in Finland were used to fund Grand Duchy expenditure.

Finland matured into a modern state apparatus much earlier than into a politically modern state. Shortly after the conquest of Finland, in 1809, representatives of the four estates – the nobility, the clergy, the burghers and the peasants – assembled in a Diet in Porvoo. This happened in accord with the traditions of the Swedish era. The next assembly of estates did not take place until 1863. Therefore, between 1809 and 1863, all the decisions concerning Finland were made by the Senate and other administrative bodies without the participation of the Diet representing the four estates. The result of this state of affairs was that the decisions did not have to be justified in public discussion in the Diet. This, again, was one reason for the low level of public discussion, which was furthered by the small size of the Finnish press and the confines set by the censorship laws. It also undoubtedly contributed to the scantiness of economic debate and argumentation, because there were no public forums in which different interests could have been presented and decisions argued for. The opinion of different corporations were sometimes taken into account in discrete, non-public ways, such as when the opinions of burghers and merchants were invited before decisions concerning their interests were made.

The situation began to change in the latter half of the 1850s after "liberal" Alexander II, liberal only compared to his predecessors, came to power. The Diet assembled again in 1863, and then regularly after that. The most important effect of this, at least from the point of view of economic thought, was that it promoted economic discussion, and formal and public formulation of economic policy decisions. At the same time, the Finnish press, first mostly in Swedish, expanded notably and contributed to the economic discussion. With the regularly gathering Diet, the political life of Finland gained new life, but the political system did not change significantly. The power of the Diet remained limited, and it did not restrict the power of the Senate, because senators nominated by the Emperor were responsible to him, not to the Diet.

This old-fashioned system with four estates and limited voting rights, which was criticized by liberals and by the young labour movement in the 1880s and 1890s, was changed abruptly in the parliamentary reform of 1906, the result of the general strike and the political turmoil of 1905. The new parliament had only one house and all adult citizens, women too, had the right to vote and to be elected. This raised the number of citizens with voting rights tenfold in one night. It is paradoxical that this very democratic reform did not give much new power to parliament, although it achieved popular legitimacy. Because the constitution (of 1772 and 1789) was not changed, the ultimate power still remained in the hands of the Emperor and the senate.

The parliamentary reform also led to the modernization of the party system. There had been no formal parties within the old four-estate system, but there had been informal party organizations within and outside of the Diet. There was a division between the so-called “language parties”. The mother tongue of the majority of the population was Finnish, but Swedish was traditionally the language of the élite groups and of higher administration. The situation began to change slowly after the 1860s, when the official status of Finnish was improved, and when the intellectual group called the Fennomans started to speak in favour of the Finnish language and culture, and of the Finnish-speaking population. The labour movement, which started in the 1880s under the leadership of liberal intellectuals, grew swiftly after the late 1890s and gained “independence” from reform-minded intellectuals. During the late 19th century too, many kinds of movements mobilized the population and also broadened the field of discussion on the problems of Finnish society. Thus there were many kinds of “prepolitical” organizations in existence before the first elections of the new parliament in 1907, which produced the party structure that, by and large, exists even today.

2.3 Intellectual Setting

The manner of Finnish nation-building and state-making, as well as the economic and social structure of the society, also affected the cultural scene, and thereby the intellectual prerequisites of economic thought. One essential element of the cultural development of 19th-century Finland was the birth of nationalistic ideology and the development of a national cultural élite. The national identity of Finland was built both in Swedish, especially by Johan Ludvig Runeberg (1804–1877), Johan Vilhelm Snellman (1806–1881) and Zacharias Topelius (1818–1889), and in Finnish, especially by Elias Lönnrot (1802–1884) and Aleksis Kivi (1834–1872). The change was particularly dramatic in the Finnish-language literature, which developed during the last decades of the 19th century from near non-existence to an established art form. Along with the creation of Finnish national culture and ideology came the formation of a Finnish-speaking intelligentsia. Nationalistic thinking was heavily influenced by Hegelianism, which was imported to Finland by Snellman in particular. This was one of the factors promoting the spread of German nationalistic, historical economic thought in Finland.

Another factor affecting the intellectual climate was the manner of Finnish state-making. As mentioned above, the Grand Duchy of Finland was gradually turned into a state in the 19th and early 20th centuries. All the prominent intellectuals in one way or another took part in this process, and most of them, at least until the turn of the 20th century, did it in the spirit of loyalty, principled or practical, towards the Russian Empire. Therefore much of the cultural and socio-political discussion was related to the problems of state-making and the delicate position of Finland within the Russian Empire. This meant that free public discussion by intellectuals was not so much opposed or counter to administrative and political discussions within the state-apparatus, but rather part of the same continuum. Consequently, it is no wonder that much of the economic discussion was state-centred too.

The economic and social structure of Finnish society also had an effect on the shape of the intellectual field. Because Finland was mostly an agricultural country, there was a strong rural flavour in Finnish, especially in Finnish-speaking, nationalism. This state of affairs did not create an abundant demand for economic experts dealing with the sophisticated problems of a modern urban and industrial economy. The other side of the coin is that there was interest in studying the economic problems of agriculture. Another feature of Finnish society was the relative small size of the urban business and middle classes. Therefore, one might say that there was not fertile soil to foster the growth of free economic discussion within business life. The universities and state administration were dominating forums for economic discussion, and even the economic associations functioned somewhat like semi-official organizations (Klinge 1988 and 1989; Stenius 1990).

3. INSTITUTIONAL SETTING

3.1 Introduction

The history of economic thought in 19th-century Finland is preconditioned by the fact that, while the internal development of economic science as such remained rudimentary throughout the period, various echelons of society made much more use of its results in arguing their case in political and social debate. This created a gradually increasing demand for economic knowledge, which in turn increased interest in economic studies proper.

The response of economic expertise to this rise in demand was also restricted due to certain specific circumstances. First, in the earlier part of the century, the nobility and the bourgeoisie, in other words the circles in society which were most likely to pursue economic debate, were very few in number. The press was next to non-existent. There were few members of independent circles of businessmen, journalists and intellectuals for example, who would have been best fitted for carrying on economic debate. Moreover, the majority of this relatively small group was more interested in "immaterial" nationalistic ideas than in concrete economic issues. Finally, the tight censorship meant that attitudes to civil society or social debate in general were not very liberal. This is illustrated in Snellman's early literary work, for example, which is discussed in more detail below.

The spread of economic expertise was also hampered by its peripheral role in the educational system of the country. Finland's foremost university, which moved from Turku (Åbo) to Helsinki (Helsingfors) at the end of the 1820s, was quite poorly organised in the teaching of the subject until the beginning of the 20th century, when the Faculty of Humanities was given a chair in economics. Before that, economics was taught as part of studies in law, and was tightly tied to the education of civil servants.

Although a more prominent role was gradually given to economic studies at the university, the status of the approach, the offshoot of which we now call modern economics, remained weak. This was due to the fact that the Finnish economic discipline of the period to a large extent imported its ideas from the German historical school or other authors more or less hostile to, or alienated from, classical political economy and its descendants. In such an academic environment, economic reasoning rather remained subordinated to history and other social sciences.

This chapter gives an overview of the institutional changes which finally gave the impetus to economics as a discipline in its own right. The evolution of academic chairs in the discipline, which remained slow throughout the period, is briefly discussed, as well as changes in the thrust of their economic curricula. The birth of economic associations and publications series is also mentioned, as well as the changing patterns of orientation towards foreign influences.

3.2 Academic Chairs

Practically-oriented economic studies gained in importance in the Royal Academy of Åbo during the last decades of Swedish rule. However, the issues in question bore no resemblance to economics in the modern sense of the term, not even business economics (although the subject of study in many cases was the individual household or firm). The approach was more akin to engineering in its focus on the material and physical management of various production processes. The chemical, technological and organisational basis of agriculture was of special concern.

The starting point of economic science in Finland may be dated in the year 1746, when Johan Kraftman (1713–1791) was appointed docent in *oeconomiae* at the Royal Academy of Åbo. During that year he lectured mostly on issues concerning agriculture, but also dealt with more general economic questions. The following year, a new professorship was established in the same discipline, but Kraftman did not get the post; it was given to Per Kalm (1716–1779), a disciple of the famous Swedish botanist Carl von Linné, who was appointed to the professorship in 1749. Kraftman left the Academy, and came back to serve three years as professor in mathematics, during which time he supervised two dissertations on economic themes. He then lived the rest of his life as an estate owner, but also wrote pamphlets on economic issues (Jahnsson 1907–1908, 159–164).

Kalm became famous for his travels to North America, his reports of which cover a wide range of botanical, zoological, geographical and ethnological observations, and were favourably cited by Adam Smith, among others. Mention should also be made of Per Adrian Gadd (1727–1797), docent in natural history and economy since 1750.

The appointment of Matthias Calonius (1737–1817), a lawyer, as docent in economic studies at the Academy in 1764 marked the beginning of a new, jurisprudential and historical approach in the subject. Calonius was interested in economic issues, his main preoccupation being with monetary institutions which, his remaining lecture notes tell us, he approached from the point of view of cameralism. He occupied the chair of law in the Academy in 1777, and became a distinguished lawyer in the Swedish Kingdom in the early years of Finnish Autonomy, before taking a central role in transplanting the Swedish tradition of law and administration to the new Grand Duchy.

Calonius also initiated the change by which the chair in economic studies was submitted, as in many other countries, to the Faculty of Law. In the Finnish case, this tradition lasted until the beginning of the 20th century. The old chair in the subject in the Faculty of Philosophy was occupied by the botanist C. N. Hellenius and was thus transformed to a chair in natural science.

The origins of economic studies were thus, in a rudimentary form, laid down in the closing period of Swedish Rule. In the reorganisation of the Royal Academy of Åbo after Russian occupation, the Faculty of Law was given a joint chair for "economic law and commercial legislation". Matthias Calonius first filled this chair, but because of his duties in the planning and implementation of the new administration, his academic input remained relatively scant in this period.

Calonius' absence was compensated by the fact that Daniel Myréen (1782–1831) held a chair in economic studies in the Faculty of Law. In addition, Wilhelm Gabriel Lagus (1786–1859) taught the subject as associate professor. In fact, he carried the main teaching responsibility, since Myréen took care of Calonius' chair from 1815 to 1818. Finally, C. N. Hellenius, mentioned above, still held the chair in the study of natural history and economy in the Faculty of Philosophy, although the subject matter became all the more distant from economics studies.

Among these early authorities on the subject during Russian

rule, Myréen and Lagus were both interested in contemporary economic thought. Myréen had studied under Lars Georg Rabenius in Stockholm and was interested in public finance, especially taxation.

When the university was moved over to Helsinki in 1828, Myréen was awarded a new chair in public law, constitution and economic studies in the Faculty of Law. For decades, this was the central chair for economic studies in Finland. It remained vacant for several years, however. Thus, after Myréen's death in 1831, it was taken over in 1834 by Johan Jacob Nordström (1801-1874), who had been acting chair previously. However, he did not serve in the post, but moved over to Uppsala in 1846. Early on he was influenced by Carl Agardh and Lars Georg Rabenius from Sweden, but his approach changed and became more liberal after a trip to Europe (in particular, Berlin, Leipzig and Heidelberg). Later on, he was well known in Sweden.

The professorship in economic studies at Helsinki remained, again, unfilled from 1846 until 1857 at the time of the strict censorship imposed by the Emperor. Lagus and Frans Edvard Florin (1816-1854) took care of the teaching responsibilities. When the University was reorganised in 1853, the chair was focused more narrowly on economics, and Axel Liljestrand (1821–1895), a moderate liberal, held it until 1877. Leopold Stanislaus Mechelin (1839–1914), a man of many political, social and intellectual activities, holder of another chair in the Faculty and the most well-known among the contemporary liberals in Finland, acted as Chair until 1882 when he became a member of the Senate. The chair was then given to Joel Napoleon Lang (1847–1905), a follower of the ideas of the German historical school, and a leading authority among contemporary social thinkers in Finland.

In the meantime, the associate professorship in economic studies in the Faculty of Law was occupied by K. J. Ståhlberg (1865-1952) and J. K. Paasikivi (1870-1956), for example, both future presidents and prominent figures in Finnish politics. At the turn of the century, this chair was divided. The holder of the associate professorship in economic studies, public finance and statistics was Karl Willgren (1865-1930) from 1901 until 1922, the first representative of marginalism in Finland.

The status of economic studies in the Faculty of Law remained relatively weak, since it was mainly considered an ingredient in the education of civil servants. It is thus understandable that claims for stronger academic representation became more frequent. Professor Lang, for instance, had suggested as early as in

Joel Napoleon Lang (1847–1905)

Juho Heikki Vennola (1872–1938)

1885 that there should be a chair in economics in the Faculty of Philosophy. The status of statistics, at the time under the umbrella of general history, was discussed in the same context, and it was taken as natural that it should be combined with economic studies. As a matter of fact, since the Faculty of Law was not considered a proper place for statistics, a proposal to institute a Faculty of Social Sciences (or Faculty of Government) was made, but this was not realised at the University of Helsinki until 1944.

In response to these partly conflicting claims, Helsinki University created a new chair in economics in the Faculty of Philosophy in 1906, while the Faculty of Law retained an associate professorship in the subject. At the same time, J. V. Tallqvist (1862–1960), an active member in the small circles of Finnish economists, and docent in statistics, became docent in economics and statistics. These changes undoubtedly strengthened the academic status of economics.

Juho Heikki Vennola (1872–1938) was nominated the first holder of the professorship in the Faculty of Philosophy, which he held until his death. He was a firm supporter of the historical

Table 1: Chairs in economic science and their holders in the Grand Duchy of Finland, 1809–1917.

	University (1) Åbo	(2) Helsinki	(3) Helsinki	(4) Helsinki	(5) Helsinki	(6) Technical University, Economics
	Economic Law and Commercial Legislation	Public and Constitutional Law and Economy	Economic Law and Economic Studies	Agricultural Economics	Economics	Economics
Chair founded	1811	1828	1853	1901	1906	1908
	Daniel Myréen (in office 1811–1828)					
		Daniel Myréen (in office 1828–1831)				
		Johan Jakob Nordström (in office 1834–1846)				
		Wilhelm Lagus (1846–48, deputy)				
		Frans Florin (1848–57, deputy)				
			Axel Liljenstrand (in office 1857–77)			
			Leo Mechelin (1877–82, deputy)			
			Joel Napoleon Lang (in office 1882–1905)			
			Karl Willgren (1906–09, deputy)			
				Karl Grotenfelt (in office 1901–1906)		
				Karl Enckell (in office 1910–1926)		
					Juho Heikki Vennola (in office 1908–1938)	
						Yrjö Jahnsson (in office 1911–1936)

school, and through his high status was able to strengthen the position of this approach in the country. Vennola, however, was so heavily occupied by his political duties – he was at times Prime Minister and Chairman of the Liberal Party – that he had no time to devote himself properly to academic studies or teaching.

At the end of the period, the Finnish system of higher education became more diversified. Although no new universities were founded before independence, specialised schools of higher education (colleges) were created for technology (1908) and commerce (1911), and in 1901 the University of Helsinki was expanded by the introduction of a new Faculty of Agriculture and Forestry. All these new institutions were given chairs in economics.

Yrjö Jahnsson (1877–1936) held the chair in the Helsinki School of Technology. He had written his dissertation on the history of economic thought in Finland, and later became known for his sharp criticism of the economic policies during the Great Slump (as well as for the foundation his wife created in the 1950s to support economics research in Finland). The chair in economics at the Helsinki School of Economics and Business Administration was held by O. W. Louhivuori (1884–1953).

Karl Johan Grotenfelt (1855–1922) served as the first Professor of Agricultural Economics in the Faculty of Agriculture until 1906, and was followed by Karl Enckell (1853–1937) in 1910. Among the economists in the Faculty, mention should also be made of Hannes Gebhard (1864–1933), docent from 1899, and later professor extraordinarie in agricultural economics and statistics until 1927. This student of Gustav von Schmoller and Adolf Wagner, a moderate synthetiser in doctrinal issues, played a key role in founding the co-operative movement in Finland. In fact, his duties as the Head of Co-operative Loan Associations, meant that he was on leave from his chair at the University for extensive periods.

Holders of various chairs in the university worked on at least some aspects of economic issues. In the Faculty of Law, mention should be made of Ossian Donner (1835–1909) and Wilhelm Chydenius (1863–1926). Among the historians, Johan Richard Danielson-Kalmari (1853–1933) and G. Z. Yrjö-Koskinen (1830–1903) were the two most distinguished representatives of the historical school in Finland and, as leaders of the Finnish Party, they were also interested in social issues from the point of view of nation building. As a disciple of Danielson-Kalmari, Ernst Nevanlinna (1873-1932, until 1906 Neovius), started as a historian, but was moved over to economic issues. He first represented the views of the historical school. Later on, in the 1920s, he turned to analytical economics as a firm follower of Gustav Cassel (Mäki 1984). Finally, Ernst Gustaf Palmén (1849–1919) was an economic historian who relied quite heavily on economics.

As far as philosophers were concerned, mention should first be made of Johan Vilhelm Snellman (1806–1881), discussed extensively elsewhere in this book, the most famous intellectual of the period in Finland. He was not given an academic chair before the 1850s, when several years had already passed since his most innovative period of scientific work and he was preparing for political activities. His biographer, Thiodolf Rein (1838-1919) was also a philosopher who was sympathetic towards the historical school, and dealt with economic issues in his work.

Table 1 sums up the changes that took place in the chairs in economic studies in the period under review. Although there was considerable expansion, particularly at the end of the period, resources remained small. Moreover, most of the holders were interested in a wide range of issues, both practical and academic, apart from economics. Under these conditions, it is understandable that the maturation of economics as a discipline was not complete. This process as such, as well as the fact that practical interest in economic issues dominated over doctrinal issues, consequently shaped the structure of the extensive discussion which follows.

Economic Studies, Curricula and Dissertations

Economic studies remained a secondary subject in the Faculty of Law. It was obligatory in only two of the three parts of the degree examination, in general law and in the civil servant examination, the so-called cameral examination. Even here, it was of minor importance, however. Nevertheless, it was through these channels that the civil servants in 19th-century Finland received their basic knowledge in economic issues, the cameral examination being especially important in this respect.

The situation was different in the Faculty of Philosophy. When the teaching of the subject was started there by Tallqvist in the 1890s, attendance at the lectures increased to around 50 persons, according to an oral account by Tallqvist himself and recounted by Hugo E. Pipping, and economics was included in the final examination by around 30 students. The popularity of economics diminished considerably, however, while Vennola held the chair (Kuitunen & Sullström 1984, 53).

Laura Harmaja (1881–1954, until 1906 Genetz) in the dining room of the Harmaja family in 1912.

Some information concerning the contents of the studies at the beginning of the century is available from the information on the curricula collected by Tero Kuitunen and Risto Sullström (1984; see also Eriksson 1978). According to this information, the influence of the German historical school was dominant. Literature in English was almost totally lacking. It is interesting that many of the most important books on the curriculum were translated into Finnish. Due to the heavy costs involved, this in turn implied that the curriculum changed very slowly: as a matter of fact, it remained practically unchanged for 30 years after the reorganisation which took place after the establishment of the professorship in 1906.

Many of the books read by several generations of students at the University of Helsinki were written by Nordic authors (e.g. Aschehoug [1903–1908] 1904). The basic text, however, was Grundriss der Politischen Oekonomie by E. von Philippovich, first published in 1893, the 10th Finnish edition of which appeared in 1914. This treatise closely followed the approach of the historical school. The only English text in the curriculum was Principles of Political Economy by J.S. Nicholson. Among other main texts were a German book by J. Conrad and a French one by C. Gide, and the rest of the books dealt with special subjects such as public finance and labour. These texts mainly followed the lines of the historical school or comparable approaches. The first Finnish textbook was by Liljenstrand, published in 1860, and the first one written in the Finnish language was written by Laura and Leo Harmaja and appeared in 1914.

The translation of foreign texts was rather sporadic. The sudden burst at the beginning of the century was due to the initiatives of the Finnish Economic Association. According to the minutes of its meetings, the choice of books to be translated seems to have been based on occasional suggestions by its members rather than on any comprehensive plan. Translation of the Great Classics in political economy into Finnish was also discussed, but nothing really came of this before the end of Russian Rule. Interestingly enough, on the initiative of Parliament, the translation of *Das Kapital* by Karl Marx was started by Professor Louhivuori in the 1910s.

Further information on the contents of studies is provided by academic dissertations, which have also been classified by Kuitunen and Sullström. The number of dissertations in the first part of the 19th century was few, and most of them are discussed more closely in forthcoming chapters. Even in the latter part of the century, when economic studies still belonged to the Faculty of Law, the number of dissertations that can be classified as in economics totalled only 11. Eight were published in the period from 1900 to 1909, and 18 from 1910 to 1919, when the professorship in the Faculty of Philosophy was already making itself felt. As a matter of fact, the total output of dissertations remained roughly at this level until the 1970s, notwithstanding the fact that the teaching of economics had begun in several new universities (see Appendix 1 and Schauman & Koskela 1992).

As far as the approaches of the dissertations were concerned, the historical school clearly dominated in the first two decades of this century. Attempts at original theoretical contributions were altogether lacking, and even works which dealt with contemporary economic theory remained few. Most of the theses dealt with the history of thought, or with concrete questions of social policy, intensively discussed in Finland at the beginning of this century.

3.3 Economic Associations and Publishing Channels

In the closing period of Swedish Rule, towards the end of the 18th century, the practical, science-based period, usually referred to as the "age of utility" or "age of freedom" in Swedish history, fostered interest in economic issues in many indirect ways. This was reflected in the founding of the society *Finska Hushållningssällskapet* in 1797 on the initiative of the scientist Johan Gadolin (1760–1852). Although this society became an agricultural consulting organisation in South-Western Finland later on in the 19th century, its original idea, drawn from the rising economic liberalism of the time, was to give impetus to economic innovativeness in the Finnish countryside. Based on physiocratic ideas, this society, which soon gained followers in other parts of the country, was conceived of as a kind of semi-public institution between the state and civil society. In a general sense, the ideas of early economic liberalism were also shared by men like Henrik Gabriel Porthan (1739–1804), Frans Michael Franzén (1772–1847) and Jacob Tengström (1755–1832), all of whom had a strong impact on the Finnish and Swedish intellectual life of the period.

The closing period of Swedish Rule witnessed an increase in social and economic debate in Finland. For many reasons, the first five decades of the Period of Autonomy did not foster these new developments. The institutional development of the subject was held back and economic pamphleteers were rather the exception. No formal economic associations existed in the early 19th century, although there were various learned societies with a wider focus, which also discussed social and economic questions.

The end of the century also marked a significant revival in the activities of economic associations (Pekkarinen 1984). This happened relatively early in Finland. There were several foreign examples to draw on, such as the Societé d'Economique Politique (founded in Paris in 1842), the Verein für Sozialpolitik (Berlin 1872), the Nationaløkonomisk Forening (Copenhagen 1872), the Nationalekonomiska Föreningen (Stockholm 1877) and the Statsøkonomisk Forening (Kristiania/Oslo 1883).

The focus of the new organisations in Finland was far from purely scientific. Like the German Verein, they were rather a combination of a scientific discussion forum, a research organisation and a social pressure group. Moreover, in the Finnish context, the language issue formed a dividing line separating the associations from one another.

Closest to the Verein für Sozialpolitik was the Finnish Economic Association (Kansantaloudellinen Yhdistys), the origins of which can be traced back to 1884. Its first chairman was the leader of the Finnish Party, G. Z. Yrjö-Koskinen, when it started more formally in 1891. Other well-known contemporary intellectuals and politicians who were active in this association included J. R. Danielsson-Kalmari, J. N. Lang, August Hjelt, Agathon Meurman, Hannes Gebhard, Ernst Nevanlinna, J. K. Paasikivi and J. H.Vennola (see Appendix 2).

The activities of this association neatly reflected the combination of thinking among contemporary Finnish intellectuals, incorporating nationalist ideology and interest in social policies aimed at improving the living conditions of the Finnish-speaking population. Both these factors in turn led them to give an active role to the state in facilitating the material and cultural well-being of the nation. In the Verein für Sozialpolitik, the Fennomans saw an organisational model of how an intellectual could promote these goals. In such a historical and ideological context, it was also natural that most of the social scientists in Finland at this time were strongly inclined towards the German historical school in their methodological approach.

The Finnish Economic Association was very active in the first decade of the 20th century. It not only organised meetings and seminars, but also sponsored empirical research projects on contemporary economic and social problems such as living conditions among the landless population in the countryside. It also acted as a scientific publisher and as a pressure group which drew the attention of the administration to social problems in the Finnish countryside in particular. It also took initiatives in the arrangement of social and economic studies. Gradually, however, the partisan nature of the Association changed and it took on the role of a normal scientific association. At the same time, the focus of its discussion turned from social policy to more conventional economic policy issues.

Given the linguistic division, the origins of the corresponding society for Swedish-speaking economists (Ekonomiska Samfundet i Finland), which was formally organised in 1894, can be traced back to certain political issues (Pipping 1944). This society drew together liberal intellectuals, politicians and businessmen, among them J. V. Tallqvist, Karl Willgren, Leo Mechelin and Wilhelm Chydenius, who took a more cautious attitude to the role of the state and tended to emphasise more strongly the self-organising potential of a market economy. According to the early historians of the Finnish Economic Association, the impetus for founding the new Society was given in a talk by Professor Lang where he criticised the proposed liberalisation of rural trade. Although the representatives of the Swedish-speaking Society denied the explicit relevance of this political issue, and emphasised the language aspect instead, it is clear that the original ideological frames of reference of these two organisations were different. Moreover, although this was later diluted and the language was given more prominence, it remained a fact that the Swedish-speaking society attracted more businessmen, whereas civil servants were more visible in the Finnish Economic Association.

Mention should also be made of the Finnish and Swedish juridical associations (founded in 1898 and 1862 respectively). Particularly during the early years of its operation, the Swedish-speaking Juridiska Föreningen i Finland gave the platform to many economists, among them Axel Liljenstrand, Joel Napoleon Lang and Karl Willgren. The younger, Finnish-speaking Suomalainen Lakimiesyhdistys, had its primary focus on juridical issues from the outset.

Up until the 18th century, the usual form of scientific publication in Sweden consisted of dissertations, normally of only a few pages. The same author often wrote several of them; moreover, it was a tradition that professors appeared as the author of the dissertations of their students. Gradually, however, the number of pamphlets aimed at a wider audience was increased. The latter part of the 18th century was particularly fruitful in this respect, and an increasing number of economic pamphlets came out in this period. Anders Chydenius was one of the most prominent contributors at this time.

Academic debate was subdued in Finland under Russian rule in the first part of the 19th century, and publication activities were again limited to dissertations. The strict censorship put tight constraints on open debate. Towards the middle of the century there were clear signs of a revival, however. The number of newspapers increased, and they dealt regularly with economic issues.

From the 1850s onwards, the number of publication channels gradually increased. The press, both Finnish and Swedish, expanded considerably. Axel Liljenstrand produced the first economic textbook in the country in the 1860s (Liljenstrand 1860), but it was largely the new scientific associations which gave a new impetus to such publishing. The Finnish-speaking association started its first series in 1884, and also began publish lectures given at its meetings. Finally, at the beginning of this century, it

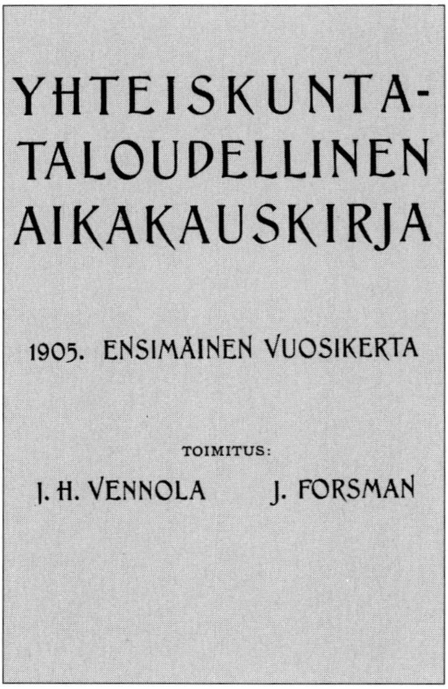

YHTEISKUNTA-
TALOUDELLINEN
AIKAKAUSKIRJA

1905. ENSIMÄINEN VUOSIKERTA

TOIMITUS:

J. H. VENNOLA J. FORSMAN

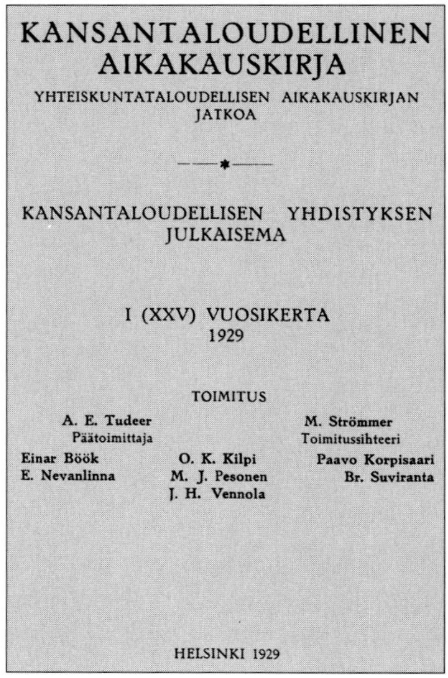

KANSANTALOUDELLINEN
AIKAKAUSKIRJA

YHTEISKUNTATALOUDELLISEN AIKAKAUSKIRJAN
JATKOA

KANSANTALOUDELLISEN YHDISTYKSEN
JULKAISEMA

I (XXV) VUOSIKERTA
1929

TOIMITUS

A. E. Tudeer
Päätoimittaja

M. Strömmer
Toimitussihteeri

Einar Böök
E. Nevanlinna

O. K. Kilpi
M. J. Pesonen
J. H. Vennola

Paavo Korpisaari
Br. Suviranta

HELSINKI 1929

The journal of Finnish-speaking economic association Yhteiskuntataloudellinen aikakauskirja started publication in 1905 and was renamed as Kansantaloudellinen aikakauskirja in 1929.

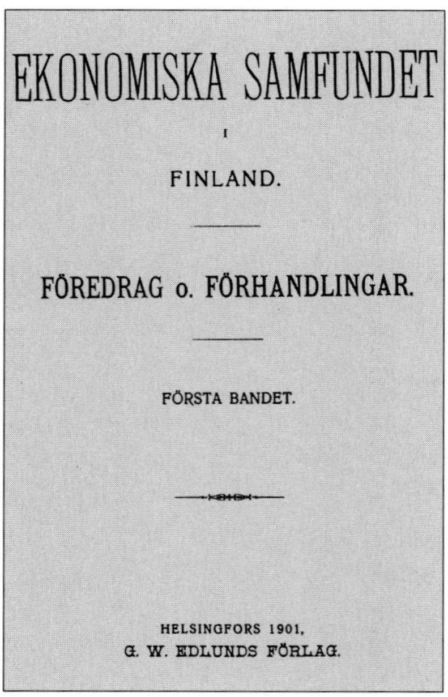

EKONOMISKA SAMFUNDET
I
FINLAND.

FÖREDRAG o. FÖRHANDLINGAR.

FÖRSTA BANDET.

HELSINGFORS 1901,
G. W. EDLUNDS FÖRLAG.

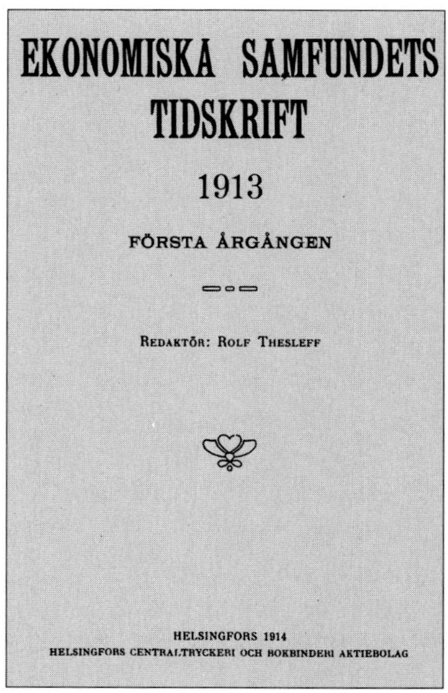

EKONOMISKA SAMFUNDETS
TIDSKRIFT

1913

FÖRSTA ÅRGÅNGEN

REDAKTÖR: ROLF THESLEFF

HELSINGFORS 1914
HELSINGFORS CENTRALTRYCKERI OCH BOKBINDERI AKTIEBOLAG

Swedish-speaking economic society started publishing the lectures at its meetings in 1901 and launched the journal Ekonomiska Samfundets Tidskrift in 1913.

started its Economic Studies series in which most economics dissertations were later to be published, and also a series with more of a focus on applied work. Its quarterly journal *Yhteiskuntataloudellinen aikakauskirja*, later on *Kansantaloudellinen aikakauskirja* (Finnish Economic Journal) was launched in 1905, since when it has been the dominant journal in the field in Finland. As indicated above, this Association also sponsored several translations which were published in Finnish at the beginning of this century.

The publishing activity of the Swedish-speaking society of Finland remained on a smaller scale. The publication of the lectures at its meetings stopped in 1912. Its quarterly journal, *Ekonomiska Samfundets Tidskrift*, started publication in 1913.

3.4 Foreign Contacts

Mapping intellectual contacts with foreigners, and foreign countries, institutions and schools of thought provides useful information on the types of influences a country like Finland, which has operated almost exclusively as an "importer" of ideas, has been subject to (see e.g. Hietala 1987). At the same time, an importing country is not only a passive receiver: it normally initiates changes in the contact network which thereby indicate a new orientation of domestic economic debate. This, in turn, may be due to factors either external or internal to domestic economic science. In the case of 19th-century Finland, a peripheral country in which economic science had not yet matured as an autonomous discipline, it can be assumed that external factors, and changes in the political and ideological situation or in the phase of economic development, were dominant.

As far as Finland was concerned, Sweden and Germany were generally the main "exporters" of influence in most fields of intellectual life, although their relative importance has changed over time and from one discipline to another. What is somewhat surprising, however, is the relatively weak direct influence from Russia in the 19th century, notwithstanding the fact that the standard of both economics and statistics was rather high there towards the end of the century.

Under Swedish rule, the role of the mother country was understandably dominant in most areas, including economic ideas; it was even through Sweden that influences from third countries were often transmitted. In particular, contacts between the universities in Uppsala and Turku (Åbo) were close, and both teachers and students moved frequently from one to the other. These contacts were not interrupted when Finland became a Grand Duchy under Russian rule, although they were weakened by the removal of the University from Turku to Helsinki – which in fact may have been partly the intention behind the operation.

In the course of the 19th century, excursions by Finns to European universities apart from Sweden were mostly to Germany or France, and more infrequently but increasingly over time, also to Britain. These excursions often lasted for years, and they were taken not only by those who aimed at a University career, but in many cases also by ambitious potential civil servants and industrialists. It was, in fact, through such "grand tours" that new knowledge and new techniques were mainly transmitted; and they seem to have served their purpose well, since Finland was relatively quick to adopt the most recent technical innovations in public utilities, for example.

According to the information provided by Björkqvist (1986), the numbers of study tours to European universities made by Finnish economists in the second half of the 19th century were as follows:

Berlin	17
Paris	10
Leipzig	3
Vienna	3
Halle	2
Heidelberg	1
Munich	1

The goal of these scientific excursions was in most cases to include several top European universities in the same trip, and the visitors had access to leading figures in their field. While Paris had been very popular earlier in the century, and to a large extent retained its position in the latter half, the University of Berlin, with Gustav von Schmoller and Adolph Wagner among its teachers, tempted Finnish academics, both doctoral students and senior scholars, particularly at the end of the century, in other words in the period in which the influence of the historical school was strongest in Finland.

As already mentioned, the number of excursions to Russia remained small throughout the period. This did not necessarily reflect any suspiciousness of Russian cultural influences as such.

The Russian university system was in fact rather underdeveloped at the time, and the academies of science there were able to accommodate only a few top scholars. Understandably, Russian excursions were more frequent among civil servants.

A further strange feature of the economic tourism of the period was the apparently small number of trips to Finland. The Finnish Economic Association, for instance, hosted only two German visitors in the period before the First World War, which is surprising since it was this association which was the closest follower of the German historical school. Visits by Nordic colleagues to the Swedish-speaking society were more frequent, but even this activity remained modest in the period under consideration. Wicksell gave lectures several times in Helsinki in his early days, but not as a well-known economist, rather as a Neo-Mathusian proponent of contraception.

Nor was much direct use made of foreign expertise in the contemporary committee work or planning of reforms. Yet there were some exceptions, such as the reliance of the Gold Standard Committee on August Wallenberg's written testimony in the 1870s. On the other hand, the committees regularly undertook surveys of foreign literature relevant to their work. Swedish expertise, as well as their experience with reforms, provided the main source of inspiration for planning reforms in Finland – a tradition which persisted far into this century. Particularly noteworthy is the almost total neglect of Russian experience. The isolation of the Finnish from the Russian civil service is also reflected in the fact that extremely few Finns took up a career in the Russian civil administration, whereas they featured relatively strongly in the Russian military service. This may partly explain the lack of interest in Russian experience.

The terms of trade thus clearly disfavoured Finland in the exchange of economic ideas, and exemplifies the peripheral position of the country. It was positive as such, however, that the interest of Finnish economists in foreign debate increased substantially towards the end of the period. This paved the way for improved domestic standards in the future.

3.5 Economic and Governmental Institutions

With the process of industrialisation in the 19th century, the division of labour went deeper and the economic structure became more diversified. There was a need to understand these new developments and, if possible, to control them. At the same time, a stronger economy gradually expanded the surplus available for such intellectual activities. In Finland, a decisive change in these material conditions took place at the end of the century. This increased governmental demand for economic expertise.

An autonomous government gradually came into being in 19th-century Finland. The number of governmental institutions, as well as the scope of their responsibilities, rapidly increased, particularly in the latter part of the century. The country was autonomous in its foreign trade and customs policy (Pihkala 1970; Heikkinen 1994). It was given a state bank, or rather a bank run by the estates which later developed into a proper central bank, from the very beginning of the Autonomy Period (1811) (Pipping 1961). In its early phase this was rather an institution providing credit to the Crown and to the public in a country where the banking system was almost non-existent. Finland had created its own currency in the early 1860s. Harsh hard-currency policies were adopted in the midst of a deep international recession and a domestic crop failure which lead to a bad famine, and the demands on the Bank of Finland as a cash bank increased considerably. The currency of the country, the markka, was first tied to silver, but a gold standard was adopted in 1877–1878.

The development of the banking system and the capital markets was not given more impetus until the latter part of the century, thus reflecting the timing of the general take-off of economic growth in that period. The first commercial bank was founded in the 1860s, and these institutions soon adopted a central role in the financial system of the country. The savings bank system also started its rapid expansion at the end of the century (Kuusterä 1995). The banking system as a whole remained in domestic hands, which turned out to be of primary significance for general economic development, too. Generally, in contrast to many other peripheral industrialisers, Finland's reliance on foreign borrowing remained modest.

Finland had an independent tax system. Since new taxes had to be accepted by the Estates, which did not gather in the first part of the century, the rise in government revenues had to be sought by increasing the rates of existing forms of taxation. This made customs duties an important source of revenue. As the Estates started to gather more regularly and the obligations of the public sector increased more rapidly towards the end of the century, the issue of enhancing tax revenue by widening the rather rudimentary tax base was naturally raised. The inherited tax base, based on wealth or rather land ownership, diminished in importance, while the revenue from indirect taxes increased due to the sharply increased income from customs duties from the 1840s and 1850s onwards. At its peak at the end of the century, before greater prominence was given to income taxes, indirect taxation accounted for 90 per cent of the state's tax revenue.

Local government remained in rather rudimentary shape in the period under review. The cities, which were extremely few in number, had their self-rule and the right to impose income tax and duties on trade. The development of the rural communities was inhibited by strict restrictions that constrained domestic trade in the cities, and by the undeveloped system of local administration in the countryside. The roots of local government, which had strengthened during the century, were set down in this period as the management of primary education and public services, for instance, previously undertaken by the parishes, was gradually transferred to the municipalities.

Gradually, the state activities which we now refer to as economic policies (largely excluding macroeconomic policies, however) occupied a central role in government. In this context, the autonomy of the Finnish government was extensive, and the activities were also considered essential for an evolving new nation. In the Senate, the person responsible for state finances was a key figure in the whole administration. The post was made still more influential by the fact that it was occupied by strong persons who kept it for several decades and enjoyed a dominant position in economic policy-making. Of these, figures such as Lars Gabriel von Haartman (1789–1859, in the Senate 1840–1858) and Herman Molander (1817–1897, in the Senate 1871–1897) cannot be omitted from the narrative which follows. Johan Vilhelm Snellman (1806–1881) also held the post for a short period (see Appendix 4).

Ministers (Senators at the time) were civil servants nominated by the Emperor, and not formally submitted to Parliament (the Estates). The role of the bureaucracy was further enhanced by the fact that the Estates did not assemble at all from 1808 to the 1860s when a regular Assembly was launched. Civil servants submitted central issues directly to the Emperor, which of course increased their influence. In the latter half of the period, the role of the Assembly was gradually increased – but there was no proper parliamentary rule before 1917 when, after the March Revolution, the Finnish Assembly adopted the mandate of the Emperor.

Lower levels of government administration were gradually expanded. As far as the economic expertise of the civil servants was concerned, the economic studies included in the cameral examination of the Juridical Faculty played a pivotal role. The teaching of the subject was concentrated on this examination targeted at civil servants.

Various civil institutions also took shape at the turn of the century, which marked the birth of the labour market, for example, and most other interest organisations. It was at that time that Finland became a stronghold for all kinds of citizens' organisations, from the fire brigade and sports associations to all kinds of societies with more or less specific economic interests (Alapuro et al 1987). The co-operative movement also gained in importance in the country, both as consumer and producer co-operatives, the latter basically in the agricultural sector.

This rise in the number of institutions of state and civil society increased the demand for economic expertise, the more so as the primary organising principle of the new institutions in many cases was, in fact, economic. The relevance of economic arguments to various interest groups was further increased by the collegial administrative system. Before the Assembly of the Estates began to function regularly in the latter part of the century, the bureaucracy listened to the voice of the citizens in accordance with acknowledged privileges: the interest groups recognised by the state as relevant to the issue in question were normally given an opportunity to express their views on it. It is natural that they tried to make use of economic arguments in this context.

Later on, the privilege tradition was reflected in an increasing reliance on committees in the Finnish administration. These made the use of economic expertise more systematic in the planning of the policy reforms of the period. As already noted, committees also undertook surveys of relevant literature. As well as providing a relatively comprehensive survey of the subject, the committee reports added to the general standard of economic knowledge in the country. Towards the end of Russian Rule, some committees organised empirical studies of their own, and thus contributed to the training of economic experts. These studies were also submitted as dissertations at the University.

Special mention should also be made here of a statistical service as an aspect of state activities. The origins of the Finnish statistical system go back to Gustavus Vasa in the 16th century. At first, use was made of tax catalogues and parish registers to collect data on the population and also, to some extent, on income. Statistics on foreign trade began to be collected in Sweden in the 17th century, and the Statistical Authority was founded in 1749, first under the Assembly and later on, at the end of the century, under the Crown. Agricultural statistics were systematised at around the same time, while collections of statistics on mining, trade and shipping started at the beginning of the 19th century.

In the Grand Duchy of Finland, the statistical activities of the Swedish authorities were first carried out through the colleges (boards) in each branch of administration. The statistical central authority was finally founded in 1870, with K. F. E. Ignatius as its active head. By the end of the century, several committees were working on the organisation of statistical activities in various fields, and although total reform of the system was not finalised in the period of autonomy, it is fair to say that the contemporary statistical service in Finland was organised quite well in comparison to many other countries (Luther 1993).

3.6 Economic Thought Outside Universities and the Civil Service

As emphasised above, it was characteristic of the immature state of economic science in the 19th century that economic aspects were not clearly distinguished or afforded separate study. Nor were economists considered as having a profession of their own. Economic issues were normally considered in a wider social context, and the arguments used by laymen, politicians, landowners, businessmen and journalists did not necessarily differ from those used by the more narrow scientific community.

In the Finnish case, however, such an intellectual community was very small. The economic structure, quite simply, was so undiversified that it did not leave much room for such a layer. Small as the body of independent intellectuals was, however, it was still responsible for some of the most insightful developments in economic ideas during the early part of the century. Moreover, towards the end of the period, as the professional community was leaning heavily towards the interventionism of the historical school, the promotion of liberal ideas to a large extent lay in the hands of businessmen and the like on the periphery of scientific debate.

In the latter half of the 18th century, i.e. during Swedish Rule, Anders Chydenius (1729–1803) was the most famous economic policy thinker in Finland who worked outside the university. Although he was capable of ingenious theoretical work of his own,

Anders Chydenius (1729–1803)

he was never appointed to an academic chair. He exercised his influence as a clergyman in a remote parish in Ostrobothnia, and was a representative of the clergy in the Assembly of the Estates. Chydenius studied under Kalm in Åbo, but most influential for his social and economic thinking was his period of study in Uppsala under a famous Swedish politician, the ideological debater and economist Anders Nordencranz. Samuel Pufendorf also exerted a strong influence on his thinking (see e.g. Patoluoto 1990).

Chydenius was an active pamphleteer. The best known of his books is *Den Nationnale Winsten* (The National Gain, 1765b), in which he defended free trade and economic liberalism, and emphasised the linkages between the free labour market, increased division of labour and economic prosperity. Chydenius also contributed to the lively debate on monetary reform in Sweden in the 1760s.

At least two outside intellectuals took part in the contemporary economic debate during the first part of the century. As already mentioned, Johan Vilhelm Snellman made his scientific contributions outside the university. The other, Michaël Tjeder (1796–1842), has remained more or less unknown. His dissertation, *Tankar om Frihet i Handel* (Thoughts on the Freedom of Trade) contains some interesting ideas, as well as comments on David Ricardo, Jean Baptiste Say and others, and is discussed more closely below. Tjeder was never offered an academic chair, and he became a humble accountant in the town of Vyborg.

From the 1860s onwards, the economic take-off as well as more liberal political conditions fostered the rapid growth of the press as well as broader economic debate. Support for economic liberalism, mostly among the Swedish-speaking community, centred on the newspaper *Helsingfors Dagblad*. Prominent members of this "Dagblad circle" included Leo Mechelin and Axel Liljenstrand, mentioned already, and businessmen such as Henrik Borgström Senior (1799–1883) and Junior (1830–1865), Otto Reinhold Frenckell (1823–1880), Lennart Gripenberg (1852–1933), Christopher Alexander Linder (1838–1868), Georg Schauman (1870–1938), Wilhelm Lavonius (1832–1897) and Axel Lille (1848–1921), the last two having written economic dissertations. Linder in turn wrote a book on monetary issues, *Om Pengar och Banker* (On Money and Banks, 1866). At the end of the century, this group of Swedish liberals, organised as a party, also launched a journal, Finsk Tidsskrift, which featured extensive comment on social, political and economic issues.

Corresponding developments in political and publishing activities took place among the Finnish nationalists, the Fennomans. After Snellman, the prominent figures included Yrjö-Koskinen, Danielson-Kalmari, Thiodolf Rein and Agathon Meurman (1826–1909). The latter, a landowner and member of the Central Bank Council, wrote several economic pamphlets. Newspapers supporting the Finnish Party included *Suometar* (from 1869 *Uusi Suometar*, later *Uusi Suomi*) and *Morgonbladet*. The party journal, called *Kirjallinen Kuukauslehti* from 1860 to 1880, and thenceforth *Valvoja*, commented on social, political and economic issues from a nationalistic point of view.

The Socialist movement in Finland was also organised around the turn of the century. It concentrated on political and, to a lesser extent, trade union activities, and genuine intellectual debate among Finnish Socialists remained subdued. Ideological debate was quite lively, however, in the context of the party programme, for example, and Socialist literature was translated quite extensively into Finnish. Kautsky took the role of the established foreign authority, but there were also influences from America, through re-immigrants, as well as from Russians such as Lenin, who was in exile in Finland.

4. VARIETIES OF FINNISH ECONOMIC THOUGHT

4.1 The Heritage of the Swedish Era

In 1747 a new professorship in economy (oeconomiae) was established at the Royal Academy of Åbo. Per Kalm (1716–1779) was appointed to the post in 1749. The domain of the new professorship was "economy", which included both private household economy of the inhabitants and the "general economy" of the country. This sounds like the modern division between micro- and macroeconomics, but the analogy is misleading. Economic science was seen first and foremost as a subdiscipline of natural history. In the regulations (1748) it was stated that the new professor had to teach students in "the sciences upon which the economy in the kingdom must actually be based", and these sciences were mineralogy, botany, zoology and chemistry, and to a lesser extent mathematics and physics. The practical spirit of the "age of utility" was reflected in the instructions, which emphasised the economic utility of the sciences mentioned above, and obliged the professor to explain "clearly and thoroughly" the four industries of which all economy actually consists, namely agriculture, mining and metal (bergverk), manufacture and trade. The regulations also advised the professor to deal with questions of the "general economy" (almänna hushålningen) "sparingly and with caution, so as not to interfere in what was the task of the High Authorities", i.e. Government (Hjelt 1896, 144–145, 153). Economic science, thus defined, was not political economy, but literally "non-political economy", which examined the physical properties of commodities rather than their "economic qualities" or, to use Adam Smith's terminology, their "value in use" rather than their "value in exchange" (Smith [1776]1974, 131) .

Kalm himself is better known to posterity for his geographical, botanical, zoological and ethnological exploration of North America in 1747–1751 than for his contribution to economic thinking. The academic titles of Kalm's colleague Per Adrian Gadd also bear witness to the kinship of economic thinking and natural sciences. He was appointed docent in natural history and economy in 1750, and in 1758 he was nominated for the professorship of chemistry, physics and economy. He became professor in chemistry in 1761 (Jahnsson, 159–162; Hjelt 1896, 256–259).

An interesting discussion of the nature of economic science took place in 1780, when Kalm's successor was elected. Henrik Gabriel Porthan spoke for Gadd's nomination in the meeting of the council of the Academy. He referred to the regulations of 1748, and stressed that chemistry and all the elements of natural history were the basis of the discipline. "Without this basis, economy as an academic discipline cannot be appropriately taken care of nor taught", he said, and reminded his audience that it was the professor's duty to take care of the botanic garden of the Academy. The council put Gadd in first place in its nomination proposal, but the Chancellor suggested Salomon Kreander (1755–1792) as professor, and although he was not among the three best chosen by council, he was nominated. The natural historians of the Academy were disappointed with the nomination, since Kreander came from a jurisprudential background; he had worked for three years (1778–1780) as extraordinary associate professor of jurisprudence. Yet he also taught economic science in the practical sense, although from a rather different angle than his "natural historian" predecessors. The title of his dissertation, published in four volumes (1775–1777), is revealing: "On the possibility, means and benefit of practising agriculture without meadows" (Om möjeligheten, sättet och nyttan att utan ängar sköta landtbruket). In the first volume of this work, a year before the publication of the Wealth of Nations, he complained that the underdeveloped state of economic science meant that there were no absolute main principles or axioms which he could use to justify his arguments. He was thinking of axioms such as "The Meadow is the mother of the field" (Äng är åkers mor), which he applied to his investigation into whether meadows were necessary for agriculture. He wrote very much in the practically-oriented spirit of utility. When he used the word "theory", it did not refer to a system of abstract economic concepts, but rather to the right method of breaking down straw for cattle feed! It is possible to distinguish a physiocratic current flowing through the work of Kreander who, like all physiocrats, regarded agriculture as the most important sector of the economy. The tide turned when Linné's disciple Carl Niklas Hellenius (1745–1820) was appointed Professor of Economy and Natural History in 1793. He concentrated on natural history and left economic science uncultivated (Hjelt 1896, 328–329; Jahnsson 167–169).

Matthias Calonius spent most of his academic career as Professor in Jurisprudence (1777–1793 and 1800–1816), but he started out as Docent in Economic Studies (1764–1777). The dissertation he wrote before his nomination as Docent dealt with the general basis of monetary economy. He lectured on economy at least in 1765–1766 and 1768–1771, dealing with the science of finance, and general and cameral economy (Björkqvist 1986, 53–55). His ideas can be traced with the help of his lecture notes from the academic year 1765–1766. The title of Calonius' lecture series was "The financial system in a well-functioning society" (Finance-inrättning i ett wälbestält samhälle).

Calonius defined "the science of finance", or in short "finance", as "science which teaches how income and expenditure can be balanced so that the former, if possible, might exceed the latter". He suggested that it was part of "the science of statehood" (stats-wettenskapen), and that it still lacked a comprehensive system. Of previously published works, the only one he felt worth mentioning was that by Jean Francois Melon (1680–1738) entitled *Essai politique sur le commerce* (1734).[1] According to Calonius, there were three reasons why the science of finance was underdeveloped. First, the world of commerce was seen as the proper place to obtain knowledge of finance. However, there was prejudice against merchants, and this prevented people of higher birth from getting involved in commerce. Second, finance was frequently left solely to the merchant, without any state intervention. The third reason was the view that the science of finance could be learned only in a merchant's office, or in a cameral or commercial college, and therefore it was almost unknown in universities. Calonius divided finance into three parts. "General finance" dealt with the income and expenditure of a state with respect to other states. "Crown finance" examined public income and expenditure. Thirdly, "private finance" (enskijlt) dealt with personal income and expenditure. Calonius discussed only "general fi-

[1] According to the Larousse encyclopedia, Melon was sometimes characterised as "neomercantilist", and sometimes as a predecessor of the physiocrats; Larousse, 7, 1984.

nance" in his lectures, dealing with four main themes: monetary standards, money supply, banking and credit, and trade balance.[2] It could be said that he started a new line in Finnish economic science, because his approach was not that of a natural or physiocratic historian, but, with its emphasis on state finance, rather resembled the cameralist approach that later became dominant in Finnish economic thought.

Without underrating the professors and docents discussed above, it is quite clear that the brightest star of Finnish economic thinking in the 18th century was Anders Chydenius (1729–1803). He was an exception in many respects. First, he was a non-academic, a clergyman from Ostrobothnia, who represented his estate in the Swedish Diet. Second, he was a "political economist" in the double sense that he was an active pamphleteer debating on economic policy matters, and he considered economic science not from the perspective of nature or state finance, but rather as the totality of various economic activities in society. Moreover, he was an exception in that he advocated a policy of economic liberalism, and was closely involved in the contemporary Swedish debate.

The most influential of Chydenius' pamphlets were *Källan till Rikets Vanmakt* (1765a, The Source of the Nation's Weakness) and *Den Nationnale Winsten* (1765a, The National Gain), both adding to the turbulent debate in the Diet of 1765–1766. Among other things, he heavily criticised the so-called principal town (stapelstad) system giving monopoly rights of foreign trade to a limited number of coastal towns, and the Swedish version of the Navigation Act (produktplakat). Both of these were cornerstones of mercantilist trade policy. Freedom of trade was Chydenius' credo.

In short, there were four distinct schools of economic thought in 18th-century Finland. First, there were the natural historians (Kalm and Gadd) dealing with the practical and "physical" economy in the spirit of utility; this actually gave rise to economic science in Finland in the 1740s. "Economy" was understood mostly as household economy, or as a concrete production process. Second, there were very feeble traces of physiocratic ideas (Kreander), but even here "economy" was treated as the practical management of agriculture. The third school was the jurisprudential one (of Calonius), which looked at state finances in the cameralist spirit of "the science of finance". Fourth, some people put for-

[2] Calonius' lectures, Helsinki University Library.

ward ideas of economic liberalism (Chydenius), in opposition to prevailing economic policy. This inheritance from the Swedish era was unevenly transferred to economic thinking in the Grand Duchy of Finland. The link between natural history and economic science had been broken during Hellenius' professorship, and there was no continuity with respect to physiocratic ideas either. Chydenius' ideas of economic liberalism found no followers during the years when the official economic policy was opposed to it. This left the jurisprudential view of the economy the most influential direct heir to 18th-century thinking in 19th-century Finland, although the transfer process was not a continuous one.

4.2 Cameralist Bias: From the 1810s to the 1840s

A Science of Government or Society?

Jurisprudence became the principal academic home of Finnish economic thinking at the beginning of the Russian period. The dominance of this approach prevailed through the 19th century in the sense that it was only in 1906 that a professorship in economics was established in the Faculty of Philosophy. Until then, economic science as an academic discipline was a minor and special branch of jurisprudence. In reality, however, approaches other than the jurisprudential one were applied to economic issues during the latter half of the 19th century, although the first half was dominated by clear jurisprudential, or more exactly cameralist, bias in Finnish economic thinking.

Cameralism, as practised in Finland in the early 19th century, was of German origin and dated from the 18th century. It was the science of government and administration, and its assimilation into the economic policy doctrines of mercantilism is misleading (Hagemann 1996). The German cameralists of the 18th century – Peter Gasser, Christoph Dithmar, Johan Heinrich Gottlob von Justi and Josef von Sonnenfelds being the most prominent – have also been labelled "new cameralists" to distinguish them from the "old cameralists" of the 16th and 17th centuries. The "old cameralists" were named "cameralists" by posterity, while the "new cameralists" used the label themselves. What was new in "new cameralism" was that a "scientific" shape was given to state administration, and to public finances in particular, in the form of cameral science (Kameralwissenschaft). The first chair for the new discipline of "Oeconomie, Policey und Kammer-Sachen" was established in 1727, and thereafter "cameral and policy sciences" became the doctrinal backbone of state administration, the "science of government", even spreading to a sort of general, undifferentiated social science to become one of the sources of the more specialised German economic science of the 19th century (Tribe 1984 & 1988; Braun 1975; Zielenziger 1923).

Cameralist bias prevailed in Finnish economic thinking from the 1810s to at least the 1840s. There were two reasons for this. First, the economic science of those decades dealt mainly with problems of public economy. In the vocabulary of the cameralists of the 19th century, "economy" usually referred to state finances in general, and to the public treasury in particular. The second reason was the fact that the main function of the academic teaching of economic science was to educate civil servants. Although Finland did not have the rank of sovereign state in 1809, it did get public finances of its own for the first time in Finnish history. It is therefore natural that economic thinkers in the newly-created Grand Duchy paid great attention to public finances.

Even though Finnish economic science was mostly the science of government in the service of Government in the early decades of the 19th century, the dominance of the narrow cameralist approach was not absolute. Understanding the economy as the "national economy", an entity different from public economy, was already part of Finnish economic thinking. Thus, there were attempts to treat economic science as a science of society as well as a science of government, as will be seen in the following. The economic thinkers to be discussed are the three professors – Daniel Myréen, Wilhelm Gabriel Lagus, and Johan Jakob Nordström – and one "outsider", Michaël Tjeder.

Daniel Myréen

The cameralist version of economic science achieved a secure, if not wide, academic position in 1811, when a professorship in economic law and commercial legislation was established at the Faculty of Law. Daniel Myréen was appointed to the new professorship in 1812. This was renamed the Professorship in Public and Constitutional Law and Economy in 1828; Myréen held it until his death in 1831. As a principal academic teacher of economic issues for two decades, he was the most prominent among the few Finnish economic thinkers in the first decades of the Finnish Grand Duchy.

Myréen, who was born in Sweden, studied at the University of

Uppsala. His dissertation on money and coins (Akademisk afhandling om penningar och mynt) was published in two volumes in 1810 and 1811, the first part under the supervision of Professor Lars Georg Rabenius. In order to get his nomination for the Professorship of Economic Law and Commercial Legislation established in 1811 he produced another dissertation on land taxes (Afhandling om jordstaxering) in 1812. That was all he published. His economic views, and those of his age, can be traced from these publications, and also from his lectures, which dealt with cameral jurisprudence (cameral lagfahrenheten) and political economy. The dissertations of his students are also informative in this respect.

In his Uppsala dissertation on money and coins (1810–1811), Myréen called his field of science "Statshushållningen" (Myréen 1810–1811, 1), literally "state economy", but actually he meant the economy as a whole, not only public finances. His terminology was thus state-centred, in the cameralist tradition, but he also spoke of "society" (Myréen 1810–1811, 37), and even of "laws of national economy" (National Economie Lagarna, Myréen 1810–1811, 38). The latter term was taken from the German scholar Friedrich Julius Heinrich von Soden (1754–1831), who coined the term Nationalökonomie ("national economy") in 1805 in the first volume of his nine-volume textbook.[3] Myréen also referred to Adam Smith, Jean Baptiste Say and James Steuart.

Myréen's short (18 pages) Turku dissertation on land taxes (1812) made no mention of foreign literature, and used only Swedish law texts and administrative decisions as his source material. He was already using the term "national economy" (National Economien) as the name of the science, and defined it as follows:

> National economy, or the science which exposes how the riches in a state shall be realised, maintained and increased, and finally consumed, therefore studies the means by which people in general, under the protection of the government, can most easily earn and increase their wealth, and put it to good use, and how to remove obstacles, which might lie in the way of useful enterprise. (Myréen 1812, 3)

Myréen seems to have viewed "national economy" or "general

[3] Jahnsson 1907–08, 30; von Soden 1805, 502.

economy" (allmänna hushållningen, Myréen 1812, 1) as separate from state finances here by speaking of "society and state" (pp 1–3), although it is not clear whether he used the words as synonyms or gave them different meanings. This ambiguousness in concept also demonstrates the fact that Myréen defined "national economy" as a "doctrine of crown incomes and *onera publica*" in his lectures on cameral jurisprudence. He saw the importance of this doctrine in analysing the effects of tax laws on the national wealth.[4] In short, the state was still Myréen's starting point.

However, the new name of the science, "national economy" (oeconomia nationalis), appeared in the university programme for the first time in 1820 as the title of Myréen's lecture series, and replaced the old name "political economy". Myréen had especially announced in the 1818 prospectus that he would lecture mainly on the basis of Adam Smith's theory (Jahnsson 1907, 189; Björkqvist 1986, 84). Carl Gustaf Bergbom (1798–1861) also pointed to this distinction between "national economy" or "general economy" on the one hand, and "state economy" on the other in his dissertation, which he wrote under Myréen's supervision (Bergbom 1820). According to Bergbom, "State economy" in the widest sense of the term was "the science of state establishment (state power) and development to importance and influence" (Bergbom 1820, 3). "State economy" (stats-hushållningen) in the narrower sense was used by Bergbom as a synonym for the concept of "cameral science" (Bergbom 1820, 3). Myréen defined cameral science in his lectures on cameral jurisprudence as being the science of "the ways and means by which the state obtains income in general, and on its collection and use".[5]

Wilhelm Gabriel Lagus

Myréen, however, was not the first academic teacher to lecture on political economy in the Grand Duchy of Finland. This accolade goes to Wilhelm Gabriel Lagus, who became Associate Professor of Economic Law and Commercial Legislation in 1813. He lectured on the "principles and theory of so-called political economy" in 1814. What he understood by "political economy",

4 Myréen's lecturers, Manuscripts, Bö III 45, Helsinki University Library.

5 Myréen's lecturers, Helsinki University Library, Manuscripts, Bö III 45, 4. "Cameral jurisprudence", the actual subject of Myréen's lectures, was, according to him, "the doctrine and knowledge of laws dealing with the Crown's confirmed right to incomes and ability to enforce these laws".

however, is not known, because no lecture notes have survived. Lagus held Myréen's professorship during 1815–1818, but then he moved to the discipline of general legislation and returned to economic matters only in 1846–1848, when he held the professorship in public and constitutional law and economy.

Thus, Lagus had quite a short academic career in economic studies, and the only text he published on economic issues was his sixteen-page dissertation on bills of exchange (Academisk Afhandling om Wäxlar, 1813), which he did only to get the nomination for the associate professorship. This short dissertation was not rated very highly in the academic world, and both Calonius and Myréen were dissatisfied with it (Björkqvist 1986, 90). Half of the text dealt with the actual theme of the paper, i.e. bills of exchange, while the other half, which is more relevant to the theme of this book, concerned the principles of economic policy and theory.

Only three books on economic issues were mentioned in the dissertation: Anders Berch's *Inledning til Almänna Hushålningen* ("Introduction to general economy", 1747), James Steuart's *An Inquiry into the Principles of Political Oeconomy* (originally published in 1767), and the second volume of von Soden's textbook mentioned above (*Die Nazional-Oekonomie*, 2, 1806). Lagus also quoted Adam Smith, but without referring to his *Wealth of Nations*. He began by characterising the mercantile system, "the oldest system in public economy (statshushållningen)" (Lagus 1813, 1), and its doctrine of a favourable trade balance. He then went on to criticise the mercantilist emphasis on precious metals as a superior form of riches:

> For if one abstracts from the property of precious metals as a species money, and examines it solely for its quality as a commodity, then it is clear that, by means of trade a nation will get no more and no fewer commodities than the value of the commodities she gives to others in exchange. (Lagus 1813, 2.)

Lagus also wrote that the mercantilist theory of trade balance could also be refuted on the basis of historical evidence. However, He did not present any such evidence, and only suggested that no nation had lost wealth because of a deficit in its trade balance, and therefore no nation could gain because of a surplus either.

Despite the fact that mercantilist theory did not make sense,

Lagus argued, almost all governments based their policies on it, and nations tried to profit from other nations' losses. He felt that this was all wrong, because states were not isolated units but rather members of a greater social organism, a system of states, the principles of which were laid down on the basis of natural law. States existed only in interaction with each other:

> The principle of national economy is cosmopolitan, and this cosmopolitanism has its clearest expression in the nature and essence of trade. (Lagus 1813, 4.)

Moreover, examples of the economic importance of trade and shipping were misleading, because it was the cities that usually profited from trade, not the countryside and its "primary producers". He concluded that the trade laws of most nations were "against the natural order", because trade was not a source of riches, but rather the means by which riches were spread around. When there was surplus production, trade followed naturally and favouring trade was therefore damaging, or at least excessive. It was damaging because it disturbed "nature's certain and even course", and it was excessive because nature itself gave the impetus for trade when there was the surplus production to facilitate it (Lagus 1813, 5–6). He presented his conclusions about trade policy, and the "theoretical contribution" of his dissertation, as follows:

> It should therefore be an incontestable truth, that the interests of the state as well as the freedom of its citizens require that, without fear or favour, trade is left to private persons and their almost always accurate and positive speculations. It behoves governments only to open up a free field to satisfy the bourgeois (verldsborgerliga) trading tendency; to abolish the obstacles that nature and human passions can put in the way of this tendency; and with the help of powerful and unbiased administration justly to maintain in credit this centre around which the trade of the modern world spins. (Lagus 1813, 6–7.)

Johan Jakob Nordström

Johan Jakob Nordström (1801–1874) was appointed to the Associate Professorship of Economic Law and Commercial Legislation in 1827, and in 1834 to the Professorship of Public and Constitu-

Johan Jakob Nordström (1801–1874)

tional Law and Economy, which he had provisionally held in 1828–1829 and 1832–1833. He left his professorial post in 1846, when he emigrated to Sweden (Björkqvist 1986).

Nordström's publications belong to the field of jurisprudence or legal history, his main works being *Bidrag till den svenska samhälls-författningens historia I–II* ("A contribution to the history of the Swedish constitution") (1839–1840) and *Skildring af municipal-författningen i Finland* ("A description of municipal legislation in Finland") (1832). What students of the history of Finnish economic thought find more interesting than Nordström's published works are his lectures, especially those on political economy in 1836. He had toured Europe the previous year – Germany, Austria, Italy, Denmark and Sweden – and had adopted ideas, especially from Germany, that he clearly utilised in his lectures (Björkqvist 1986, 131–132).

His lecture series was entitled "Political Economy" (politisk oekonomie), which he used as a synonym for "state economy" (statsoekonomi). However, he also used the term "national economy" (national oekonomie), which is no wonder because his main source was Lars Georg Rabenius' book (Rabenius 1829). He even used two German textbooks, by Karl Heinrich Rau (1826–1837) and Johan Friedrich Lotz (1821–1822). He also referred to the works of von Soden and Jacob.

Following the lines of thought of Rabenius, Nordström divided economic science into two parts: the pure or theoretical part and the applied (använd) or practical. The former concerned the "natural" laws of economy, while the latter focused on the influence of the government or state on those "natural" laws. Nordström reserved an interesting place for political economy in his family of "state" sciences (the word should perhaps be interpreted as "the society the head of which is the state"). History concerned its past; statistics (statistiken), which should not be equated with modern statistics, was more to do with the present condition of the state at a certain moment; and political economy, which examined the "laws of the internal material life of the state" was the science for studying the future.[6]

Nordström's transition towards the paradigm of classical political economy was a prolonged developmental process. This process reached fruition just after his migration to Sweden in the latter half of the 1840s, where he did not have to worry about the restrictive influence of censorship. The introduction to his book *Afhandlingar rörande läran om crediten I, Credit och bankväsendet* reveals his new views. He examined central concepts of the economy, keeping his eye on its circular flow, where demand and supply meet, and where both exchange values and prices are determined. Money serves only the role of a medium of exchange in this circular flow. It is the value of the commodities rather than the amount of money available – as in mercantilist thought – that is the basis of the wealth of the nation.

Nordström was influenced theoretically, mainly by French classical economists, as the names mentioned in the introduction of his book reveal: Frédéric Bastiat, Michel Chevalier, Joseph C. Garnier, Pellegrino L. Rossi and Jean Baptiste Say. In line with the classical economists he emphasised the division of labour and increased efficiency of production as the driving force behind economic development. The division of labour and trade were not only internal factors, but expanded to become international phenomena. Nordström accepted Say's law, according to which

[6] Nordström's lectures, Helsinki University Library.

supply always creates demand in the economy. If this is true, overproduction crises are not possible. However, overproduction may occur now and then in the course of history because of a variety of institutional problems.

Johan Jakob Nordström criticised Adam Smith's division into productive and non-productive labour. According to Smith, it is only material production that increases the wealth of societies, creating physical products that can be exchanged. Nordström emphasised the significance of non-material production such as science, art, education and government, where the same basic facts hold true as in material production. Non-material production is necessary to maintain social order.

Nordström dealt with credit in the second chapter of his book. He saw credit, like money, as an intermediary link between production and consumption. The institution of credit is based on trust. The dynamics of the credit institution are related to tradability on secondary markets of forms of credit such as bills of exchange or government bonds, which greatly intensify the use of credit instruments. Nordström's authorities on economic theory were Henry Carey, Charles Coquelin, Henry Parnell (*On paper money*, 1829), Pinto (*Traité de la circulation et du credit*, 1771) and Adam Smith.

Nordström devoted the third chapter of his book to banking and the credit system, the significance of which was based on the gathering of capital and channelling it to meet different needs in the economy and society. Banks were divided into deposit banks and note banks. The latter could be either public or private, and had the right to issue bank notes, although this was strictly controlled by the authorities. The money in circulation represented only coins, and there was no possibility of having a fixed exchange rate between coins and paper money. In this, Nordström appealed to Ricardo's views and to Peel's Banking Act, translated into French in 1844, suggesting that the relation between circulating currency and reserves must be defined on the basis of practical experience, because there was no scientific theory to lean on.

He illustrated the practical significance of banking with a comparison between the English, Scottish, Irish, French and North-American banking systems. As far as the English system was concerned, he referred to Thomas Tooke's writings on the disadvantages of Peel's Banking Act.[7] According to Tooke, the central

[7] Tooke, Thomas: *An Inquiry into the Currency Principle, the Connection*

bank had to have the possibility to stop fund orders during times of crisis in order to avoid worsening the recession by cutting the amount of money in circulation. This remark reveals Nordström's knowledge of the ideas of the new banking school in monetary theory.

Nordström pointed out the significance of credit from the point of view of the individual actor and society. Credit enables the individual actor to start or widen production despite the lack of accumulated capital. It is a question of timing the use of capital. The significance of credit in society lies in the fact that it enables the removal of capital from passive owners to active entrepreneurs, thus paving the way for entrepreneureship and the development of entrepreneurial skill. It also facilitates exchange in many ways, and thus causes an increase in production. Moreover, it economises on the use of money, because a smaller amount is needed in the circular flow.

Michaël Tjeder

Among Daniel Myréen's students can be counted Michaël Tjeder (1796–1842), who studied at the Faculty of Law in 1816–1822. His dissertation, *Tankar om Frihet i Handel* ("Thoughts on the Freedom of Trade") was published in 1826. When Tjeder's application for publication of his thesis was discussed in the meeting of the Academy Council, Myréen spoke strongly in his favour. Some members of the Council, Wilhelm Gabriel Lagus among them, did not want to give Tjeder permission to publish, so without Myréen's strong affirmation it may never have seen the light of day.[8]

Although only 57 pages long, Tjeder's dissertation, with its fresh views, made a major contribution to the meagre economic litera-

of Currency with Price and the Expediency of a Separation of Issue from Banking, 1844; Tooke, Thomas: *A History of Prices and of the State of the Circulation from 1793–1837 I*, 1838.

[8] The arguments of council members against publication permission were formal. Tjeder wanted to present his dissertation alone without a teacher ("praeses""), which was rather unusual (Liljenstrand 1890, 61). The normal practice was that the academic teacher was presented as the main author, and was also present when the dissertation was examined. Tjeder did get permission to present his dissertation alone, and only his name is printed on the title page. It is of course not impossible that Tjeder's topic and his opinions might have contributed to the negative attitude of the opposing members of the university council.

ture of Finland. In his support of Tjeder's thesis, Myréen stated that it was of good quality and "showed evidence of close acquaintance with works of recent authors".[9] One of these recent authors was David Ricardo, from whom Tjeder had taken the motto for his dissertation, that the fulfilment of individual interests is good for the well-being of the whole society.[10] An even stronger influence was "the immortal work of the famous Adam Smith" (Tjeder 1826, 21), *The Wealth of Nations*, and to Jean Baptiste Say and his *Traité d'Economie Politique*. As the names of Smith, Say and Ricardo indicate, Tjeder's work was firmly based on the doctrine of economic liberalism. He did not analyse the question of trade from an impartial point of view, but argued strongly for free trade, and ended his dissertation with a utopian appeal for a society in which trade would be free and "the interests of an individual are united with the general good of the whole society" (Tjeder 1826, 57). He even honoured practical businessmen by dedicating his dissertation to the Trade Society of Turku.

Tjeder took as his starting point the postulation that the riches and welfare of a nation grow along with the freedom of action allowed to its members. This was "not just a hypothesis, an idea born of reason, an assumption of Theory, but a fact proved by experience and accepted by most positive legislators" (Tjeder 1826, 1). Tjeder himself presented historical evidence (Tjeder 1826, 1–16) which, in his opinion, proved his postulation: freedom in trade and industry was the basic source of national welfare (Tjeder 1826, 17). However, if the advantages of free trade were so obvious, then how could the persistence of the mercantile system be explained? Tjeder gave two reasons. One was the underdevelopment of economic thought, the lack of proper knowledge on the essence of wealth and value. The other was the government's lacking insight into the functioning of the economy, and the priority of state finances over the welfare of the whole society in decisions concerning economic policy (Tjeder 1826, 17–21).

In Tjeder's opinion, the first reason, the underdevelopment of

[9] University of Helsinki Archives, Record of the meeting of the University Council 12.6.1826 ("vittnade om närmare kännedom af nyare författares arbeten").

[10] Tjeder obviously read Ricardo in German translation, because he quoted him in German: "Die Rücksichten des individuellen Intresses vertragen sich auf's Beste mit dem allgemeinen Wohl der ganze Gesellschaft" (Tjeder 1826, 1). Ricardo's *Principles of Political Economy and Taxation* (1817, 2nd ed. 1821) was translated into German in 1821 (Björkqvist 1986, 97).

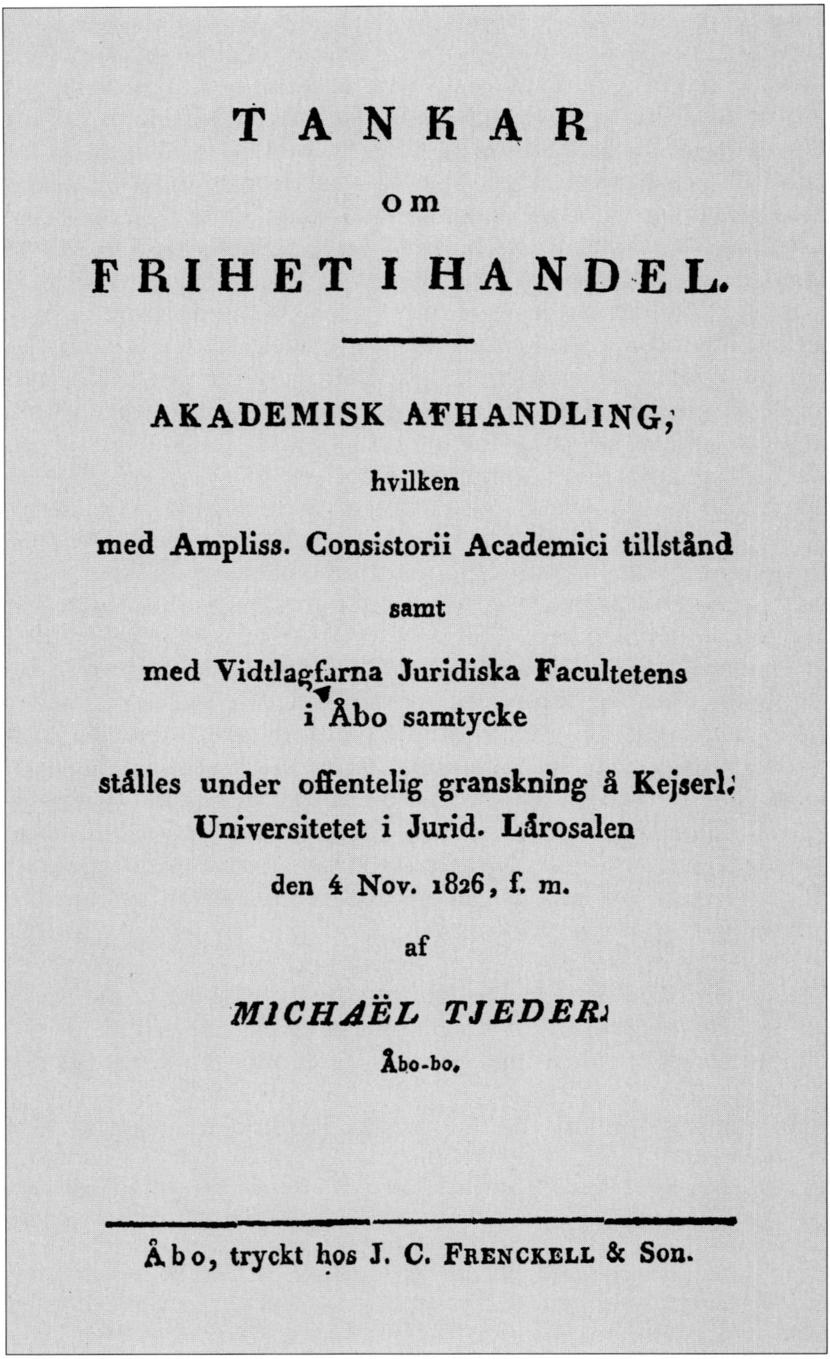

TANKAR

om

FRIHET I HANDEL.

AKADEMISK AFHANDLING,

hvilken

med Ampliss. Consistorii Academici tillstånd

samt

med Vidtlagfarna Juridiska Facultetens
i Åbo samtycke

stålles under offentelig granskning å Kejserl.
Universitetet i Jurid. Lårosalen

den 4 Nov. 1826, f. m.

af

MICHAËL TJEDER,

Åbo-bo.

Åbo, tryckt hos J. C. Frenckell & Son.

The title page of Michaël Tjeder's dissertation.

economic thought, was not a relevant explanation in the 1820s, because Smith, Say and Ricardo had already developed the principles of political economy to "the completeness of a scientific system" (Tjeder 1826, 22). However, even though economic thinkers had proved the usefulness of free trade, the state trade policy was still based on old and false arguments. Trade between nations was still weighed down with import restrictions or high customs duties (Tjeder 1826, 22–23). Tjeder argued that this prohibitive or protective trade policy was based on false premises, which he heavily criticised.

Tjeder used a sardonic tone to criticise the mercantilist doctrine on trade balance. Whenever imports exceed exports, people start to talk about a "highly unfavourable trade balance which threatens to ruin the state if the government does not intervene with prohibitive measures" (Tjeder 1826, 24). In Tjeder's opinion, the basic misunderstanding leading to this false conclusion was ignorance of the functions of money. Those worrying about an unfavourable trade balance had not yet understood that money (specie) "is value representing another value, which again does not exist outside products" (Tjeder 1826, 23).

The basic premise of the mercantilist trade policy was the assumption of one nation's gain in trade being another nation's loss. It followed from this that every country needed to maximise her exports and minimise her imports. The logical but absurd conclusion would thus be that all countries would want to export and no country would want to import, which would, of course, make all export impossible (Tjeder 1826, 38–41). Such an extreme state of affairs, which would lead to the stagnation of all trade, was of course untenable. The actual mercantilist trade policy was based on a less severe version of the import minimisation principle. Tjeder formulated the policy as follows: the only commodities that should be imported from other countries were those that could not be produced in the home country. This did not only apply to commodities already being produced in the home country, but also to those which could be produced if production was stimulated and protected. This would be attained with the help of production premiums and high import duties, or even prohibitions (Tjeder 1826, 42). Tjeder criticised this principle sharply on various grounds.

It was evident that the only kind of production that needed protection was that which was not competitive with foreign products. The consequence of protection, if carried out through import duties or prohibitions, was that the consumer "has to pay more for the commodity than its value" (Tjeder 1826, 42). Moreover, if production were to be stimulated with the help of government subsidies, the result would only be that "one citizen paid taxes to another" (Tjeder 1826, 43). The net result would be a plain welfare loss to the whole nation.

The mercantilist counter-argument against this kind of reasoning was that, even though protected commodities did cost more than corresponding foreign goods, the income received from them at least stayed in the home country and stimulated her economy. However, according to Tjeder, this led to the inefficient use of capital. Capital should not be used to produce commodities that were produced more cheaply in foreign countries. Tjeder appealed to the authority of Smith, Say and Ricardo:

> These writers had proved that it was always most profitable for a country if her producers were engaged in such production in which they succeed better than a foreigner and not in that in which the foreigner succeeds better than they do. (Tjeder 1826, 46)

Even though Tjeder did not formulate his argument in Ricardian terms of comparative advantage, his thoughts seem to have run along the same lines. Prohibitive or protective trade policy makes "national capital unproductive" (Tjeder 1826, 46) by allocating it to sectors in which the country is not internationally competitive. It would be better for a country to have only one profitable production sector than ten sectors with no preconditions for success (Tjeder 1826, 47).

Tjeder criticised advocates of mercantile policy for their lack of comprehension of the totality of the economy. Every producer is also a consumer, he wrote (Tjeder 1826, 49), and therefore the effects of trade policy must be studied on the level of the economy as a whole. Referring to Smith, he argued that the industriousness of society grows only in proportion to the growth of capital, while the growth of capital depends on savings, and savings depend on income. A protective trade policy would thus allocate capital for non-optimal purposes and hamper the growth of the national income and national welfare.

The greatest merit in Tjeder's dissertation was that he brought the ideas of economic liberalism of Smith, Say and Ricardo into Finnish economic literature.[11] He also succeeded in examining

[11] Harmaja 1925, 78.

the economy as a totality of dependent variables such as "national income", "capital" and "welfare",[12] and he made a distinction between state and society, between public finances and the economy as a whole. His own interest was clearly in the last-mentioned: society and the economy. He was not a cameralist, but rather a political economist.[13] It is therefore ironic that, after publishing his dissertation, he spent the rest of his career mostly in state finance and did not fill any academic post.[14]

Cameralist Bias

The "Economic sciences" practised in Finland during the 1810s–1830s have been characterised above as cameralist in spirit. Following the natural historically-oriented economic science of the 18th century, which understood "economy" mostly as practical household economy, state finances became the main object of jurisprudentially-orientated economic studies at the beginning of the 19th century. In the vocabulary of Finnish economic science from the 1810s to the 1830s, "economy" most often referred to state finances in general, and to the public treasury in particular. Economic science was taught in the Faculty of Law, its main aim being to train civil servants to administer public finances.

Although there were strong institutional factors promoting the cameralist approach, its dominance should not be exaggerated. The economy was not understood as only limited to the sphere of public finances. Even in the 18th century, the object of economic science was divided into two, "general economy" and "private economy", or into three as Calonius did in his division of "the science of finance" into "general finance", "crown finance" and "private finance". During the period from the 1810s to the 1830s, new terms were adopted to describe the division of economic science. Instead of "general economy", the word nationalekonomi, "national economy", a translation from the German Nationalökonomie, was taken as the name of both real economy and

[12] Tjeder used the terms "national-inkomsten", "nationens kapital" "nationens välmåga" (Tjeder 1826, 46–47).

[13] Tjeder used the term *statshushållningslära*, literally "doctrine/science of state finances", as the equivalent of "political economy". He described it as "the economic side of political science (statslära)" (Tjeder 1826, 19, 22).

[14] Tjeder worked for short periods as a translator of Russian in various offices (1824–1829), and for a longer period (1829–1842) as a deputy (or assistant) accountant (varalääninkamreeri) in the Chancellery of the Province of Vyborg.

the science of studying it. At the same time, economic science, the "general" part of it, was also called "political science" or "state economy". "State economy", however, was also used in a more limited sense, as a synonym of "cameral science", the object of which was public finances, especially state income.

We may thus conclude that Finnish economic thought followed the German model, in which the new science of Nationalökonomie supplemented and competed with the old cameralism (Tiber 1988). These new ideas came directly from the works of German scholars and via Swedish writers, of whom Lars Georg Rabenius was the foremost. Finnish economic thinkers also referred to British and French authors, but as the 19th century advanced, the influence of German Nationalökonomie grew in importance at the expense of British-type political economy. In the 1820s, a committee making plans for the reorganisation of the academic teaching of economic matters, among other things, plans that were not put into practice in their entirety, took their models from Germany (Björkqvist 1986, 94–95).

As the diffused terminology discussed above suggests, the division between state and society was not made clear in Finnish economic discourse. We might say that economy in general was examined from the point of view of public finances. Therefore, economic concepts analysing the economy as a system differing from the state – concepts such as "value" or "capital" – were seldom used; it was more general to use the cameralist terminology of legislation and public account keeping. There was no use worth mentioning for explicit theories. Finnish economic science did not have much to say about the Finnish economy either; no empirical research was conducted.[15] Finnish economic thinkers were more at home in the normative world of legal texts, administrative instructions and public accounts than in the world of positive economic theories and empirical research. It may be significant that the "mother science" of Finnish economic thinkers during the early decades of the Russian era was not philosophy, which might have encouraged theoretical speculation, but jurisprudence, which focussed attention on judicial and administrative taxonomies of public finance, especially since history or statistics did not yet exist in the form which later enabled them to give stimulus to empirical economic research.

[15] The only exception was Bergbom's dissertation (Bergbom 1820), which contained statistical material, although limited, on prices of "tax commodities", i.e. prices which were used when tax payments in kind were calculated in money terms.

4.3 Johan Vilhelm Snellman – a Finnish Listian

Introduction

Johan Vilhelm Snellman (1806–1881) is best known as a Finnish Hegelian national philosopher. A wide variety of literature on Snellman and his philosophical work[16] exists, but there is no comprehensive evaluation of his writing on economic questions, although one can say that he was one of the most important thinkers and writers during the autonomy period. This study concentrates on the interpretations of Snellman's work as presented by Björkvist (1986), Jahnsson (1907–08) and Harmaja (1925). According to Jahnsson, Snellman's thoughts developed in the direction of economic liberalism until the 1860s, while Harmaja does not identify any extensive changes in his ideas concerning customs policy issues, at least. We will question these interpretations and present Snellman as a nationalist thinker, influenced by List but later guided by practical experience from his own career as the Head of the Office of Financial Matters at the Senate. Snellman turned from a young rebel philosopher and journalist into an elder statesman. We will try to avoid exaggerating his importance as an economist, because after all he is best known for his most influential work as a philosopher, journalist and politician.

Snellman was influenced in his own economic thinking by the German nationalist and romantic economic thinker, Friedrich List (1789–1846). Other writers of influence included List's German contemporaries, Friedrich Schmitthenner and Karl Heinrich Rau, the American Henry C. Carey, and the Swedish professors Lars Rabenius, Per Bergfalk and Jacob Lundell. Friedrich List has been characterised as a man with great vision, and as one of the most important and influential German economic thinkers of all times alongside Karl Marx and Gustav von Schmoller (see e.g. Lenz

[16] Manninen (1984) published a catalogue on Snellman research which covers the time up to 1984. Snellman's economic thought has been examined, for example, by Alf-Halonen (1954), Becker (1905), Björkqvist (1986), Jahnsson (1907–1908), Harmaja (1925), Heinonen (1996b), Patoluoto (1986), Pihkala (1981, 1984 and 1990), Rantakari (1910) and Savolainen (1989). Important sources for studying Snellman's social and political philosophy are the works of Airas (1956), Lehmusto (1923), Manninen (1987), Pulkkinen (1982 and 1989), Teljo (1934) and Wilenius (1978). A good source dealing with Snellman's life and activity is the biography written by Rein (1895 and 1899). We have used the new edition of Snellman's collected works *Samlade arbeten* (Snellman 1992–1998, from now on SA).

Johan Vilhelm Snellman (1806–1881)

1946, 17, Roscher 1874, 978 and Schumpeter 1955, 504). Rather than being a theoretical thinker, however, he was a practical reformer. His infant industry argument[17] has been one of the most powerful justifications for using customs duties to protect developing domestic industry. According to this argument, a country could protect its industry from foreign competition with the help of customs duties, the level of which should be independently determined in every individual case. However, he supported this only until "manufacturing power was strong enough no longer to

[17] On List's influence in European countries, see Wendler (1996). According to Jacob Viner (1937, 71–72) Bindon, Dobbs, Hamilton and Wood had presented the infant-industry argument as early as in the 18th century. From the time before Adam Smith, Viner mentions only five economic thinkers who consistently supported free trade: Gervaise, Jocelyn, North, Paterson and Whatley (Viner 1937, 92).

have any reason to fear foreign competition..." (List 1950, 272). Thus, for List, customs duties were only a provisional weapon to protect the developing industry of a country, and the ideal remained international free trade.

Friedrich List wanted to replace the Smithian theory of value, and suggested instead a theory of productive forces. According to him (List 1950, 322), the productive forces of a nation consisted of all individuals' intellectual and physical forces and the common environment of a society, its institutions, and the natural resources and means of production possessed by the nation. Such means of production were products of former intellectual and physical efforts. Thus, the present and future success of a nation was based on the development of its productive forces rather than on accumulated material wealth. List strongly criticised the views of Adam Smith, J. R. MacCulloch, and especially Jean Baptiste Say. He thought that their ideas were too materialistic and individualistic. List himself described economic development as evolving through successive stages, each characterised by a specific kind of interaction between material forces of production and broader civilisation.[18]

Snellman's Social Philosophy and the Main Features of his Economic Thought

It seems to us that distinguishing between the thinking of the young and the old Snellman may be useful in tracing the development of his economic ideas. He constantly emphasised the gain of the nation and the importance of civilisation in his writings. He was an advocate of the rising force of capitalism. He was a faithful disciple of Hegel, although he did not accept all Hegelian ideas as such. According to Lehmusto (1923, 169), in social and political matters Snellman represented the "right wing of the centre" in the Hegelian school of thought. Hegel was the only German philosopher before Marx who was familiar with British political economy. He had been widely influenced by Adam Smith, Adam Ferguson, John Millar and James Steuart (see Sive-

[18] List received his stage theoretical ideas from 18th-century thinkers (Schumpeter 1955, 505). His stage theory was quite similar to Adam Smith's. Smith developed his ideas of materialistic stages at the same time, in the 1750s, as the French physiocrat Turgot (Meek 1977). Smith identified four stages of development in human history: hunting, pasturage, farming and commerce. Private and state ownership were constituted in the farming stage.

nius 1984, 135; Pulkkinen 1989, 32). He separated the concepts of the state and society as Ferguson and Schlözer did before him (Teljo 1934, 9).

There was a significant difference between Hegel and Snellman: Hegel based his discussion of civil society on the system of needs to express the relationship between the people and the classes: for him, civil society (die bürgerliche Gesellschaft) was society as an economic system, and the state was society seen from an ethical angle (Pulkkinen 1989, 128). Snellman based his concept of civil society on the order of justice (Teljo 1934, 23–26). He suggested that the national spirit was the intermediating factor: this integrated into the state all aspects of social life which were independent of the state's immediate influence. In Snellman's terminology, civil society was a "law-abiding society" (Pulkkinen 1989, 129), and engaged in actions in which private interests rather than individual ethical intentions and autonomy were centrally positioned.[19]

In defence of economic liberalism, Hegel presented an argument according to which an individual had the right to act freely within the economy. This argument also exists in Snellman's writing as an argument for the freedom of industry and trade. Snellman presented a philosophical argument supporting liberalism. He saw the struggle for economic freedom in the context of the wide movement for freedom which advocated as broad an interpretation as possible in the fields of religion, the state and civilisation (Patoluoto 1986, 271). In analysing civil society, Hegel discussed the problem of poverty and pauperism, but did not propose any solution. According to Patoluoto (1986), Snellman attempted to solve the problem.

Snellman was a moderate thinker in his views on social issues. Becker described his economic views as follows: "When discussing economic matters in general Snellman floates high in the air of absolutism but is brought down by his sanity and actual circumstances" (Becker 1905, 207). Many writers – Becker (1905), Teljo (1934) and Pihkala (1981) – have pointed out the roots of Snellman's thought: English and French liberal heirs of Adam Smith on the one hand, and precursors of the German historical school such as Friedrich List on the other. Of the Swedes, Lars Rabenius, Per Bergfalk and Jacob Lundell were of particular influence.

[19] On the differences between Snellman's and Hegel's social theory, see also Pulkkinen (1989, 59–72 and 124–131).

"Young" Snellman looked for general principles to solve economic problems. In the 1840s he concentrated on writing newspaper articles dealing with practical economic questions. Abstract and philosophical Hegelianism was replaced by his own practical reasoning. The tension between universal economic liberalism and the Listian emphasis on national gain was reflected in Snellman's thoughts in an interesting way.

"Young" Snellman: Snellman as a Social Philosopher and Journalist

Snellman travelled to Stockholm in November 1839 after graduating from the University of Helsinki. In Stockholm he actively participated in public discussion and wrote articles for the journal Freja. He met the Swedish journalist Johan Johansson,[20] who seems to have influenced his thoughts (Manninen 1976, 280). He published two articles: *Nationalekonomi* (SA I, 328–331) and *Individens förhållande till lagen* ("An Individual's Relationship to the Law") (SA I, 354–357). The articles were labelled by their Listian views, although it would be too hasty to jump to the conclusion that Snellman was an unreserved Listian only on that basis. Listian influence is recognisable, but List was not the only theorist who had those kinds of ideas (Patoluoto 1986, 299).

Snellman's first article deals with Johansson's translation of List's book (List 1850a, see also Manninen 1976). Snellman followed Listian ideas opposing the Swedish Customs Committee that had supported freedom of trade (SA I, 328–331). He emphasised the importance of developing national manufacturing, twice citing List:

> Prof. List, a man who had to leave his country because of his liberal thoughts and action, openly declared his conviction that "the Colbertian system" extended by wisdom and insight could "through reforms" have been able to influence "the formation of public liberty" in such a way, that "France had not experienced any revolution". (SA I, 330)

He continues on the following page:

> We confess our embarrassment upon the statement that in the latter writing (Införselsfrihet och Skyddsförfattningar)

[20] Johansson was a supporter of Listian ideas and translated List's works into Swedish.

> the free North America is seen as a state which has mostly suffered from the unavoidable consequences of free trade. The truthfulness of Prof. List's knowledge and his ability to evaluate circumstances in a country, where he has spent years in exile, cannot be suspected. (SA I, 330)

In the other article, *Individens förhållande till lagen* (Law and the Individual) Snellman appraises Johansson's translation of List's book that was published in Swedish under the title *Om vigten och betydelsen af slöjder och manufakturer för ett samhälle* ("On the Weight and Importance of Home and Manufacturing Industries for a Society") (List [1840], 1850b). His support for Listian ideas[21] is again quite clear. His only remark concerning the translation was his own formulation of the "basic principle of the public finances" presented by the translator in the preface of the book (see List 1840, XII and Snellman SA I, 356).

Snellman connected List's work with the criticism of the absolute position of the police and economic legislation, which, according to him, was the main message. In his article Snellman also wrote: "This work of Professor List includes a number of general conclusions. These are based on facts which he has mentioned in the book *Införselsfrihet och skyddsförfattningar* (Freedom of Import and Protection Codes) that has been translated earlier. Thus one should read both books together." (SA I, 357.)

When he came back to Stockholm from his Central European study tour, Snellman prepared his principal work, *Läran om staten* ("A Treatise on the State") (SA III, 298–498). Published in 1842, this book presents Snellman's philosophical defence of liberalism as the basis of his claim for freedom of trade and industry (Teljo 1934, 105). However, he did not consistently take a liberal stand.

Economic issues are dealt with especially in chapter 38 (SA III, 387–391) of the book. Snellman maintained that national independence also paved the way for economic independence. He analysed the following representatives of various schools of economic thought: the mercantilists Mun, Child and Davenant, the physiocrat Quesnay, the founder of the "theory of industrial systems"[22] Adam Smith, and Jean Baptiste Say. Following Friedrich

[21] Jahnsson (1907–08) and Harmaja (1925) have also pointed out Snellman's Listianism in this context, but they did not mention the exact references.

[22] This term was presented by the German economic thinker Schmitthenner.

List, Snellman heavily criticised the Smithian theory of value.[23] He emphasised the fact that free trade presupposed that the trading nations were on an equal level of economic development (compare List 1950, 213). He felt that the mercantilistic justification of protectionism as a source of state income was invalid, and that it was only the protection of domestic industry by the imposition of customs duties that was justified.

Snellman's Listian infant-industry view may come from the German thinker Friedrich Schmitthenner[24] (1796–1850), who was List's contemporary and shared many of his opinions. The main difference between List and Schmitthenner was primarily that Schmitthenner attempted to formulate a general social theory in his main work, *Zwölf Bücher vom Staate oder systematische Encyklopädie der Staatswissenschaften* – the first part was published in 1839 – while List restricted his own examination to the economy. Another difference linked with foreign trade was that List saw a possibility for free trade in the future, while, according to Schmitthenner, "general free trade is only an ideal, like everlasting peace" (Snellman SA III, 390–391; see also Patoluoto 1986, 284, and Roscher 1874). Thus, Snellman approvingly quoted Schmitthenner. This gives reason to believe that he agreed with Schmitthenner and saw free trade only as a theoretical possibility and as a utopia. It is rather surprising that Snellman did not mention List at all in his *Läran om staten*.[25]

[23] List wanted to replace the Smithian theory of value with his own theory of productive forces.

[24] Schmitthenner is historically positioned between Adam Müller and Friedrich List by Wilhelm Roscher (1874). He represented German nationalist and romantic thinking. Snellman also referred to Karl Pölitz (1772–1838) as a source of influence. The unoriginal social thinker Pölitz was a writer of lesser importance (Roscher 1874, 841).

[25] According to Jahnsson (1907–08, 256) the reason was that Snellman was not yet familiar with List's main work *Das nationale System der politischen Oekonomie* (List 1950), originally published in 1841. This is likely. Perhaps more important was the fact that List had already begun to develop his ideas on protection in his earlier works *Outlines of American Political Economy*, published in 1827 during his stay in the United States, and *Das natürliche System der politischen Oekonomie*, published in 1837. I am grateful to Professor Erkki Pihkala for pointing out that in 1845, shortly before his death, List was attacked by an anonymous writer in *Oberpostamtszeitung*. The writer claimed that List was not an original writer at all but had copied Professor Schmitthenner's ideas in his main publication (Häusser 1850, 359–361). This false charge was very grave. List, whose health was deteriorating at the time, took it seriously. However, there is some reason to believe that the

On the basis of *Läran om staten* and the journal articles, Snellman could be characterised as a potential Listian thinker. He continued his journalist's career after returning to Finland in 1842. He worked as the headmaster of a school in Kuopio, and as editor of the journals Maamiehen Ystävä ("Farmers Friend") and Saima. (Rein 1895, 259–404.)

Snellman published a series of articles in his journal Saima (Snellman SA IV, 60–70), in which he discussed whether Finland could have an export industry and large-scale industry serving the domestic market. He was sceptical with regard to the possibilities of a Finnish export industry. He quoted the German economist Karl Heinrich Rau[26] (1792–1879), who divided the productive forces into capital, labour and natural resources. Finland was abundant with the last-mentioned, and only lacked the machines, skilled labour and a financial system (SA IV, 62). The creation of industry was only possible with the help of import restrictions or high customs duties. It was Snellman's view that the disadvantages to consumers and merchants that resulted from the imposition of customs duties limited the popularity of manufacturing and industry. However, it was difficult to assess the optimum position of customs or restrictions (SA IV, 63). This seems a rather Listian, view and can be interpreted as promoting the infant-industry argument.

Snellman had a debate with the journal Borgå Tidning early in 1845. He had expressed his opinion that exports and imports had to be in balance in his own journal, Saima. He wrote three articles on the issue: *Lyx och import* ("Luxury and Imports"), *Lyxen och tullen* ("Luxury and Customs Duties") and *Kan tullen reglera handelsbalansen?* ("Can Customs Regulate the Balance of Trade?") (SA IV, 456–458, 475–476, 495–498). In his first article, Snellman argued that his contemporary economists approved of restrictions to free trade being imposed only to protect domestic industry, or as taxation to get money for the state. Thus, he maintained that the views expressed in Borgå Tidning against free

truth could have been the opposite: List had begun to develop his ideas in the United States in the 1820s. One thing is certain. As a university professor, Schmitthenner was a much higher authority than the political activist, journalist and rebel Friedrich List. Yet, if we accept the view that List was the original father of the system of protection, we are quite near the conclusion that Snellman's real authority on the issue was actually Friedrich List. List committed suicide in 1846.

26 According to Roscher (1874, 851), Rau was a follower of Adam Smith, but as a young man he used to be "close to the historical school".

trade and the import of luxury items were old-fashioned protectionism. He did not think luxury was to be condemned as such. It is possible that he had in mind a division between useful and harmful luxury.

In his second article *Lyxen och tullen* ("Luxury and Customs", SA IV, 475–476), Snellman explicitly denied that he relied on the ideas of the economic liberalists in the issue of free trade. He emphasised that he had nothing against customs that were aimed at protecting domestic industry or state finances (SA IV, 476).

Snellman published excerpts of one chapter of List's *Das nationale System der politischen Oekonomie* in the journal Saima, issue numbers 44 and 45 in 1846, originally titled *Die Manufacturkraft und die persönlichen, socialen und politischen Produktivkräft*' (List 1950, 294–306). Ilkka Patoluoto (1986) assumed that the introduction of the article was written by Snellman, and also claimed that the text had been translated by him, although it is not totally identical with List's original.

Snellman's introductory words are as follows:

> During this time of finding solutions to the problems of making sure that a country's expanding intellectual and material culture will promote the national good, which is one of the issues of the day, and is close to the hearts of our statesmen and patriots, we think we can give joy to the reading public by focusing on an issue which foreign economists and thinkers have already clarified. It is with this in mind that I would like to present the meritorious work of Dr. List from the German Customs Union, "Das nationale System der politischen Oekonomie".
>
> The writer explains in the introduction his most pressing reasons for publishing this work. His theoretical knowledge no less than his practical experience had convinced him that the usefulness of the theses he imposed on his readers lay in their references to the nature of things. He gives a historical review of agricultural and industrial journal articles covering the rise and subsequent fall of the culture and well-being of the higher strata of the population. He then paints a convincing picture of the shortcomings of the founders of the older political and economic systems, especially Adam Smith. The misguided aspects of these systems disappeared, and the useful ones survived, and the writer puts forward his own historically-based theories for this. He presents his views in an accessible and understandable way.

This is followed by a translation of List's original text. It all seems to be rather strong evidence of Snellman's interest in List and, combined with the views presented in the journal articles, also of Listian influence on him.

The authorities decided to prohibit the publishing of the journal Saima in 1846. The main reason for this seems to have been the rather radical views about the problem of poverty expressed on its pages. The Governor of Vyborg County, Baron von Kothen, was especially irritated with the radicalism expressed in Saima. (Rein 1895, 503–511.) However, Snellman carried on his journalist writing and started a new journal, *Litteraturblad för allmän medborgerlig bildning* ("A Literary Newspaper for the General Civilian Education of Citizens") in May, 1847. The tightening of censorship signified new limitations on journalism: articles dealing with political and socially important issues were not allowed to be published.

In 1849, Snellman published an interesting small article, *Om små nationers handel och industri* ("On the Trade and Industry of Small Nations", SA VI, 599–610), in his new journal, Litteraturblad. He gave a prediction according to which the products of agriculture, home industries and animal husbandry would, in the future, be even more important as export articles of the Finnish economy than the products of forestry (SA IV, 604–605).

Snellman was appointed professor of philosophy at the University of Helsinki in 1856. His journalist's career was overshadowed by his new duties as a university instructor, and thus he did not write as much as previously. However, his Listian influence can be perceived in his commentary on the statement the authorities had issued concerning the potential of the Finnish iron industry, published in the Litteraturblad in 1858 (Snellman 1895, 370–380). According to Snellman, most iron products in Finland were produced abroad, and the Finnish iron industry had been based on the iron ore imported from Sweden. The customs duty, which increased the price of iron, was meant to exist only until the domestic production of iron had become established. Thus, it seems that Snellman supported the infant-industry argument. He continued by mentioning that the most severe obstacles to the development of the Finnish economy were the backwardness of the monetary institutions and the transportation network, the ever-changing economic and customs legislation, and the customs-free import of manufactured products from Russia when Finland did not have the same privilege on the Russian market (Snellman 1895, 371–372).

The writings of the US economist Henry C. Carey (1793–1879) were given considerable attention by Finnish economists in the mid-19th century. Carey himself based his support of protectionism on Listian ideas. Snellman also commented on Carey, and in 1849 had already appraised the Swedish translation of Carey's book *Past, Present and Future* (Carey 1849–1851) in Litteraturblad. In his appraisal he dealt mainly with Carey's criticism of the Ricardian theory of rent. Eleven years later, he reviewed a translation of another book by Carey (*North American Politics and its Effects on the People and the Affairs of the State*). Snellman wrote:

> If the manufacturing industry is not successful without the imposition of high customs duties when, at the same time, agriculture does not need them, it is evidence of the superiority of the latter, which means that more capital and labour must be invested in it... When there is no fruitful wilderness anymore in the United States, people will turn to another kind of agriculture, which will increase production costs and decrease profits. Capital and labour will then also move over to manufacturing. (SA IX, 320.)

Thus, according to Snellman, the time was not ripe for a manufacturing industry boom in Finland: the resources should be reallocated to industry as profits from agriculture diminished. He thought that the former supporter of free trade, Carey, ended up as a protectionist partly because of the slavery question in the United States – the southern states promoting slavery and free trade.

Snellman's career as a Senator began in the 1860s. As the head of the office of financial matters, he first saw through monetary reform, and then struggled during the famine years of 1867–1868. His solution to the monetary problems, as well as his theoretical thoughts, are presented in detail in Chapter 5. It is enough to say here that he was quite well acquainted with the theoretical aspects of these questions, and his solutions revealed his philosophically-oriented thinking.

Snellman as a Finnish Listian

We have emphasised the influence of List on young Snellman, and the growing pragmatism of his views as the Head of the Office of Financial Matters in the Senate. It seems that Snellman was influenced both by Listian ideas of economic development and by Smithian views received through Hegel. Jahnsson (1907–08) proposed that Snellman's stand was shifting towards liberalism until 1860. This view is not very tenable. We might rather say that Snellman's views did not change extensively, but that the general orientation of economic policy shifted slightly towards increased liberalism during the régime of Alexander II. Thus, the social and economic background changed gradually in the direction that Snellman aimed at. He himself practised some pragmatism as the Head of the Office of Financial Matters. This is reflected, for example, in his rather cameralist concern about the balance of state finances. Klinge (1975, 16–17) has characterised Snellman as a combiner of national and social thinking, who was in opposition during the rule of Nicholas I and in the government during the reign of the more liberal-minded Emperor Alexander II in the 1860s. This characterisation is quite an apt overall appraisal of Snellman.

Snellman's hovering between economic liberalism and some form of state intervention is seen in his position towards liberalism: the reductionist idea of taking the individual as a starting point when talking about society was theoretically very disagreeable to him, although he agreed with almost every social demand of the Liberals of his age (Pulkkinen 1989, 45). Thus, on the one hand, he supported civic freedom, freedom of the press and abolition of the guild system and trade restrictions, and followed the liberal tradition in this respect. On the other hand, a strong state was an essential feature of his political philosophy. He saw possibilities for state intervention in managing economic life though temporarily carrying out a customs policy, which did not apply to exports, and taxing the wealthier classes to provide training and social security for old age among the wider population (Pulkkinen 1989, 16). However, he was aware of the possible growth of pauperism as a result of growing economic freedom, and thus of the need for a social policy. The liberal features of Snellman's thought seem to be manifested most clearly in his work in carrying out the liberal monetary reform in the 1860s. Altogether, his liberalism seems to have been rather instrumental.

The character of Snellman's writings dealt with in this context differs in several aspects. His book *Läran om staten* ("A Theory of the State") was an academic piece of work written for the academic audience, while the articles published in the press were addressed to wider circles. His statements in the Senate were addressed to the other senators.

Although Snellman did not declare himself a Listian, List's influence on his economic thinking was obvious. Pihkala's (1981, 43) conclusion thus seems to be right: Snellman's economic thought was a mixture of Friedrich List's and Adam Smith's ideas pragmatically applied to the Finnish circumstances. In this respect he was not alone. He did not write any independent economic treatise, and most of his views were expressed in his journalistic writings. It seems that he himself considered his philosophical work central and most important, and was interested in the practice of economic policy rather than in the theoretical issues.

4.4 Between Economic Nationalism and Liberalism

Axel Liljenstrand

Axel Wilhelm Liljenstrand (1821–1895) has been classified as a student of legal history by Klami (1977, 22).[27] This classification is based on the historical character of the main works written by Liljenstrand, and on his activity as a university teacher. He was appointed to the new Professorship of Economic Law and Economic Studies in 1857, and held the post for 20 years. He was an important person because he was responsible for the teaching of economic science at the university, and he wrote the first Finnish text book on the subject. However, he cannot be credited with having produced any genuine and independent contributions to economic theory.

Axel Liljenstrand passed his matriculation examination in 1836. He became Master of Arts in 1844 and Master of Laws in 1847. He practised in the legal profession and took the post of secretary in the Senate in 1849. He then travelled to Germany, France and England in 1850–1851 to familiarise himself with the European streams of economic thought. In 1851 he presented his licentiate thesis on the influence of canonical law in Swedish legislation. Two years later, together with Frans Edvard Florin, he applied for the new chair and wrote his doctoral dissertation (Liljenstrand 1853), but was declared unqualified and was only given a lectureship. His second dissertation in support of a professorship *Om Finlands strömrensningsverk* ("On the cleaning of Rivers in Fin-

[27] I think that the characterizations of Liljenstrand by Harmaja (1925) and Björkqvist (1986, 295) as a strict and convinced liberal are exaggerated. More justifiable is Jahnsson's (1907–08, 402–403) view according to which Liljenstrand was a liberal who had been influenced by the historical school.

land") failed as well. He managed to get his professorship after having submitted a third dissertation (Liljenstrand 1857).[28] Liljenstrand resigned his office at the university in 1877. He continued to write and to participate in the public discussion in the press.

Axel Liljenstrand's doctoral dissertation (Liljenstrand 1853) is interesting from the perspective of the development of his economic views. In the first part he dealt with economic science and its history. His most important source on the history of economic thought was the Frenchman Jérôme Adolphe Blanqui's (1798–1854) *Histoire de l'économie politique en Europe.* Following the mainstream of European economic thought during the late 1840s and 1850s, and probably as a result of his European tour in 1850–51, he highly regarded the ideas of the French economic liberalists Michel Chevalier (1806–1879), Joseph Garnier (1813–1881), and especially Frédéric Bastiat (1801–1850). He wrote: "it is through Bastiat economic science (National-Ekonomin) has gained in harmony and completeness, and has gained ground, even if his philosophical reflections sometimes uncover a certain Kantian dualism characteristic of French study" (Liljenstrand 1853, 22). Bastiat was well known as a strong advocate of free trade and economic liberalism. His work *Les harmonies économiques* was published in Paris in 1851.

Bastiat appreciated Adam Smith as the founder of economic science, and his French follower Jean Baptiste Say, who gave more scientific grounds to the Smithian doctrines. Liljenstrand criticised the Ricardian theory of rent, and based his criticism on the arguments of the American economic writer Henry Charles Carey. Liljenstrand respected Carey, who had added "important truths" to the theory.

An important detail is Liljenstrand's high appreciation of Friedrich List, whom he even considered one of the most remarkable contemporary economists (Liljenstrand 1853, 6). On the issue of freedom of trade, Liljenstrand wrote:

> Without wishing to deny that suitable protective customs can be justified and necessary at certain times, we cannot examine this necessity otherwise than as temporary or as noteworthy careful nursing. (Liljenstrand 1853, 7.)

[28] Liljenstrand's rivals for the office were doctors *Knut Ferdinand Lagus* (1824–1859) and *Johan Wilhelm Rosenborg* (1823–1871). The former died soon after and the latter was appointed Professor of Cameral and Public Legislation. He wrote about the problems of the rural proletariat for example, and was a supporter of economic liberalism.

Axel Liljenstrand (1821–1895)

Liljestrand's view was not far from the Listian infant-industry argument. He warned his readers about the idleness and unwillingness that lay hidden behind the protective customs duties, but his justification of temporary trade protection gives us a reason to interpret him as a potential Listian, or at least to note the tension in his thinking. Thus, Björkqvist's (1986, 295, 304) view of Liljenstrand as "a convinced liberalist" is somewhat too exacerbated. Liljenstrand's views should rather be seen against the background of strongly centralised bureaucracy and very limited economic and other freedom in the Grand Duchy of Finland in the 1840s during the rather reactionary rule of Nicholas I.

Axel Liljenstrand published the first Finnish economic textbook (Liljenstrand 1860) only a few years after being appointed to the professorship. Over 50 pages of the book are dedicated to an account of the history of economic thought, and supporters of various schools are listed. John Stuart Mill's (1806–1873) work *Principles of Political Economy* is cited in several places, and

Adam Smith is given credit for his original and independent theoretical system. Other British economists and their works that Liljenstrand mentioned include James Mill (1773–1836) and his *Elements of Political Economy*, Nassau Senior (1790–1879), who had published *An Outline of the Science of Political Economy* in 1836, and John R. MacCulloch (1789–1864), whose *The Principles of Political Economy and A Dictionary Practical, Theoretical and Historical of Commerce and Commercial Navigation* he thought worthy of mention.

Again, he repeated his appreciation of the French liberalists, especially Jean Baptiste Say as "a refiner of Smithian ideas", and Frédéric Bastiat as "a French defender of free trade". Liljenstrand thought highly of Bastiat's battle for free trade, and mentioned his book *Cobden et la ligue* as an example. He explicitly wished success to French supporters of freedom of trade[29] (Liljenstrand 1860, 81).

Liljenstrand considered protectionism a relic of the old system of mercantilism (Liljenstrand 1860, 40). His appreciation of Friedrich List seems to be summed up in the following quotation:

> List, who was quite well-appreciated during his lifetime, was in one way a supporter of the mercantilist system, because he tried to show that protective customs were necessary for all nations with no developed industry. (Liljenstrand 1860, 62.)

However, Liljenstrand did not see the Listian difference between infant-industry protection and ordinary protectionism. He named Wilhelm Roscher (1817–1894), the founder of the German historical school, as the most influential German economist, and even said that Roscher had "abandoned the above-mentioned approach in his praiseworthy work recently published" (Liljenstrand 1860, 62). Although Liljenstrand was somewhat unclear, he presumably meant the British classical economists. Roscher's *Grundriss zu Vorlesungen über die Staatswirtschaft nach geschichtlicher Methode* was published in 1843, and the first volume of the System der Volkswirtschaft in 1854.

Axel Liljenstrand gave two examples of the protectionist economists of his age. The first was the above-mentioned H. C. Carey,

[29] Liljenstrand's wish soon came true: In 1860 England and France concluded the so-called Cobden – Chevalier Treaty, which was the symbolic victory of the free trade supporters in the 19th century.

who had apparently become as keen a supporter of protectionism as he was of free trade before. The other was the German Karl Marlo[30]. Liljenstrand's own stand on the issue of the freedom of trade remained somewhat unclear, since he came up with a rather Listian formulation, drawing a parallel between the freedom of trade and civilisation:

> ...free trade, which is an inseparable part of a true civilisation. But it is no more arbitrary than freedom in general. Moreover, this is not the same as freedom from all customs duties, as many people think. (Liljenstrand 1860, 82–83.)

He did not specify his view of freedom of trade. What else could it be, if not the absence of customs?

In a rather long list of economic treatises, he (1860, 83–87) mentioned the works of Smith, Say, Ricardo, Malthus, MacCulloch, von Soden, Storch, Rabenius, List, H. C. Carey, Mill, Rau and Roscher, among others. Such a well-informed literary survey was not common in those days.

Although Liljenstrand criticised mercantilist thought in several connections, and supported the French economic liberalists, he also recognised the need for an historical approach in the study (Jahnsson 1907–08, 392). Compared with the foreign models, his liberalism was rather moderate and could be interpreted as influenced by the mainstream economic thought in the mid-19th century, especially in England and France. He was not at all systematic, and did not produce any genuine independent contributions. His text book was sympathetically reviewed by J.V. Snellman, however.[31]

It must be remembered that Liljenstrand was a lawyer, and his main area was economic law. However, he gave a lecture course in economic science shortly after being appointed to the professorship in 1858–59. He began another lecture series in 1862, this

[30] Karl Marlo's true name was *Karl Georg Winkelblech* (1810–1865). He was a chemist and held a professorship in Kassel from 1839. He had published his main work *Untersuchungen über die Organisation der Arbeit oder System der Weltökonomie* in 1850–58. Winkelblech was a supporter of protectionism in trade policy, and of state intervention in the economy. He had received some ideas from the socialists and tried to develop an intermediate stand between liberalism, mercantilism and socialism. (Björkqvist 1986, 310–311.) According to Marlo, mercantilists emphasized nationality too much, while liberalists exaggerated cosmopolitanism (Liljenstrand 1860, 62).

[31] Snellman 1860.

time following the French economist Joseph Clément Garnier's (1813–1881) book *Traité d'économie politique*, first published in 1846. Later he gave lectures on topical issues surrounding French and English theories of free trade. (Björkqvist 1986, 317.)

Liljenstrand participated in the controversy over liberalism in the press in the 1870s. He responded to the critique of economic liberalism of Axel Fredrik Granfelt (1815–1892), Professor of Dogmatics and Moral Philosophy. Granfelt was a Swedish-speaking supporter of the rising Fennoman movement. A series of his articles (Granfelt 1873) was published in the newspaper Morgonbladet,[32] in which he aimed his critique at the Manchester school. He heavily criticised the theories of economic liberalism presented by Adam Smith and Frédéric Bastiat. His criticism was largely ethical, since he did not approve of Smith's and Bastiat's idea of basing an economic system on pure egoism.

Liljenstrand criticised Granfelt in an article (Liljenstrand 1873) published in the journal of the Juridiska Föreningen i Finland.[33] He claimed that the internal disagreements within economic science arose from a false interpretation of liberalism. As he put it, "immature ideas of free competition" had resulted in ignorance of agriculture, the birth of 'unnatural" industries, and even trade wars (Liljenstrand 1873, 151). He again mentioned his idol Frédéric Bastiat at the end of the article.

The above-mentioned tension between the Listian and historical perspective and economic liberalism in Liljenstrand's thinking is again perceivable in his other article (Liljenstrand 1878–79), published in the same forum as the first. Liljenstrand described the meeting arranged to honour the hundred-year anniversary of the publication of Adam Smith's work *The Wealth of Nations* in London at the Political Economy Club in May 1876. The English pioneer of neoclassical economics, William Stanley Jevons (1835–1882), was one of the speakers. Liljenstrand made a methodological commitment in this article. He openly opposed the Jevonsian bisection into inductive and deductive inquiry, and Jevons' wish to separate these methods strictly from one another. Liljenstrand

[32] Björkqvist 1986, 334. The newspaper Morgonbladet was published in 1872–84 in Helsinki, and it was the organ of Swedish-speaking educated Fennomans. Its chief editor was August Hagman.

[33] Juridiska Föreningen, the Finnish Association of Lawyers, was founded in 1862 as the second Finnish professional society (Konttinen 1991, 256). Its journal *Juridiska Föreningen i Finlands Tidning* was founded in 1865, and published articles mainly on issues concerning the interpretation of the law (Konttinen 1991, 227).

seemed to think that both inductive and deductive methods were always needed. He stressed the fact that Adam Smith had based his own inquiry on rich historical experience (Liljenstrand 1878–79, 306).

According to Liljenstrand, the use of the sentence "laissez passer, laissez faire" was damaging. He emphasised the fact that the sentence was used by physiocrats and not by Smith (Liljenstrand 1878–1879, 309):

> Every day, scientific theories of freedom are often confused with individual disadvantage. When an economist recommends freedom of trade, do many people understand that the customs institution, and even all taxes, have to be abolished, although the same people in no way drop their demands for a share in every benefit that society provides through taxes. (Liljenstrand 1878–79, 310–311.)

He then went on to suggest that an examination of the historical facts on the basis of a nation's political situation and cultural development as well as the development of its legislation would be appropriate if it was based on political economy (Liljenstrand 1878–1879, 313). Björkqvist (1986, 338) exaggerated this by claiming that Liljenstrand had introduced the Jevonian marginalist theory to Finland, and only briefly commented on Jevons' words spoken at the Adam Smith anniversary.

This seems to be quite clear evidence of the fact that Liljenstrand was in no way a supporter of extreme forms of liberal ideas. Although he took liberal positions on many questions concerning economic legislation, his methodological statements support the view that he was a thinker influenced by the historical methodology of his age. It must always be remembered that the bulk of his writings are classified as legal history, and economic science was only his secondary concern.

In his third article (Liljenstrand 1875) he presented his views on questions of taxation. He felt that taxation in the form of customs duties had had harmful effects on industrial freedom (Liljenstrand 1875, 270). As he saw it, the advantages of customs duties and other indirect taxes were in the free choice of the time of payment, and in the incidence of taxation: the tax was to be paid by consumers.

Soon after having resigned from the professorship Liljenstrand published his second book (Liljenstrand 1880), a legal study of the legislation surrounding credit and its development. It was almost entirely legal in character and can be classified as a study of legal history. Liljenstrand was not an independent or genuine economic thinker, although his first Finnish textbook of economic science made a significant contribution. It is an exaggeration to claim that he was the first Finnish scholar who knew English economic literature (Klami 1977, 58). Michaël Tjeder[34] before him had mentioned Smith, Ricardo and John Nickols, and classical economic thought was frequently referred to by Daniel Myréen, Johan Jakob Nordström and Johan Vilhelm Snellman, among others.

Axel Liljenstrand was responsible for the teaching of economic science at the Faculty of Law for twenty years. However, he was more a historian of law than an economist. The naivety of his views and shallowness of his knowledge sometimes shone through. However, his interest in economic issues must be acknowledged. He died in 1895 at the age of 74.

Two Practical Liberalists: Reinhold Frenckell and Henrik Borgström

In the late 1850s and early 1860s, ideas of economic liberalism were propagated with a vigour not seen before. Outside the academic world there were practically-oriented thinkers with a business background promoting liberalist ideas. The most prominent of these were Reinhold Frenckell and Henrik Borgström Jr., both of whom are to be counted among the so-called Dagblad circle, named after the leading liberal newspaper Helsingfors Dagblad, founded in 1862.

Otto Reinhold Frenckell (1823–1880) was the son of a businessman who owned a printing house and later also a paper mill. He ran the family firm in 1844–1856 before leaving it to his brother and concentrating on public affairs. He became the first editor of Helsingfors Dagblad (1862–1863), a member of the board of the Mortgage association in 1860, and its chairman in 1863, when he was also appointed a director of the only commercial bank in the country (Föreningsbanken). He changed roles in 1866, and the businessman was transformed into a civil servant, becoming a member of the board of the Bank of Finland. He became the first general director of the State Treasury in 1879 (Blomstedt 1976, 157; Björkqvist 1986, 325; Pipping 1961, 432).

[34] However, Liljenstrand did not mention Tjeder in his textbook (Liljenstrand 1860).

Otto Reinhold Frenckell (1823–1880)

Henrik Borgström Jr. (1830–1865)

As an economic thinker, or writer, Frenckell was most active at the turn of the 1850s and 1860s. In 1858 he published a book on the Paris stock exchange, its history and organisation, and a more theoretical work dealing with industrial labour and its relation to national wealth in 1860. The inspiration for both works came from the current problems and plans surrounding business life and economic policy. Not surprisingly, both were published and printed by the family firm.

The book on the Paris stock exchange was the result of Frenckell's visit to Paris. He gave a short history of the exchange and described its functioning. It is probable that existing plans to establish a stock exchange in Helsinki was one reason for Frenckell's interest.[35] He clearly saw the stock exchange as an institution contributing to economic development by increasing the circulation of capital, although he settled for putting forward only "positive facts and explanations", and leaving readers to "draw conclusions of a national-economic kind themselves" (Frenckell 1858, iv).

While Frenckell's book on the stock exchange was a descriptive

[35] The stock exchange was established in Helsinki only in 1912.

empirical presentation, his second work on industrial labour had more of the flavour of economic theory. However, this was not a theoretical work in the strict sense of the word either, but rather like an essay utilising, and extensively quoting, international economic literature. The impact of Frenckell's stay in Paris is again evident in that he referred most frequently to the works of French economists such as Jean Baptist Say and Michel Chevalier. Adam Smith and other British writers were also frequently quoted.

Frenckell's book on industrial labour was divided into eight chapters dealing with the necessity for labour, the freedom, definition and division of labour, wages, commodity prices, profits and the progress and power of labour. The most extensive chapter was devoted to the freedom of labour. There, Frenckell distinctly argued against the restrictions imposed, and against a protectionist customs policy as well. In both respects, and although he discussed the question on a general level and with the help of international literature, Frenckell dealt with matters that were highly topical in Finland. In the late 1850s, when the book was written, freedom of trade was still largely restricted, while the liberalising process had already begun in the tariff policy. Thus, Frenckell's work might be considered an address in a contemporary discussion dealing with fundamental questions of the future of the Finnish economy. As mentioned above, he in no way hid his liberalist faith in the beneficial effects of economic freedom and competition, and he defined economic studies (nationalekonomi) as the "science of material interests" (Frenckell 1860, 197). He called his concluding chapter "The progress and power of labour", and ended it with the following optimistic statement: "Everything must be done to improve the productive power of industrial labour in order to create a bigger and bigger capital base, with the help of which social welfare can gradually be realised" (Frenckell 1860, 242).

Practical businessmen have often played a significant intellectual role, alongside academic scholars, in monetary and banking issues. In this respect, Finland follows the international tradition. Henrik Borgström, Jr., born in 1830, was a good example of a businessman interested in economic issues. As the son of an influential commercial counsellor and a wealthy owner of a merchant house he was quite well aware of the regularities of business life. Financial security enabled him to undergo versatile academic training (M.A. 1853, Master of Laws 1857). His study tour to France and Scotland, and working in the newly-established Stockholms Enskilda Bank, complemented his theoretical studies.

Borgström's career remained short, however, because he died in an accident at the age of 35 years in 1865. Thus, his work with monetary and banking policy issues lasted for less than a decade. However, his achievements were noteworthy.[36]

He was well known as a founder-member of the liberal discussion group that was the starting point of the so-called "Dagblad circle" during the 1860s. These supporters of economic liberalism had as their organ the newspaper Helsingfors Dagblad, founded in 1862. They were followers of the Smithian tradition represented by French scholars such as Jean Baptiste Say and Michel Chevalier, and transmitted to Finland through Sweden. This group actively directed attention to questions of constitutional law as well as to economic issues.

Borgström participated in the rather heated discussion on monetary and banking in the late 1850s. He was among the most active debaters with J. V. Snellman, Otto Reinhold Frenckell and Ernst Linder. While Snellman came from academic circles, Frenckell, Linder and Borgström were independent intellectuals. The debaters focused on questions concerning the establishment of private banks, and on the problems caused to the Finnish monetary system by the fact that the Russian rouble abandoned the metallic standard (Pipping 1928).

Henrik Borgström Jr. crystallised his views in his two books on mortage associations and private banks (Borgström 1858 and 1859). The second one was partly made up of newspaper articles written in preceding years. His starting point was free competition in business and banking. "State officials do not have such special know-how or training that they can handle the banking business better than private businessmen. If the securities needed for establishing a bank are available, the concession should not be refused." (Borgström 1859, 129)

He saw economic activity as a totality, where everything influences everything. Analysis of economic conditions and arriving at a reliable conclusion requires wide-ranging real-time information on conditions in the most important sectors such as agriculture, manufacturing, foreign trade and monetary transaction. On the other hand, this kind of information requires the availability of systematic annual statistics based on scientific inquiry.

Borgström Jr.'s influence was central to the planning and organising of private banking in Finland. As was seen above, he also played a crucial role in the preparations for the monetary reform

[36] Kansallinen elämäkerrasto I Osa A-E, 1927.

of the 1860s, such as through his influence on Fabian Langenskiöld who was in charge of fiscal affairs in the Senate as the preparations for the reform began. Against this background, it is interesting to note in passing how he motivated his suggestions and on what intellectual sources he drew.

He opposed the existing paper rouble standard on two grounds. First, relying on well-known liberal arguments, he insisted that a paper standard undermined the overall stability of the monetary conditions by subjecting them to the vagaries of civil servants. Second, he pointed to the fact that the existing attachment to the Russian paper standard subjected the monetary conditions in Finland to developments in Russia, which were often unstable and did not reflect the underlying economic developments in Finland.

From these starting points, Borgström came to two main conclusions. First, Finland should create its own currency tied to silver, and second, although minting silver could be left as the monopoly of the Bank of Finland (central bank), private banks should also be given the right to issue notes, convertible to silver. (Borgström 1859)

In arguing for these views, Borgström relied on short references to a rather extensive list of contemporary monetary analyses, mostly English and French, but he was also well aware of Nordström's book on credit issues (Nordström 1853). Among his main sources, Michel Chevalier stands out with his work *La Monnaie* (1853), but he also cited James Mill (through a French translation from 1823), Adam Smith and MacCulloch. In defence of the right of private banks to issue notes, he drew on critiques of the Currency school, including Thomas Tooke, John Stuart Mill, who was not well known in Finland at the time, as well as McCulloch. Notwithstanding the fact that his references were mostly brief, they provided evidence that Borgström Jr. was well aware of contemporary monetary thought. His organisational skills were taken into use when the first commercial bank in Finland was launched, a process with which he had become acquainted while working in the Stockholm Enskilda Bank in Sweden. It was undoubtedly his early death that prevented him from leaving an even more weighty imprint on intellectual and business life in the latter half of 19th-century Finland.

In the late 1850s and early 1860s Borgström had a disagreement with Snellman on the causes of the current depression. According to Snellman, the economic imbalance was caused by excessive imports and the Bank of Finland had no reason to alleviate the situation. Borgström considered this as an attack on private business. He was of the opinion that the depression had several exceptional causes, which had led to the excess of imports. Therefore there were no grounds to accuse businessmen of recklessness. Instead, a more active monetary policy by the Bank of Finland was needed to stimulate the economy. (Pipping 1961, 312–314)

However there remains a black spot in Borgström's thinking. He was sympathetic to the views of the Banking school, while defending the flexible attitude of the Bank of Finland to the 7:15 cover rule during the crisis in the aftermath of the Crimean war in the late 1850s. This raises the question why Borgström was not openly critical of the rigid credit policies pursued in Finland in the context of the silver standard reform. Did he feel that, through his influence on Langenskiöld in the early phase of the reform, he was so committed to it in that it was in line with his long-term aims, that he was not willing to rock the boat as difficulties were met during the transition? Or was he simply on the sidelines? Borgström's views on monetary policy are further discussed in Chapter 5.

The "Workers' Question" and the Controversy over Liberalism

In 1874, G. Z. Forsman (later Yrjö-Koskinen) published an influential article series in the journal Kirjallinen Kuukauslehti,[37] in which the position of industrial labour was discussed. Industry was still quite undeveloped in Finland in the 1870s, and social problems caused by industrialisation and urbanisation had not affected the country seriously. Yrjö-Koskinen had taken part in the public discussion on poor relief at the turn of the 1850s and 1860s.

Yrjö-Koskinen criticised Smithian, Manchesterian and general liberal views of the state, and discussed the problems caused by uncontrolled free competition. The starting point in his critique was Hegelianism.[38] He felt that communism and its lighter ver-

[37] Name Yrjö-Koskinen was taken in use when G.Z. Forsman was raised to the nobility. Previously, he used the pseudonym Yrjö Koskinen in his writings. Kirjallinen Kuukauslehti was the central organ of the Fennomans. It was published between 1866 and 1880 in Helsinki. The articles published in Kirjallinen Kuukauslehti dealt with many kinds of social, cultural and scientific issues. Yrjö-Koskinen was its chief editor.

[38] According to Yrjö-Koskinen, the state is a manifestation of the national spirit. Its purpose is to ensure a nation's economic and intellectual develop-

sion, socialism, shook the basis of the social order in its questioning of property rights. Yrjö-Koskinen takes the position of *Kathedersozialismus*:

> But exactly this kind of sharp conflict has always been harmful in history, and luckily a transitional party has lately been established in Germany in order to study on the basis of science and Christianity what concessions to its own good society can make to allow the claims of labouring people... Of course it is difficult to say beforehand how soon *die Kathedersozialisten* will find the right means to level out the hills and valleys in contemporary European societies. The laying of grounds that are based on something other than mere free competition already seems to us to be an unforeseen step forwards, and therefore we welcome this 'historico-ethical school' in the science of political economy with optimism. (K[oskinen] 1874, 96–97.)

Yrjö-Koskinen proposed public support measures to encourage working people to save. Drawing on his French experience, he recommended the founding of provincial savings banks and the issuing of specific bonds to finance poor relief. All in all, he was in favour of moderate social reform and was particularly concerned about the position of rural workers, labour protection and other social measures.[39]

Thus, Yrjö-Koskinen saw German social policy as a possible answer to the problematic questions raised by industrial capitalism, and as a weapon against the threat of rising socialism and communism. He thought that social policy could heal the wounds of social structural change and prevent the growth of social misery.

Wilhelm Lavonius[40] (1832–1897) published an article called *Kateder-socialisterna* (Lavonius 1874) in the journal of the Juridical

ment. Free competition that is wholly unlimited leads to enmity among people. (Heinonen 1987, 149–150.)

[39] Björkqvist (1986, 227–228) mentioned Yrjö-Koskinen as a supporter of the Schulze-Delitzschian co-operative movement. Evidence of Yrjö-Koskinen's social reformism was his rather positive attitude towards Kyröskoski Tehdasyhtiökunta, the first Finnish experimental production plant led by workers (Björkqvist 1986, 480).

[40] Wilhelm Lavonius published his dissertation *Om tull-lagstiftning i Finland* ("On Customs Legislation in Finland", Lavonius 1873) in 1873, the first Finnish dissertation dealing with customs policy and theory. Together with

Georg Zacharias Forsman, later Yrjö-Sakari Yrjö-Koskinen (1830–1903)

Karl Gabriel Thiodolf Rein (1838–1919)

Association at the same time as Yrjö-Koskinen's article series appeared. Lavonius' article is a descriptive presentation of *Kathedersozialismus* and the constitutive meeting of the Verein für Sozialpolitik held in Eisenach in 1873, and cites the speeches of Gustav von Schmoller and Lujo Brentano. It is written from a rather positive point of view. Lavonius maintained that social reforms were needed in Finland to improve the position of the rural population.

There was controversy in the press in the 1870s about the interpretation of liberalism. The Fennomans who had been influenced by the German *Kathedersozialismus* were on one side, and the Swedish-speaking liberals Liljenstrand and Mechelin (Heinonen 1987, 68–70 and Appendix 3) were on the other. The liberalism controversy began with the above-mentioned presentation of the

Leo Mechelin (1839–1914), he applied for Liljenstrand's professorship at the Faculty of Law at the University of Helsinki. When Mechelin, the leading person in the Finnish liberalist movement, was given the Chair, Lavonius moved to Vyborg where he became Justice in the Court of Appeal (Björkqvist 1986, 323).

ideas of *Kathedersozialismus* by Professor Granfelt, with Liljenstrand's quick response to Granfelt's critique of liberalism, and with articles written by Lavonius and Yrjö-Koskinen.

The "second round" of the liberalism controversy started with Professor Karl Gabriel Thiodolf Rein's (1838–1919) article published in Kirjallinen Kuukauslehti (Rein 1878). Rein was appointed Professor of Philosophy at the University of Helsinki in 1869. Later he was also rector and vice-chancellor of the university. He was a very active essayist and a supporter of the Finnish nationalist movement. (Björkqvist 1986, 480.)

Rein's article can be characterised as a philosophical essay on the ideological content of liberalism (Björkqvist 1986, 485). He heavily criticised economic liberalism:

> For freedom as understood in liberalism is a wholly negative concept; it is not a productive force, because it is realised only by removing obstacles which harm the appearance of productive forces. If such forces do not exist, freedom cannot create them. It must be admitted that these productive forces, which exist and seem to lie dormant, can often be revived and develop when given the chance to show what they can produce; otherwise they must be revived and developed by force, and it is one-sided to decide in advance that freedom always has a positive influence, and compulsion a negative one. (Rein 1878, 77.)

Rein opposed liberalism, which he thought would lead to everyman's war against everyman. He was also opposed to socialism, which he saw as being based on materialism and "hatred of all the idealist struggles of human life – religion, family, fatherland" (Rein 1878, 179). He felt that socialism had gone too far in its opposing of individualism and limiting of personal freedom. He thus took the transitional position of *Kathedersozialismus*.

Rein's views have a clear Listian flavour: he used the Listian notion of forces of production, and emphasised the differences between different nationalities (Björkqvist 1986, 487). He also mentioned the juxtaposition of the Fennomans writing to *Kirjallinen Kuukauslehti* and the Swedish-speaking liberals who wrote to *Helsingfors Dagblad*.

Another important article published by Rein was entitled *Kansantalouden uusi oppikunta* (A New School of Thought in the Economic Discipline, Rein 1879a), in which he criticised the liberalist notion of free competition. According to him, a rise in prices and rents, different consumption habits and speculation caused uncertainty in workers' conditions of living. He thought that socialism had found a better solution to the problem than liberalism: socialists aimed towards a more equal society.

> There is no equality where there is not only inequality in the possession of property, but also the possibilities to acquire wealth are as a matter of fact different, because both chance and order in society favour one person and one social class more than others in struggles to acquire wealth. This must be addressed, but it can only happen if society exclusively controls the acquisition of wealth and its distribution. (Rein 1879a, 4.)

According to the socialists, the formation of capital should be arranged by the state. Only labour income should be private by nature. Rein approved of many ideas of the socialists, but not of the means to achieve their ends. It was his opinion that the collectivisation of the whole economy and the striving for instantaneous social change rather than historical evolution were the mistakes of the socialists (Björkqvist 1986, 482).

Under *Kathedersozialismus*, individual freedom and private property should be maintained. Its proponents tried to combine collective and private economy. The accumulation of capital into the hands of a small minority was supposed to be prevented by progressive taxation. Rein also dealt with the following issues: social policy, social legislation, state intervention in the economy and customs protection. In many senses, he followed the lines of thought of the Belgian *Kathedersozialist*, Émile de Laveleye.[41]

The above-mentioned Swedish-speaking leading liberal Leo Mechelin opposed Rein's views in an article published in Finsk Tidskrift (Mechelin 1879).[42] Mechelin was mainly looking at is-

[41] The Professor of Economic Science at the University of Liége de Laveleye visited Finland in summer 1877 (Björkqvist 1986, 445). He was well known because of his versatile publications on economics, on the history of social policy, on socialist thought and on monetary theory. He belonged to the left wing faction of *Kathedersozialisten* in the Historical School.

[42] Finsk Tidskrift is the oldest cultural journal in the Nordic countries that is still published today. It was founded in 1876 as a counterbalance to the journal *Kirjallinen Kuukauslehti* that was the main organ of the Finnish-minded nationalists, the Fennomans. Finsk Tidskrift was aimed at the liberal-minded Swedish-speaking intelligentsia. Its first chief editors were C. G. Estlander (1876–1886) and M. G. Schybergson (1896–1907).

sues of language and nationality. He felt that liberalism was a protest against despotism (Mechelin 1879, 132) rather than an idea going back to the age of reason when freedom was considered to be guaranteed to all in society, as Rein believed. He remarked that Rein was mixing up freedom of association with decentralisation and autonomy. He emphasised that liberalism did not preach abstract freedom without any contact with the state or without the notion of solidarity.

Rein published a series of articles (Rein 1879b) in the newspaper Morgonbladet as a response to Mechelin. He maintained that Mechelin had misunderstood his ideas by assuming he wanted to eradicate liberalism from Finland. He only tried to show that liberalism alone was an inadequate principle of statesmanship. By liberals, Rein meant the heirs of Adam Smith, and classical political economy and the Manchester School.

To conclude, we would like to emphasise the divergent interpretations of liberalism by the participants in the controversy. Liljenstrand and Rein wrote about liberalism as an economic school of thought, whereas Yrjö-Koskinen and Mechelin rather meant it as a political movement. According to Liljenstrand, the controversies in economic science were based on mistakes in interpreting liberalism. Yrjö-Koskinen, Lavonius and Rein confessed their support of *Kathedersozialismus*.

4.5 Towards the Hegemony of the German Historical School

Introduction

This section examines the influence of the German historical school in Finland. The central theme is the period of organisation of the economics profession at the turn of the century, in which the Finnish Economic Association[43] played an important role. The association was founded in 1884 after the model of the German Verein für Sozialpolitik. It was a combination of scientific forum, research organisation and political pressure group (Pekkarinen

[43] For literature on Kansantaloudellinen Yhdistys and the Society for Swedish-speaking Finnish Economists, *Ekonomiska Samfundet i Finland*, founded in 1894, see Björkqvist (1986, 517–527), Eriksson (1978), Eskola (1962), Harmaja (1934), Heinonen (1987), Koskenkylä et al. (1984) and Pipping (1944).

1984, 19). According to Esa Konttinen (1991, 217), two factors, above all, separate a modern profession from a premodern one: 1) expertise that is based on specialised science is organised as a central basis of qualification and justification in practising a modern profession and 2) a modern profession is institutionally specialised and organised as a professional organisation. In Finland, the economics profession had just begun to specialise and organise in the last decades of the 1900s and at the turn of the century. An independent professorship of economics was founded in the Faculty of Philosophy at the University of Helsinki in 1906. Before that, economic subjects were taught in the Faculty of Law.

The German historical approach dominated Finnish economics for many decades. For instance, the first professor of economics in the Faculty of Philosophy was Juho Heikki Vennola (1872–1938), who was a supporter of the German historical school. Many of the leading members of the Finnish Economic Association adopted the ideas of the historical school during their study tours to Central Europe and Germany. This school was not replaced by neoclassical Casselian economics until the 1930s and the 1940s.

The German Historical School

Adam Müller (1779–1829), Friedrich List (1789–1846) and Friedrich Schmitthenner (1796–1850) were predecessors of the German historical school.[44] Wilhelm Roscher (1817–1894), who taught at the University of Leipzig, is usually considered to be

[44] On the German historical school of economics see Boese (1939), Eräsaari (1976), Gide & Rist (1953), Lindenlaub (1967), Schüller (1899), Hagemann (1996) and Schumpeter (1986). Müller has been characterized as "romantic". He examined society as an organic totality, introduced historic continuity as a factor of production and criticized Adam Smith's views from an ethical point of view (Eriksson 1978, 15). List can be characterized as a "nationalist". He proposed his own "theory of productive forces" as a supplement to Adam Smith's "theory of values' in his principal work *Das nationale System der Politischen Oekonomie* published in 1841. List is best known for his *infant-industry argument* in the theory of international trade, but he also proposed a theory of development stages: according to him, every society develops through the following stages 1) barbarian, 2) nomadic, 3) agrarian, 4) agrarian and industrial and 5) agrarian, industrial and commercial (List 1950, 63). Schmitthenner can be characterized as a transitional writer between Müller and List. His *Zwölf Bücher vom Staate* is actually a general theory of society. See Rosher 1874.

the proper founder of the historical school. He was the leader of the so-called older generation of this school of thought. Alongside him, Bruno Hildebrand (1812–1878) and Karl Knies (1821–1898) are the most prominent names of the older historical school.[45]

From the 1870s on, the "newer" historical school strongly influenced economic science in the German-speaking world. Its outstanding figure was Professor Gustav von Schmoller[46] (1838–1917), who held a professorship first at the University of Halle (1864–72), then at Strasburg (1872–82), and finally at Berlin (1882–1913). He was one of the founders of the German Association of Social Policy (Verein für Sozialpolitik)[47] in 1873, and for a long time held the chairmanship of the association. Members of the Verein were called *die Kathedersozialisten*.

Apart from von Schmoller, the other representatives of the new historical school were Adolph Wagner (1835–1917), Lujo Brentano (1844–1931), Albert Schäffle (1831–1903) and Karl Bücher (1847–1930). Werner Sombart (1863–1941), Arthur Spiethoff (1873–1957) and Max Weber (1864–1920) were considered to be the critical members of the 'newest' generation of the historical school of thought.

Wagner was a professor at the University of Berlin in 1871–1918, and became known as a theoretician of public finance. Brentano was the social policy modernist of the German historical school. He sympathised with the sociology of Max Weber and was a friend of the reformist social democrat Eduard Bernstein. Brentano taught in several universities including Strasbourg, Vienna and Munich. (Eräsaari 1976, 55–58.) Karl Bücher is best known as an economic historian, and Sombart and Spiethoff

[45] Roscher's most important publications were the five-volume *System der Volkswirtschaft* (1854–1894) and *Geschichte der Nationalökonomik in Deutschland* (1874). Bruno Hildebrand's chief work was Die Nationalökonomie der Gegenwart und Zukunft (1848). Knies was a great teacher who "made Heidelberg a center of study and research". His chief publication was *Geld und Credit* (1873–79). (Schumpeter 1986, 507–8 and 850.)

[46] Among Gustav von Schmoller's most influential writings were *Zur Literaturgeschichte der Staats- und Sozialwissenschaften* (1888) and *Grundfragen der Sozialpolitik und Volkswirtschaftslehre* (1897). He also founded a periodical journal named *Jahrbuch für Gesetzgebung, Verwaltung und Volkswirtschaft im deutschen Reich* that became known as *Schmoller's Jahrbuch*. (Schumpeter 1986, 809.)

[47] For instance, the Finnish association *Kansantaloudellinen Yhdistys* was founded after the model of the *Verein* in 1884.

were disciples of von Schmoller. Max Weber is best known as one of the founders of sociology.[48]

The rise of socialism in the second half of the 19th century gave young German economists a reason to search for solutions to social problems to prevent revolution. They became strong proponents of social reforms, and critics of economic liberalism. Incidentally, the Verein für Sozialpolitik was founded as a reaction to the German free-trade school. (Lindenlaub 1967, 1–2.) *Kathedersozialisten* shared the following features in their economic thinking:

- historical relativism
- a holistic approach
- evolutionism
- an emphasis on empirical research and the inductive method
- seeing human motives as complex and even irrational phenomena
- an emphasis on the ethical point of view
- consideration of cultural and sociological matters
- the linking of economic action and the institutional framework.

Kathedersozialimus had advocates in many other countries besides Germany. In Great Britain, W. J. Ashley (1860–1927), W. Cunningham (1849–1919), W. A. S. Hewins (1865–1931), J. K. Ingram (1823–1907) and T. Cliffe Leslie (1826–1931), and in Belgium Émile de Laveleye (1822–1892), were representatives of the

[48] Wagner's well-known works are his four-volume *Finanzwissenschaft* (1877–1901) and *Grundlegung der politischen Oekonomie* (1876). Brentano's *Die Arbeitergilden der Gegenwart* (1871–72) and *Wie studiert man Nationalökonomie* (1912) are his main publications. Schäffle's *Bau und Leben des sozialen Körpers* (1875–78) is perhaps the best known of his works. Sombart's important work is *Der Moderne Kapitalismus* (1902) which, according to Schumpeter (1986, 817), was in a way the culmination of the historical school. Spiethoff was assistant to von Schmoller for a long time, and later on a professor in Bonn. He is known as a researcher of business cycles. Max Weber started his academic career as an economist and economic historian (see Clarke 1982 and Hietaniemi 1987). The posthumously published *Wirtschaft und Gesellschaft* and the essay *Die protestantische Ethik und der "Geist" des Kapitalismus* in *Archiv für Sozialwissenschaft und Sozialpolitik* (1904–05) are the best known of his works. Weber accepted the Mengerian theory of marginal utility as a theory of price, but his relationship to marginalist economics was problematic (Gronow 1987, 18–19).

historical approach. Outside Europe, the historical school held quite a strong position in the United States and Japan for even longer, into the last decades of the 19th century. Students travelled to Germany to study economic science under the leading teachers of the historical school.

The Reception of the German Historical School in Finland

Social policy and the ideas of the *Kathedersozialismus* evoked increasing interest in Finland in the 1870s and 1880s. Their reflections in the debate on economic liberalism were discussed above. Later on, the ideas of the German historical school were more systematically introduced by Joel Napoleon Lang (1847–1905). He published his doctoral dissertation in jurisprudence in 1880, and qualified for the professorship with his other dissertation (Lang 1882). Before that he had studied economic science in 1880–1881 in Germany. He held the economics professorship at the Faculty of Law in 1882–1905, and later became dean of the Faculty. He was the chairman of the Finnish Economic Association in 1895.

As mentioned earlier, economics was solely taught at the Faculty of Law until 1905. As part of a reorganisation process, the teaching of economics, finance and statistics was moved to the Faculty of Philosophy (Björkqvist 1986, 528–530). After that, the assistant professor could still arrange examinations for the degree of Master of Laws in these three subjects with the help of the professor of economics. However, the former professorship at the Faculty of Law was turned into a professorship of economic law.

Juho Heikki Vennola was appointed to the new independent chair of economics that was founded in the Philosophy Faculty at the University of Helsinki in 1906. Vennola (1900) published his historical dissertation in 1900.[49] He studied history and statistics in Sweden in 1897, and economics in Halle and Berlin in 1903. He became a docent in statistics and economics in the Philosophy Faculty in 1904 and a full professor in 1908. He travelled to Berlin and Leipzig to study again in 1906 and 1908, and to Berlin and Vienna in 1907.

[49] Vennola's teacher was Professor Ernst Gustaf Palmén (1884–1911), who was a historian specialized in administration and economic history. Palmén started the first large historical research project studying ownership in the Finnish countryside. Vennola's study was the only doctoral dissertation prepared in the project. (Lilja 1993, 542–543.)

In his studies, Vennola showed interest in agricultural economic research, and published a research report on the relative prices of corn and bread in 1904 (Vennola 1904). The statistical data was from the years 1889–1895, and Vennola followed the example of the German professor Johannes Conrad (1839–1915), who was a student of Bruno Hildebrand and followed Gustav von Schmoller as professor in Halle. Part of the study was carried out under the leadership of Johannes Conrad in 1903. (Björkqvist 1986, 532–533.)

Vennola published a study in economic history (Vennola 1908) as well, in which he applied the theory of economic stages presented by the German economists of the historical school. He used historical data from the 16th-century Swedish Kingdom. He also published studies dealing with the corn trade between Finland and Russia, and on economic and agricultural policy problems.

Commenting on the "Methodenstreit"

The Austrian pioneer of marginalist revolution Carl Menger (1840–1921) published his methodological work in 1883 (Menger 1883), and this started the famous methodological controversy[50] (Methodenstreit). Gustav von Schmoller criticised Menger's work, and Menger responded by writing a pamphlet (Menger 1884). The controversy also attracted attention in Finland, although the Finns did not analyse the arguments systematically. Mäki (1984, 112) pointed out that, as early as in November, 1885, Joel Napoleon Lang gave a lecture at The Finnish Economic Association in which he (Lang 1893, 4) presented the same division of economic science as Menger had done two years before, but without mentioning Menger's name.[51] Lang, however, did not explicitly cover the methodological controversy.

Agathon Meurman gave a lecture (Meurman 1897) in the same

[50] Gustav von Schmoller criticized Menger's work, and Menger answered this criticism by writing a pamphlet entitled *Die Irrthümer des Historismus in der deutschen Nationalökonomie* (Menger 1884). *Eugen von Böhm-Bawerk* (1851–1914) as a supporter and *Heinrich Dietzel* (1857–1935) as an opponent of Menger were among those who took part in the dispute (Schumpeter 1986, 814).

[51] Menger divided economic science in the following way: 1) historical sciences (history and statistics), 2) theoretical economic science that examines the general features of economic phenomena, and 3) practical economic science (economic policy and finance). (Willgren 1893, 332.)

Ernst Nevanlinna (1873–1932, until 1906 Neovius)

Agathon Meurman (1826–1909)

forum in December, 1894 in which he criticised the "Manchester school fanatics" of dogmatism and trust in general laws of national economy. He also criticised Henry George, whom he considered an extreme representative of the Manchester school, for ignoring historical and geographical matters.[52]

Meurman wrote about the mathematical methods of the Manchester school. Because he did not use references, it remains unclear whether he meant British marginalists – Jevons, Marshall, Edgeworth, Wicksteed, Sidgwick – many of whom, like represen-

[52] The influence of Henry George reached Finland via the Tolstoyan thinker and writer, and Young Fennoman opinion leader, *Arvid Järnefelt* (1861–1932), who translated some of George's works into Finnish during his student days in the 1880s. Järnefelt even visited Tolstoy in 1899. See Järnefelt (1980). The so-called Manchester school was actually not a genuine economic school of thought: it did not have any consistent theoretical basis (Grampp 1960, 2). It was formed by a group of businessmen, pacifists and different kinds of radicals opposing the corn laws and led by *Richard Cobden* (1804–1865) and *John Bright* (1811–1889) in the1830s and 1840s (Grampp 1960, 5–15). In Finland, the name Manchester school was often mistakenly used for all supporters of free trade at the turn of the century.

tatives of the Manchester school, were supporters of free trade. On methodological questions, Meurman clearly took the position of the historicists, which was a common position among members of The Finnish Economic Association.

After the turn of the century, methodological discussion in Finland took place mainly in Historiallinen Yhdistys, the association of historians, where the collectivist conception of history of the historian Karl Lamprecht (1856–1915) was discussed (Mäki 1984, 114).[53] The young historian Ernst Nevanlinna (1873–1932) (until 1906, Neovius) took part in this discussion. Nevanlinna was a trained historian, but soon became interested in economic science. He studied in Germany, in Berlin and Leipzig, in 1899–1900. He wrote his dissertation on the Finnish financial system (Nevanlinna 1899) just before the turn of the century, and in 1905 he was the chairman of The Finnish Economic Association. Later in 1924 he became professor of public finance at the University of Helsinki.

Nevanlinna published a booklet (Nevanlinna 1913) in which he examined Gustav von Schmoller and Adolph Wagner and their work.[54] Von Schmoller was Menger's main opponent and object of criticism in the methodological controversy, in which the difference between the two approaches, the Schmollerian historicist approach and the Mengerian approach, was often perceived as a "difference in or different emphasis on the deductive and inductive methods" (Mäki 1984, 114). The core of the controversy was exactly in this methodological difference: on the one hand a historical and empirical approach in research, and on the other hand an approach aiming at an abstract universalist theoretical system. Nevanlinna posited two clearly different and conflicting methodologies:

> Schmoller's whole training and his disposition have affected him, and he has always been a strong supporter of induc-

[53] See Viikari 1983, 82–83, e.g.

[54] The leading figure of the second generation of the German historical school and Chairman of Verein für sozialpolitik, Gustav von Schmoller emphasized historical and institutional matters in his thinking, which had a relativistic tone. He did not see any permanent features in the economy, and so he gave empirical research a central position. Wagner respected theory, and in this respect was in opposition to historicism. Together with *Johann Rodbertus* (1805–1875), *Ferdinand Lassalle* (1825–1864) and *Eugen Dühring* (1833–1921), he belonged to the so-called state socialists, who supported the workers movement and state intervention but did not go as far as *Karl Marx* (1818–1883) and *Friedrich Engels* (1820–1895).

> tion... Menger subordinated the means and the ends of research as practised by the historical school of economics under strict criticism, and wanted to give deduction more or even decisive importance in examining economic problems. (Nevanlinna 1913, 31–32.)

Nevanlinna considered von Schmoller's methodological point of view moderate. He felt that Menger's critique aimed at von Schmoller was not wholly justified because "...Schmoller sharply denies the claim that he or his approach would mean one-sided support of the empirical method and induction... he is wholly aware of the necessity of deduction" (Nevanlinna 1913, 33).

German socialists such as Marx, Engels and especially Rodbertus had influenced Adolph Wagner (Nevanlinna 1913, 73), who was ready to give recognition to representatives of British classical political economy, because they have "...rightly examined and taught us to understand the skeletal structure of private economic connection and the basic features of its statics and dynamics" (Nevanlinna 1913, 76). According to Wagner, their mistakes were their false conception of the state, and seeing society and the economy as mechanical and unhistorical phenomena.

Nevanlinna described Wagner's views: the deductive method was the right one, but the English had misused it. Nevanlinna left open the possibility of deep divergence between the views of Wagner on the one hand, and both the historical school and the English and the Austrians on the other. (Nevanlinna 1913, 102–103.) Here he was perhaps anticipating his own methodological turn to becoming a supporter of Gustav Cassel's (1866–1945) neoclassical economics (Mäki 1984, 115–116).

The representatives of the youngest generation in the German historical school, Sombart and Weber, criticised historical economics inside the Verein für Sozialpolitik in the value judgement controversy (Werturteilstreit) in 1909–1914 (Eräsaari 1976, 172). They were representatives of a radical wing at the Verein, and were supporters of value objectivity as a guiding principle in social scientific research. The value judgement controversy was about the old scientific dispute about value objectivity. The controversy culminated in the session of the Verein für Sozialpolitik in Vienna in 1909. Max Weber, Werner Sombart and the Englishman Joseph Nicholson (1850–1927) were among those supporting value objectivity, while Adolph Wagner, Eugen von Philippovich (1858–1917), Albert Schäffle, Johannes Conrad (1854–1915) and the Englishman Alfred Marshall (1842–1924) held the position that values were part and parcel of social scientific discussion.

In Finland, Oskar Kaaleb Kilpi (1878–1937) presented and briefly commented on the standpoints in the controversy in his article (Kilpi 1915) in a journal published by the Finnish Economic Association. He raised two questions: Is Weber's and Sombart's critical position going to be purely methodological? Will it lead to the birth of a kind of neoliberal school? In answer to the first, he wrote that criticism could lose its meaning as an independent position if the *Kathedersozialisten* took it seriously. To the other question he responded that the birth of a new school was not impossible because many journals were already in the hands of critics (Kilpi 1915, 255). Kilpi saw the criticism presented by Sombart and Weber as aimed at establishing a new school of thought. About the case of Finland he wrote in strongly social-reformist tones:

> In Finland social reforms are just beginning. Here we have a lot to do with the land question and labour legislation. There is no room for counteraction, if it is connected to resistance of social reforms. (Kilpi 1915, 257.)

He acknowledged the fruitful influence of the "critical position", and thus seemed to be a true reformist in the spirit of *Kathedersozialismus*. That was the dominant position among members of The Finnish Economic Association.

Kilpi had studied in Germany at the University of Berlin under the supervision of Wagner and von Schmoller in 1906–1907. He was a docent of statistics at the University of Helsinki in the 1920s, and then became professor of economics at the Helsinki School of Economics and Business Administration. (Alapuro & Alestalo 1973, 97–101 and 110–111.) Kilpi's dissertation on the structure of the economically active population in Finland in 1815–1875 was pioneer work based on careful scrutiny of the population statistics. Kilpi (1917) represented a more theoretical perspective on economic dynamics in his study on the economic and social causes of migration. All in all, his work in economics was quite extensive by contemporary Finnish standards.

Empirical Social Research

In the second half of the 19th century, the German historical school also provided a model for empirical social research in Finland. Social problems caused by industrialisation, urbanisation and transformation of the social structure were addressed. This line of research was intertwined with the development of social statistics (Alapuro & Alestalo 1992, 78).

The rise in empirical social research was preceded by a debate on the "workers' question" and socialism. The problems of the landless rural workers were closely tied to this. The "land question" was the biggest social problem in Finland at the turn of the century (Soikkanen 1961, 36–39; Haatanen 1968, 36), and the driving force behind the increase in empirical social research.

The strongly nationalist Finnish intelligentsia saw enlightenment and the education of the lower social classes as its common goal. Before the political parties were organised at the turn of the century, the Finnish Economic Association was an especially important forum for social discussion and the planning of reforms. Alapuro and Alestalo (1992) divided the empirical research done by the Finnish Economic Association into two parts: that on the rural population and, on the other hand, that on the worker population.

As early as in the 1880s, an investigation into the land ownership and circumstances of the rural population was carried out by the Finnish Economic Association. A series of research reports on the economic conditions in the Finnish countryside was published. Axel Warén's (1869–1899) study on the crofters' living conditions was a comprehensive empirical study in which he used statistical data, interviews, and many kinds of documents (Warén 1898). In the true mood of the German *Kathedersozialismus*, he believed that the problems could be solved by legislative reforms (Alapuro & Alestalo 1992, 86).

Waren's work was continued by Hannes Gebhard, originally a historian but later an agricultural economist and one of the founders of the Finnish co-operative movement. He had studied in Germany in 1893–94 under the tutelage of the famous German agricultural economist Max Sering (1857–1940), and the leaders of the younger generation of the German historical school Gustav von Schmoller and Adolph Wagner (Paasikivi 1986, 209). His dissertation (Gebhard 1889) was a historical study.

Gebhard was a pioneer of agricultural economics in Finland, and the chairman of the "Subcommittee of Landless People" (Tilattoman väestön alakomitea) that was founded at the turn of the century to plan and research the "land question": the conditions of the landless rural proletariat which was increasing quickly in numbers (Alestalo & Alapuro 1992, 86–88; Paasikivi 1986, 210–11). This committee carried out the most influential studies on conditions in the Finnish countryside around the turn of the century (Alapuro & Alestalo 1992, 88).

Gebhard was appointed to a docentship in agricultural economics and statistics in 1899 and, finally, to a special professorship in agricultural economics and statistics in the Faculty of Agriculture at the University of Helsinki in 1909. As a university teacher, he was inspiring. Edvard Gylling, Yrjö Jahnsson, O. K. Kilpi, Sulo Wuolijoki, and Martti Kovero were among his pupils. He also acted as chairman of the Finnish Economic Association in 1900. His main interest, however, lay in co-ordinating the activities of the Finnish co-operative movement – especially managing the Central Co-operative Bank in Finland. That is why he left the University in 1911, and directed his intellectual efforts towards practical and ideological questions concerning the co-operative movement. He quite actively corresponded with the famous French economist Charles Gide, for instance, but the correspondence was strictly limited to co-operative matters.

Jaakko Forsman (1867–1946) was the first subeditor of the first Finnish social scientific journal, *Yhteiskuntataloudellinen Aikakauskirja* (the Finnish Economic Journal), founded in 1905. He was one of the best experts on socialism and the labour movement in the circles of the Finnish Economic Association, and wrote several articles on these issues.

One of his booklets (Forsman 1912) is particularly interesting and includes a clear reference to Schmollerian historical methodology. He wrote:

> ... although the logical deduction was carried out quite correctly in itself, it can lead to mistakes nevertheless, because, in fact, there is rather little logic and consistency in human life and action. You feel yourself moving into a quagmire in this kind of mass psychological study. Be that as it may, you have to get some impression of the interaction between external conditions and people's mental lives to understand historical development at all. Without this kind of inquiry, sudden phenomena like large national movements, which bounce up from underground, will stay inexplicable mysteries. (Forsman 1912, 6–7.)

Here it is possible to identify several characteristics of the methodology of the German historical school listed above. Moreover, Forsman's views were not very far from the modern notion of the history of mentalities.

The first initiatives for the study of conditions among the Finnish working class were taken by the Workers' Association of Helsinki in the late 1880s, and the need for broader study was expressed at the second meeting of representatives of the labour movement in Tampere in 1896. The collection of statistical data was started, particularly at the Workers' Association of Helsinki (Alapuro & Alestalo 1992, 102–103). Oskar Groundstroem (1868–1940), G. R. Snellman (1864–1922) and Vera Hjelt (1857–1947) carried out pioneering work on the economic conditions of working people.

Oskar Groundstroem had had a statistician's training and worked as a registrar in the Finnish Statistical Central Office. He gave several lectures at the Finnish Economic Association and the Swedish-speaking Economic Society in Finland. His study (Groundstroem 1897) was the first survey on the issue (Alapuro & Alestalo 1992, 103). The question of the working class was the largest social problem, according to Groundstroem. His study was a standard statistical study and he dealt with problems of data collecting, the representativeness of the data and the calculation of statistical parameters as well.

As registrar, G. R. Snellman compiled twelve of the sixteen Labour Statistics research reports published between 1903–1914. These studies were basic empirical inquiries into the working conditions of industrial workers in Finland in different environments such as tobacco factories, bakeries and machine workshops. Their importance was equal to that of the reports of the Subcommittee of Landless Population. Together with Leo Ehrnrooth and Oskar Rosenqvist, Snellman represented radical social policy orientation in the Swedish-speaking economic society (Pipping 1944, 38–40; Björkqvist 1986, 524).

One of the above-mentioned sixteen reports was Vera Hjelt's survey (Hjelt 1912). This study was the first empirical survey on the living conditions and consumption of working people in Finland. Hjelt used account books filled in by worker families over one year as her data. Her study was the first thorough empirical study of consumption carried out in Finland.

Eino Kuusi (1880–1936) was a typical example of a representative of the German historical school, and had a brilliant career both as a civil servant and as an academician. Among other things, he was minister of social affairs (1922) and professor of practical economics at the University of Dorpat (1928–1931).

Kuusi's dissertation about winter unemployment was published in 1914. In his thesis he clearly revealed his intellectual roots. His

Vera Hjelt (1857–1947)

starting point was how the liberal economic policy of the last decades of the 19th century had provided the conditions for the then current massive unemployment. At the same time, the supporters of this doctrine had not comprehended the fact that it was only by public intervention that it was possible to alleviate the burden of unemployment. Kuusi's study was based on comprehensive empirical data about unemployment among outdoor workers in the biggest towns during the period 1890–1911. He deliberated about the causes of the unemployment, and about the means by which it could be prevented or alleviated. Although Kuusi was a typical representative of the German historical school, he introduced new ideas to Finnish economics. One innovation was the systematic use of British research and he referred to W.H. Beveridge's book *Unemployment, a Problem of Industry* (1911) and Sidney & Beatrice Webb's *The Prevention of Destitution* (1912).

Kuusi's later orientation towards social policy is evident already in this study, and he soon became a pioneer in this new field in Finland. His translation of R. van der Borght's textbook on social policy was published in 1909. Later he wrote in two volumes the first Finnish handbook on "Social Policy" (Kuusi 1931). His views about social policy dominated Finnish thinking in the first two or three decades of independent Finland.

Some members of the Finnish labour movement contributed to the empirical social research literature on the living conditions of the industrial working population. Social-reformist-minded people, such as Hannes Gebhard, August Hjelt and Jaakko Forsman, participated in the activities of the Finnish so-called "Wrightian" labour movement before its radical orientation in the 1890s and adoption of a socialist programme at a meeting in Forssa in 1903 (Alapuro & Alestalo 1992, 101).

Edvard Vilhelm Gylling (1881–1938) defended his doctoral dissertation in 1909 (Gylling 1909). The nature of the study was legal historical. The following year he was appointed a Docent in statistics at the University of Helsinki. His research methodology was historical and statistical, and he took part in the activities of the so-called "Subcommittee of Landless People" mentioned above. Martti Kovero's (1882–1955) dissertation (1909) also dealt with the historical background of the highly relevant "rural question". His theme was the settlement policy in Finland in the 18th century.

The Success of the Historical School

The influence of the German historical school among Finnish economists can clearly be seen as methodological: most of the academic dissertations written before 1920 were empirical studies. Eriksson (1978) examined those dissertations in detail in his valuable study. The 22 dissertation studies published in 1859–1919 under the general category of economics were classified by him as follows (Eriksson 1978, 41–64): Nevanlinna – who later on became a critic of the historical school – and Vennola (economic history), Martti Kovero, Edvard Gylling and Topi Kallio (social history), Leo Harmaja, Eino Kuusi and O. W. Louhivuori (social policy), Heikki Renvall, Yrjö Jahnsson and Georg Schauman (history of economic thought), Oskar Lundell, O. K. Kilpi, T. T. Kaila and A. E. Tudeer (statistics), Rolf Thesleff, Åke Dalberg and Paavo Korpisaari (money, credit and insurance), F. M. Pitkäniemi and K. Mannelin (commerce and industry), Ilmari Kovero (business) and Kyösti Järvinen (finance). Paavo Korpisaari and Rolf Thesleff were actually the only scholars who consciously took distance from the historical school in their academic dissertations (see Appendix 1).

The main reasons for the strong support of the historical school were: i) the training system – economic subjects were taught at the Faculty of Law until 1906 when an independent chair was established, and most scholars were trained lawyers or historians; ii) strong cultural and scientific ties to Germany; iii) the practical and policy orientation of Finnish social scientists at the turn of the century; iv) the authoritarian society of economists; and v) the poor ability of scholars to follow the international discussion taking place in Great Britain, Italy and France, and also in Austria, in an era when economists were beginning to use new concepts and mathematics in their writing.

It took until the 1930s and 1940s before neoclassical economics began to overshadow historically-oriented economics. Professor J. H. Vennola at the University of Helsinki was busy with politics in the 1920s, and did not have time to follow the developments in economic science. A new generation – names such as Bruno Suviranta, Arthur Montgomery, Lauri af Heurlin, C.-E. Knoellinger, C. A. J. Gadolin and Matti Leppo – emerged in the years between the wars. An economics profession was becoming institutionalised and finding new approaches to research.[55]

4.6 The Influence of the Austrian School

The term marginalist revolution refers to the paradigm change that occurred in economic science during the last decades of the 19th century.[56] This paradigm shift started with the works of the Englishman William Stanley Jevons (1835–1882), the Frenchman Léon Walras (1834–1910) and the Austrian Carl Menger (1840–1921). The main features of the marginalist revolution were characterised by Craufurd Goodwin as follows:

> ...: first, a new emphasis on the place of the individual utility function in the theory of price, and second, use of precise incremental analysis for the study of human behavior and markets. (Goodwin 1972, 551.)

Mark Blaug (1972) emphasised the interpretation of the term

[55] See Bergholm (1987 and 1988).

[56] Issue 1972:4 of A *History of Political Economy* contains valuable articles concerning the marginalist revolution and the development of marginal utility theory in economics. Other important sources are Stigler (1950), Howey (1960) and Kauder (1965).

marginalist revolution as rational reconstruction. It was rather more a process than an event. The success of the marginalist revolution was closely connected to the professionalisation and institutionalisation of economics as a science.[57] The institutionalisation of economics led to a specialisation which reduced the layman's participation in economic discourse. Fisher (1986, 209–210) suggested that specialisation in economics was a consequence of the emergence of a marginalist research programme.

Mark Blaug (1983, 314–318) divided the explanations of the genesis of marginal utility theory into four categories: i) explanations that take the autonomous development inside the discipline of economics as the starting point; ii) explanations that see marginalist revolution as a product of philosophical currents; iii) explanations that appeal to the fundamental institutional changes in the economy; and iv) explanations that see the marginalist revolution as an answer to the socialist movement and Marxism. The explanations in none of the categories are sufficient in themselves, and they are not mutually exclusive. One category that is missing in Blaug's list concerns explanations that consider the breakthrough of marginalism in connection with the inner changes of the community of economics in issues such as professionalisation and specialisation. Another is the influence of natural sciences that, interestingly enough, was reported by Philip Mirowski, for instance.[58]

This section examines the reception and initial comments on marginalist neoclassical economics in Finland before the Civil War of 1918. The new approach introduced in economic theory in the last decades of the 19th century received quite limited attention during that time. Some individual scholars made comments on marginalist writers in a few journal articles and lectures. Most attention was given to Karl Willgren, who was the most influential interpreter of marginalism in Finland. He was a Doctor of Jurisprudence, who was interested in the Austrian version of marginalism and wrote several articles upon the subject. Ernst Nevanlinna and the statistician Oskar Groundstroem also commented on the writings of the Austrian theorist von Böhm-Bawerk.

[57] See, for instance, Coats (1972).

[58] Philip Mirowski's interesting and powerful thesis about the development of economic science and the adoption of metaphors of 19th-century physics without full understanding of their substance (Mirowski 1984, 1987 and 1989) is beyond the scope of this article. See Heinonen 1993.

First Reactions to Marginalist Theory

Professor Johan Leffler (1845–1912) introduced the marginal utility theory to the Swedish audience,[59] and marginalism very soon acquired prominent representatives in Sweden. Knut Wicksell (1851–1926) published in Germany books on the theory of capital and interest (Wicksell 1893 and 1898).[60] Another important and influential Swedish theoretician was Gustav Cassel (1866–1945), who was influenced mainly by Walras and Jevons. Cassel published a book on the theory of interest in 1903 (Cassel 1903).[61] The third Swedish marginalist economist was David Davidsson (1854–1942), a monetary theoretician from Uppsala.[62]

In Finland, Professor Axel Liljenstrand was the first to call attention to one marginalist, namely W. S. Jevons, in his article (Liljenstrand 1878–79). Liljenstrand just mentioned Jevons, who had defended the universalism of economic laws and the tight division of deductive and inductive research in the speech that he gave at the hundredth anniversary of Adam Smith's Wealth of Nations. Liljenstrand did not write about the marginalist ideas of Jevons in his article.

A Swedish professor from Gothenburg, Gustaf Steffen (1864–1929), in fact presented Jevons' economics to readers of journals in an article (Steffen 1890) that was published in Finsk Tidskrift. He mentioned several English representatives of the new economic school at the beginning of the article, and of the predeces-

[59] Björkqvist 1986, 609. On Leffler, see Olofsson & Pålsson Syll (1998). Björkvist's view is problematic. Knut Wicksell published his works at the beginning of the 1890s, in German, and another Swede, Gustaf Steffen, published his article in 1890 in Swedish, although in a Finnish journal (Steffen 1890).

[60] Schumpeter (1986, 913) thought that Wicksell, whom he called "Nordic Marshall", presented the best formulation of the Austrian theory. Wicksell was influenced especially by Eugen von Böhm-Bawerk (1851–1914). On Wicksell, see Uhr (1991a) and Pålsson Syll (1998, 212–218).

[61] Cassel's international reputation was based on his contribution to the discussion on monetary policy during and after the First World War. Cassel published an influential book entitled *Theoretische Sozialökonomie* in 1918 (Schumpeter 1986, 862). He was very influential among the Finnish economists in the 1920s and 1930s. One could even talk about a "Casselian turn" in Finnish economics. This can be seen clearly, for instance, in the change of course in the thinking of Ernst Nevanlinna, who became a true Casselian (Eriksson 1978, 87–89 and Mäki 1984, 127). On Cassel, see Magnusson (1991) and Pålsson Syll 1998, 218–222.

[62] On Davidsson, see Uhr (1991b).

sors of marginalism he picked out the German Gossen and the French Cournot. According to Steffen, the theory of consumption was the main interest of the "Jevonians". The difference between the old and new schools of thought in English economics lay in the theory of value: the Jevonians did not accept the labour theory of value of the old school (Steffen 1890, 5). Steffen crystallised the Jevonian theory of value as follows:

> Following Jevons, let us call this lowest subjective use value, or lowest subjective value that has significance, briefly "marginal utility". This gives the following form for Jevons "theory of value":
> *Use value is the marginal utility, and its magnitude is determined by the quantity of the good.* (Steffen 1890, 12, italics G. S.)

Steffen addressed the question of how the exchange value of the good depended on its quantity in the market. He used as an example the market for sewing machines. As he saw it, the equality between the exchange value of goods and the cost of production held true only for industrially produced goods and only in circumstances of wholly free competition. Like Jevons, Steffen emphasised the universal character of the equality of the subjective use value of commodities:

> The exchange value is only a condition characteristic of our societal circumstances, a phenomenon that characterises all human economy: *there is an equality between the subjective use values of the commodities.* (Steffen 1890, 17, italics G. S.)

Thus, Steffen saw the new theory of value as the core of the new English economic theory. The Swedish professor was thus the first to present marginalist economics to Finnish economists.

Why was a Swedish professor willing to present Jevonian economics to a small crowd of Finnish economists? He was influenced by the rising socialist labour movement, as well as by Knut Wicksell in Lund and Gustav Cassel in Stockholm. Steffen had studied under Wagner and von Schmoller in Berlin, and moved to London in 1887. There he became involved with Philip Wicksteed and the Fabian Society, and his political opinions were influenced by them. He soon became an exponent of neoclassical and Fabian criticism of the Marxian labour theory of value in the Swedish press. He even gave lectures at London University in 1892 about labour economics and the labour movement, arguing for social reform, and published the lectures in the form of articles in the Swedish social democratic and liberal press (Lönnroth 1991, 37).[63] Thus Steffen was interested in Jevonian value theory as an alternative to the labour theory of value which he considered to be unable to explain a commodity's value in exchange. His enthusiasm did not seem to have been reciprocated in Finland.

Karl Willgren: a Finnish Interpreter of Marginalism

The doctor of jurisprudence Karl Salomon Willgren (1865–1930) first presented Austrian marginalism in an article that was published in Finsk Tidskrift (Willgren 1893). He had received his doctorate a year before, and his jurisprudential dissertation was presented in 1891. Apparently, his interest in marginalist economics began during his study tour to Stockholm and Uppsala in 1890, and to Copenhagen and Berlin in 1891. His second dissertation (Willgren 1899) was defended in the Faculty of Philosophy at the University of Helsinki, and concerned his main field of interest, namely, public finance.[64]

Willgren held the professorship in economic law and economic studies in the Faculty of Law at the University of Helsinki. He has been mentioned as the founder of Finnish administrative law, at the side of Kaarlo J. Ståhlberg (Klami 1977, 77). He taught economics to students of law, and also published a textbook of statistics (Willgren 1905–1907). He can actually be considered the only Finnish expert on marginalist neoclassical economics before the Civil War of 1918.

In the article mentioned above, Willgren concentrated on the Austrian contribution to marginalism. According to him, the most important representatives of the Austrian school were Carl Menger, Eugen von Böhm-Bawerk and Eugen von Philippovich (1858–1917) [65], who were professors at the University of Vienna, Friedrich von Wieser (1851–1926) and Emil Sax (1845–1927)[66]

[63] In 1900, Steffen published a substantial work entitled *Lönearbetaren och samhället* (Wage Labour and Society), bringing together his ideas presented earlier in the form of articles and lectures.

[64] On Willgren, see also Heinonen (1996a).

[65] It is problematic to call von Philippovich marginalist. He was sympathetic to the ideas of German historical economics. His main publication was *Grundriss der politischen Ökonomie*, published in 1893–1907.

[66] Emil Sax published *Das Wesen und die Aufgaben der Nationalökonomie* in 1884 and *Grundlegung der theoretischen Staatswirtschaft* in 1887.

from the University of Prague, and the head of the statistical department at the Austrian Ministry of Commerce Victor Mataja (1857–1934)[67] (Willgren 1893, 325–326).

The Austrian school was generally interested in finding out the psychological motives behind people's economic activity (Willgren 1893, 333). Thus the theory of value was a key element in Austrian theory, in which the value of commodities was considered to depend on the needs which were meant to be satisfied with the help of those commodities. The marginal utility theory, which was given its name in German[68] by von Wieser, was at the core of Austrian value theory: the source of value of the goods was the marginal utility that they yielded in consumption. The representatives of classical political economy had ignored consumption when they directed their attention to the costs of production as the source of value (Willgren 1893, 336–337). All this is problematic. One has to add that, for Menger, marginalism was a side issue compared to his subjectivism, for instance. Erich Streissler (1972, 426–427) stressed the nature of Menger's theory as "basically an *information theory*, economic theory under uncertainty and not under certainty" (italics original).

On the question of labour, Willgren wrote the following:

> Laisser-faire, laisser-passer is not the solution of the Austrian school; on the contrary, its representatives seem to be very sympathetic to the modern reforms in society. (Willgren 1893, 338.)

According to Willgren the economic policy views of the Austrian school seemed to be rather close to *Kathedersozialimus*,[69] the German representatives of the historical school who founded the Verein für Sozialpolitik under the leadership of Gustav von Schmoller (1838–1917) in 1872.[70]

[67] Victor Mataja published his *Der Unternehmergewinn* in 1884.

[68] The German word *der Grenznutzen* means marginal utility. The word was used for the first time in Friedrich von Wieser's book *Über den Ursprung und die Hauptgesetze des wirtschaftlichen Werthes* published in 1884 (Howey 1972, 295).

[69] Von Wieser especially sympathized with the economic policy of *Kathedersozailismus*. Menger declared in his book *Die Irrthümer des Historismus in der deutschen Nationalökonomie*, published in 1884, that he was in favour of social reforms, and his famous socialist brother Anton Menger had some influence on him, but Carl Menger was not a socialist (Kauder 1965, 64).

[70] A possible interpretation is the following: the minimisation of the role

According to Willgren (1893, 330) the Austrians had the following aims:

- reformation of economic science, and especially
- close observation and description of the facts of social life,
- the theories should be based on a more solid foundation than those of classical political economy, which according to the Austrians was based on an untenable "mechanistic way of thinking", and
- the theories should be based on a more solid psychological foundation, the reason for calling the Austrian school "the psychological school of economics".

The Austrians certainly aimed at the reformation of economics. Here the second point about the observation and description of social facts is especially problematic. Menger's attack on the German historical school is clear evidence of his ideal of theoretical science aiming at the examination of the essence of economic categories such as value, profit and the division of labour: Menger opposed the naive empiricism and gathering of facts of the historical school. The psychologism of the Austrian school was more acceptable. According to Kauder (1965, 120–121), most Austrians used some kind of introspection, meaning "the ability of the observer to reconstruct events which go on in the mind of another person with the help of self-observation".

Despite their rather radical programme, the Austrians did not foster any revolution in economic science, according to Willgren. They built on the foundations laid by the Physiocrats and Adam Smith (Willgren 1893, 341).[71] Thus Willgren emphasised continuity in economic theory, and did not think that there was a gap between classical political economy and Austrian marginalism. The Austrians, and Menger especially, saw themselves as a genuine new school of thought in economics, a view which is still held

of the state had perhaps been against the interests of many representatives of the Austrian school because they were civil servants and some of them worked in the administration (for example Mataja and von Böhm-Bawerk).

[71] Willgren's view is problematic. As a matter of fact, Carl Menger was critical of Smith. He considered himself to be a continuator of the heritage of the founder of the "older" historical school, Wilhelm Roscher (1817–1894). Menger even dedicated his *Grundsätze der Volkswirtschaftslehre* to Roscher. Kauder (1965, 95) emphasized the Aristotelian legacy of the Austrians.

today. Willgren did not emphasise the heterogeneity of the Austrian school enough.

Willgren was interested in the ideas of the Swedish marginalist Knut Wicksell. In the 1890s he published two articles appraising the works of Wicksell (Willgren 1895 and 1897) in the journal Finsk Tidskrift. The first one dealt with a book published by Wicksell (1893) who, according to Willgren (1895, 158), had developed Eugen von Böhm-Bawerk's ideas and so contributed to the more solid foundation of economic theory. The difference between Wicksell and the Austrians lay in the attitude towards the use of mathematics.[72] Wicksell did not share the Austrian resistance towards mathematics as a way of presenting economic ideas. Willgren (1895), however, felt that the Austrian way of thinking was completely mathematical, and referred to the book written by John Neville Keynes (1891). It remains unclear what he meant by that statement. He himself did not use mathematics, but he wrote approvingly about its use:

> The symbolic language of mathematics makes it possible to easily follow the complex way of thinking that characterises economic theory... Besides this, symbolic language offers, as Wicksell shows, the advantage that wrong conclusions and inconsistencies otherwise difficult to notice are revealed when the economic ideas are formulated mathematically. (Willgren 1895, 164.)

Willgren's other article reviewed Knut Wicksell's book *Finanztheoretische Untersuchungen* that had been published a year before. Wicksell emphasised both the traditional fiscal effects and the distributional effects of taxation (Willgren 1897, 358). The general trend of the taxation system in Finland towards the end of the 19th century was the heavy shift in emphasis towards indirect taxation, and at the beginning of the 20th century, the proportion of indirect tax revenue of the whole tax burden exceeded 90 per cent. This meant a rise in social inequality: a problem that was much discussed from the 1890s onwards (Kuusterä 1990, 55–56, see also Kuusterä 1989b). This may partly explain Willgren's interest in marginalist economics.[73] Perhaps he

[72] According to Kauder (1965, 90–91), Menger was "a fanatical opponent of mathematical analysis" in his creative years.

[73] Marginal utility and the law of diminishing utility were used as a justification for progressive taxation until the 1920s (Kauder 1965, 138–139).

was looking for a model for treating the practical problems of taxation.

Willgren examined different principles of taxation in this article. The first, the "interest principle", based the taxes payable by a person on the utility or revenue received from the state. According to another principle, the taxation should be based on the taxpayer's ability to pay. Wicksell saw his new fiscal principle as both a method which guaranteed justice in matters of taxation, and a development of the old interest principle (Willgren 1897, 360). The tax system must be based on the unanimous decision of the groups in society whose interests are related to the state budget which is financed by tax income.

Willgren examined the problems connected with the measurement of the utility the various interest groups received. Wicksell had proposed that the state budget should be divided into parts in such a way that part of the whole state income would be allocated to every expense or group of expenses. Willgren thought that this arrangement would make the budget more complicated, and used the Finnish state budget as an example.

Wicksell described and criticised the Swedish system of taxation in his book. Willgren agreed, and stated that it must be possible to reform the system of taxation "since this science [finance] has progressed so much lately" (Willgren 1897, 366). This statement can be interpreted as a reference to the application of marginalism to the theory of public finance. Willgren did not name marginalist authors, so the issue cannot be settled with certainty. According to Willgren, Wicksell's research work had the lasting result that the interest principle was given more emphasis in theories of public finance. He also showed the close connection between political institutions and taxation (Willgren 1897, 368). Willgren would have preferred to see theory and practice coming closer to each other in the theory of public finance, following the example of Knut Wicksell. So his appraisal of Wicksell's book was very positive.

It seems that Karl Willgren found the economics of the Austrian school and its Wicksellian version scientifically somewhat more convincing and persuasive than the German historical economics of von Schmoller, Wagner and others who dominated so strongly among the Finns. However, he was alone in his sympathy towards Austrian economics. As an Associate Professor the Faculty of Law he had an extensive obligation to teach and could not devote himself to scientific research.

Karl Willgren's interest in Wicksell's economic ideas is indisput-

Karl Salomon Willgren (1865–1930)

able. Apart from the articles mentioned above, he published a review of the first part of Wicksell's famous textbook (Wicksell 1901; Willgren 1903). He began by characterising "economic science in its modern form" as based on the ground laid by Smith, Ricardo, Malthus and Mill, and went on to refer to the problem with many textbooks of popularising the ideas of past masters without presenting the new contributions. Another problem was the complex and difficult forms of expression which were one reason for the "bad reputation" of the so-called mathematical school, and had resulted in neglect of their work. Willgren named Alfred Marshall's work *Principles of Economics* as an exception.

Willgren wrote that Wicksell's book had served Swedish economic literature in introducing the "more and more territory taking" mathematical and graphic methods of expression. However, he thought that a mathematical introduction had been necessary in Wicksell's work, because many potential readers were not at all familiar with differential and integral calculus. He wrote: "It is a pity that the mathematical basis of so much that is meant to clarify economic notions in this way must be passed-by by most readers..." (Willgren 1903, 282).

Willgren pointed out that Wicksell used the same ceteris paribus method as in his previous book (Wicksell 1893), reviewed by Willgren in 1895. According to Willgren, the theory of income distribution was, for the first time, clarified in such a thorough and satisfactory way by Wicksell, although the presentation would have been even clearer had he emphasised the different functions of an entrepreneur and analysed the components of entrepreneurial profit (Willgren 1903, 283). Nevertheless, Karl Willgren found Wicksell's book "one of the best" presentations in the economic textbook literature of those times.

Willgren's Theory of Income Distribution

In the Finnish context, Karl Willgren was exceptionally well aware of the development of economic theory. Two articles (Willgren 1916a and 1916b) published in the journal Ekonomiska Samfundets Tidskrift are clear manifestations of this. Willgren took the transitional stand between the Russian Mikhail Tugan-Baranowsky[74] and the German Rudolf Stolzmann[75] on the one hand, and the marginal utility theoreticians on the other. The articles contain many references to the works of the leading marginalists: in addition to the Austrians, these included Walras, Marshall, John B. Clark and Frank Taussig.

According to Willgren (1916a, 152), the distribution of the national income was "a complex result of the interest struggle between different groups in society". He emphasised the difference between pure economic exchange and income distribution. Equal individuals meet in exchange, but in income distribution the agents are members of different classes of society. The problems of price formation cannot be examined as fully analogous to the problems of income distribution theory, although the distributional shares of different factors of production can to some extent be seen to be dependent on price formation. Willgren modified his surprisingly radical position, however, in stating that

[74] Tugan-Baranowsky was the best-known Russian economist of his time (Schumpeter 1986, 1126). He was a theoretician but did a lot of empirical work as well. He had been very much influenced by Marx, and Schumpeter (Schumpeter 1986, 879) called him a "semi-Marxist Marx critic". His most important works were the history of Russian industrial capitalism *Die russische Fabrik* (The Russian edition was published in 1898), *Theoretische Grundlagen des Marxismus* (1905) and *Soziale Theorie der Verteilung* (1913).

[75] Stolzmann published *Die soziale Kategorie in der Volkswirtschaftslehre* in 1896 and *Der Zweck in der Volkswirtschaft* in 1909.

"the difference between the laws of production and the laws of distribution is only a gradational difference, however" (Willgren 1916a, 154).

John B. Clark, in the Austrian spirit, stated that the problem of income distribution could not be settled without clarification through "imputation", what share of the output belonged to every single factor of production.[76] Willgren summed this up: "The results of the production will be directed (imputed) to every factor of production in the same ratio as it has contributed to the production" (Willgren 1916a, 156). According to Willgren, the Austrian von Wieser was a strong supporter of the 'imputation theory".

The Swedes Knut Wicksell and Gustav Cassel had criticised von Wieser. Wicksell had remarked that there was nothing new in von Wieser's thoughts: in circumstances of free competition, one factor of production must get approximately the same compensation regardless of the transaction which was in question. Cassel had criticised the assumption of the law-like character of the "imputation" that had been von Wieser's starting point.

Willgren addressed many critical points to von Wieser. He suggested that the harmony between factors of production and products postulated by the "imputation theory" was an illusion. It was not possible to separate a certain part of the output, and then show that it was the result of the influence of a certain factor of production (Willgren 1916a, 161). The main mistake of the "imputation theory" of von Böhm-Bawerk was the underestimation of the influence of the forces of nature in the formation of the output. The interesting feature in the "imputation theories" lay in their emphasis on the connection between production and distribution. Willgren looked at marginal productivity as a norm of income distribution:

> Thus it can theoretically be maintained that *the rise in production of the last hired worker* becomes decisive both up and down for wages in general. (Willgren 1916a, 173, italics original.)

He saw the issue as a kind of exchange of employment performance and the corresponding wage. The marginal productivity of labour determined the wage, which was an analogous case to the

[76] Clark's ethical conclusions went further than those of the Austrians. He maintained that distribution according to the law of marginal productivity was "fair" (Schumpeter 1986, 870).

correspondence of marginal utility and price in the commodities market. He referred to Wicksell's Lectures (Wicksell 1901), suggesting that rent was also determined by marginal productivity (Willgren 1916a, 175).

Willgren presented his own contribution to the theory of income distribution in the article (Willgren 1916b). His solution is closely connected to Mikhail Tugan-Baranowsky's theory of income distribution (Tugan-Baranowsky 1913), thus making him an exception among Finnish economists: he admitted that Russian economic theory had influenced him (Willgren 1916b, 349–350). Tugan-Baranowsky had emphasised the interdependence of power relations and income distribution between capital and labour, and the independence of rent. He also suggested that income distribution did not depend on the exchange of the products. Although Willgren did not accept all the main theses of Tugan-Baranowsky, he considered the theory of income distribution to be independent of the theory of price (Willgren 1916b, 349). This was clearly not a marginalist stance.

Willgren maintained that a historical point of view was needed as a counterbalance to the rather abstract framing of the question by the "classical" and "socialist" schools of thought. He wrote:

> ... it is a remarkable economic and historical fact that wages, interest and rent are determined more or less by law and habit after the determination of the prices of commodities in the market through free competition. (Willgren 1916b, 374.)

He also referred to Henry Sidgwick's (1838–1900) book (Sidgwick 1883). When the influence of institutions and societal factors is omitted, the productive impact of the factors of production can be examined as services the prices of which are determined by the law of demand and supply.

The distribution of income in the economy seems to be a system which aims at equilibrium between the different forces that influence demand and supply. Willgren mentioned Stolzmann and emphasised that the distribution of income had to happen on the grounds of "societal organic appropriateness" (1916b, 376).[77] Thus the capital revenue had to serve capital formation. Interest could be compared to the wage of the workers: it was

[77] This expression resembles the language of the German historical school.

the compensation that capitalists and landowners received for their action in society. According to Willgren, the predominant income distribution was based on the achieved societal condition and could essentially be changed only if co-operative production displaced capitalist production.

An interesting detail in Willgren's writings is his essay (Willgren 1915a) about Joseph Schumpeter's book on economic development (Schumpeter 1911). Willgren brought out Schumpeter's well-known ideas concerning a dynamic vs. static economy, business organisation and the role of entrepreneurs on the one hand, and economic crises on the other, as creative forces in economic development. He also referred to W. S. Jevons' famous "theory of sunspots" as an explanation of economic crises (Willgren 1915a, 348–349). He criticised Schumpeter's theory of economic development for excessive generality and a lack of "contact to reality", and thought that it should be developed to deal with long-term depressions. In this context, Willgren pointed out the importance of mass consumption which balanced the gap between rising production and consumption and prevented the appearance of crises due to under-consumption (Willgren 1915a, 353). He proposed that the problem could be solved by raising the ability to consume of the "lower social strata", which was reminiscent of the social policy thinking of the German historical school.

Willgren's own contribution to the literature on taxation was his extensive research report published by the Tax Committee.[78] The report (Committee Report 1911: 12b) is actually a comparative study of the tax systems in European countries. Willgren supported the general subjective income taxation system (Committee Report 1911: 12b, 585), as well as property taxation, as a way to additionally burden a stable income. He did not use marginal analysis in his study.

Willgren's contribution can be summarised in the following way. His articles reveal his exceptional knowledge of new economic theory in the Finnish context at the turn of the century, but

[78] The Tax Committee was appointed in 1908 and it was formally disbanded in 1915 (Wikström 1985, 76–82). The committee could not present any proposals on the execution of the general income and property tax, but it issued three publications. One was the report written by Willgren (Committee report 1911: 12b). The committee published the Finnish translations of the Prussian, Danish and Norwegian tax laws, and the French and Russian proposals for tax laws (Committee report 1911: 12c). The work of the Tax Committee did not lead to immediate changes in legislation.

he did not use marginal analysis in his works at all, even though he referred to foreign authorities on many issues. Nevertheless, his introduction of Austrian marginalist ideas and the economics of Knut Wicksell and Gustav Cassel to the Finnish audience was a valuable contribution.

The Influence of Austrian Capital Theory

The ideas of the Austrian economist Eugen von Böhm-Bawerk received very much attention at the beginning of the century, and were presented in one published lecture (Groundstroem 1903) and two articles (Willgren 1914 and Nevanlinna 1914). The writer of the published lecture, Oskar Groundstroem (1868–1940), had had a statistician's training and was a registrar in the Finnish Statistical Central Office. He gave lectures at the Swedish-speaking society Ekonomiska Samfundet. Ernst Nevanlinna (1873–1932) was trained as a historian, but he was interested in economics. In 1905, Nevanlinna was the Chairman of the Finnish Economic Association, founded in 1884. He was appointed Professor of Financial Economics at the University of Helsinki in 1924.

What was the reason for the special interest in von Böhm-Bawerk? One apparent reason was the German influence on Finnish economics and the fact that the Finns usually travelled to Germany and Austria to study economics. Another reason was perhaps that the practically-oriented Finnish economists shared von Böhm-Bawerk's ideas because of his experience in practical economic matters. He had served three times as Minister of Finance in Austria. According to Nevanlinna (1914, 274), "he [von Böhm-Bawerk] had given the most easily understandable form to the marginal utility doctrine". The Finnish economists, who were trained as jurists or historians, must have appreciated this non-mathematical form of economic theory. That was perhaps the third reason.

The capital theory and the theory of interest were the main research areas of von Böhm-Bawerk. In methodological questions he followed Menger's "abstractive and deductive" style of analysis, and he was one of the most ardent advocates of marginal utility in the theory of value. (Nevanlinna 1914, 264–265 and 274 and Willgren 1914, 198–199.)

According to Willgren, von Böhm-Bawerk admitted the role of the cost of production in the determination of the value of the commodity in an article published in the journal Zeitschrift für Volkswirtschaft, Socialpolitik und Verwaltung (Willgren 1914, 203). However, he considered them to be "indirect causes' of value (von Böhm-Bawerk 1909, 299). Willgren referred to the critique of marginal utility theory, that marginal utility alone could not determine the value of a commodity because the costs of production limited the diminishing marginal utility. It had also been stated that marginal utility could not explain the value of unique objects. Willgren wrote:

> It is a characteristic of rare objects that the utility of every additional unit is rising – contrary to what marginal utility theory teaches – until the required quantity is fulfilled. (Willgren 1914, 205, italics K. W.)

Willgren himself took the position of a moderate critic in relation to marginal utility theory.

Nevanlinna's attitude towards von Böhm-Bawerk was highly respectful rather than critical. Nevertheless, he referred to Wicksell's and Marshall's critical remarks concerning von Böhm-Bawerk's principal work, *Kapital und Kapitalzins* (Nevanlinna 1914, 268).

Both Nevanlinna and Willgren concentrated their attention on von Böhm-Bawerk's theory of interest and capital. Nevanlinna referred to the point of departure that was common to von Böhm-Bawerk and the German historical school, namely the critical attitude towards Jean B. Say (Nevanlinna 1914, 269). Von Böhm-Bawerk strictly distinguished the concept of productive capital from the concept of capital that yielded interest. Like Wagner and Rodbertus, he called the former "social" and the latter "private capital". He denied the classical political economy view of capital as a factor of production that could be compared with natural forces and with labour. Instead he stressed its character as an intermediate product.

Von Böhm-Bawerk emphasised the significance of the extension of the production period in his theory of production. In the capitalistic production process, the loops of production made larger and better quality production possible than in production without capital, but the production time was necessarily longer.

The theory of interest presented by von Böhm-Bawerk was also related to the concept of time. He thought that there were both psychological and technical reasons to value present goods more than future goods. He called the difference between the present value and the future value "agio": this was exactly the interest on capital (Willgren 1914, 212).

Karl Willgren on the Labour Issue

Like many of his contemporaries, Willgren was also influenced by German social policy thinking. At the beginning of the 1890s he had already written about limitations on working hours in Finland (Willgren 1891), and about workers' sharing in business profits (Willgren 1892). In his first article he examined the discussion about possible limits on working hours internationally and in Finland.

Willgren's conclusion was that without a reduction in common working hours, all other social reforms would fail (Willgren 1891, 431). The nature of the criticism against such reduction had been partly economic and partly moral (Willgren 1891, 190). In his article, Willgren responded to the economic aspect by pointing out that it did not necessarily result in reduced production. The same held true for the alleged negative effect on wages (Willgren 1891, 421). He did not think that a reasonable reduction in working hours would reduce the productivity of labour but, on the contrary, that it would increase it. In any case, the worker's ability to consume would rise, which would lead to a rise in production:

> It is consumption that runs production; it is consumption that is the goal of production. A worker plays a role not only in production but also in consumption. But now it has been shown everywhere that a reduction in working hours has improved the worker's position, developed his physical and intellectual powers, and he has also advanced technically and risen to a higher moral standpoint; it has even been shown that his needs have diversified at the same time as his ability to consume has risen. (Willgren 1891, 200.)

Thus, Willgren concluded that a moderate limitation on working hours would not cause any harm to the Finnish economy. In those days the length of the working day could still be over 12 hours.

From the point of view of well-being and health, Willgren's view is clear: reduction in daily working hours was necessary (Willgren 1891, 265). In answer to the alleged bad influence on the morals of the working class, he pointed out that associations, the development of public libraries and raising the level of workers' education were the best ways to help people to spend their increasing leisure time. However, he also emphasised that any reduction in working hours should be made prudently and gradually to avoid possible economic disturbances. Willgren's view was that working hours should not be exactly the same in every industry, but should vary according to the specific conditions, the difficulty of the work and the effects on the workers' health.

In his article on workers' shares in business profits, Willgren pointed out that experience in France, Germany and other countries had shown that giving workers a share in profits was an effective incentive, and a better incentive than piecework. A bonus could be given once a year to industrious and skilful workers and to those with long service, or it could be distributed on the basis of saved raw materials (Willgren 1892, 95).

According to Willgren, incentive systems had their drawbacks as well. When the amount of the incentive depended on incidental factors, and its distribution to the workers was arbitrary, it could result in dissatisfaction and spoil the working atmosphere. He also referred to the productive units owned by workers, but thought that the Finnish workforce was not civilised enough to perform their jobs independently, especially in the area of business management. Nevertheless, the Finnish co-operative movement became an important economic force after the turn of the century, and remained one for several decades.

These two articles are clear examples of Willgren's social and politically oriented thinking. Like many other Finnish scholars of the time, he shared the reformist spirit of many members of the economic and political élite. The Finnish élite perceived the same danger as the German *Kathedersozialismus*: the rising labour movement and socialist ideology. Their response was in empirical social research and in the demand for social reforms.

Willgren made a contribution to empirical social research in his lecture for the Society for Swedish-speaking Economists on April 29, 1907. An enhanced version of the lecture "Arbetarklassens ekonomiska framåtskridande" (The Economic Progress of the Labour Class) was published two years later (Willgren 1909). The article is a rather thorough examination of the economic conditions of the Finnish labour force at the turn of the century. Willgren's problem was whether the industrialisation process had brought improvement or misery to the working people.

Willgren examined the development of workers' economic conditions in Finland under the period 1876–1905. He showed that their material conditions had improved steadily in previous decades in spite of occasional setbacks (Willgren 1909, 43). Finland had experienced rather rapid urbanisation: in 1870, 7.5 per cent of the Finnish population lived in towns, and in 1905 the percentage was 13.7. Emigration from Finland was rather extensive in the last decades of the 19th century, as well.

However, during those decades and around the turn of the century, the Finnish economy and its industry experienced a "take-off stage" in Rostowian terms, with the wood-processing and engineering industries being the leading sectors. Wages were increasing rather rapidly in industry and manufacturing, as well as in agriculture. Moreover, working hours had been reduced: under the period in question they were generally no more than ten per day. Real wages had also increased because of a decrease in the price of corn. Willgren concluded that even farm labourers lived better than at the beginning of the period, in the 1870s. (Willgren 1909, 64–69).

Although it had been claimed "from the side of the social democrats" that the conditions of industrial labour had worsened, Willgren pointed out that an "impartial examination" did not support such a claim (Willgren 1909, 77). He particularly emphasised the fact that an overview of the period 1876–1905 did not uncover a single branch of business in which wages had not basically increased (Willgren 1909, 80). He concluded:

> Although the costs of living had risen somewhat, especially after the turn of the century, we can find an even larger increase in wages in most occupations. Generally, you could say that, in the whole country, industrial workers and artisans are now better off than 30 years ago. (Willgren 1909, 87.)

It was only five years from the publication of Willgren's lecture to the outbreak the First World War. Finland, as part of the Russian Empire, was also involved, although no fighting took place on Finnish soil. However, the economic situation worsened. There was already a lack of food in 1917. In Russia, the revolution broke out in October. Amidst this unstable situation, the Finnish Government published its Declaration of Independence in December, and the dramatic civil war broke out in January, 1918.

In 1917, Willgren contributed to the debate on the eight-hour working day. He did not share the Social Democratic majority's view in the Diet: they wanted a universal reduction in working hours to eight, and believed this was a general international development.

In his article (Willgren 1917, 106) he referred to the endangered competitiveness of Finnish industry, because against the Social Democrats' optimism, he did not believe that other countries would apply the general eight-hour working day. He rather felt that rival countries would have the "self-control, discipline and the overall perspective on the economic conditions" that was lacking in Finland. He thought that the international social democratic plan for an eight-hour working day would lead to unemployment and deteriorating economic conditions.

Karl Willgren and the History of Thought on Public Finance

Willgren's second dissertation (Willgren 1899) for the Faculty of Philosophy dealt with public finance. His main jurisprudential work (Willgren 1906) was his basic university textbook, which was on the curriculum for several decades. As was pointed out previously in this context, he was involved in the work of the Tax Committee in 1908–1915, and also published two articles in which he theorised on the origins of public finances and financial institutions (Willgren 1910 and 1915b). Both articles can be classified under the history of economic thought, although the emphasis in the second one was strongly on the history of financial institutions and taxation. It is very likely that the two articles were biproducts of Willgren's work for the Tax Committee.

The first article (Willgren 1910) was a rather wide survey covering theories of public finance in past centuries. He emphasised the absence of economic study in Sweden and Finland until the 18th century. The model that was adopted for the study of public finance came to these countries from Germany in the form of cameralism. Willgren named Anders Nordencrantz as a representative of Swedish mercantilism in the 18th century (Willgren 1910, 174).[79] Physiocratic thought and the idea of a single tax on the agricultural net product was represented by Carl Fredrik Scheffer, Lars Ekmarck, A. G. Barchæus and Anders Wappengren during the final decades of the 18th century (Willgren 1910, 178–179). Willgren concluded that the impact of physiocracy was not very strong in Sweden or Finland.

In spite of the rise of Adam Smith's economic liberalism in many countries, and Anders Chydenius' critique of mercantilist commercial policy in the Diet, cameralism dominated thoughts on public finance. In Sweden, Professors Anders Berch and Lars

[79] On Swedish mercantilists, see also Magnusson 1987.

Georg Rabenius of the University of Uppsala gave lectures on public finance in a cameralist spirit. Rabenius in particular influenced Daniel Myréen, Wilhelm Lagus and Johan Jakob Nordström. Thus, the predomination of the cameralist principle of equivalence between state income and expenditure lasted a long time in Swedish and Finnish public finances. Cameralist writers thought, for example, that taxation should be based on several types of taxes, and that the tax burden should be evenly imposed among taxpayers. Karl Willgren concluded that cameralism brought about the birth of public finance as a subject of scientific scrutiny in Sweden and Finland (Willgren 1910, 218). However, he emphasised that it was no ready-made science at first, but rather an embryo of a scientific field.

Willgren concentrated on the history of economic institutions and legislation in his other article (Willgren 1915b). He examined the early development of economic legislation and institutions of public finance, especially the period from antiquity to the Middle Ages. He mainly relied on the works of the German writers Adolph Wagner and Johan Friedrich Lotz as his sources, but he also referred to Giuseppe Ricca-Salerno's history of Italian financial thought, J. K. Ingram's history of economic thought, William Cunningham's economic history, and Edwin Seligman's studies on taxation

The Reception of Neoclassical Economics on the Periphery

Marginalist economics was presented to the Finnish audience relatively early in the 1890s. Thus one is perhaps allowed to say that marginalism was imported into Finland, but that it in no way became embedded in Finnish economics. The German historical school was highly respected by the Finns, and it reigned supreme over the turn of the century. Before the Civil War and into the 1920s and 1930s, Finnish economic research had a rather strong practical and empirical emphasis, and theoretical work remained on the sidelines. Marginalist economics was normally seen as a continuation of classical political economy, and its significance as a paradigm shift was not emphasised.

Why was marginalist economics imported into Finland? One answer to this question is simple: because it was there. Marginalism was a new approach to economic questions. Its position was strengthening in large European countries, although the reign of the historical school was very strong in German-speaking areas. Almost the only one to follow and comment on marginalist economics was the Swedish-speaking economist and jurist Karl Willgren. However, this may be explained by factors related to training. The lack of communication between societies of Swedish- and Finnish-speaking economists, and the strong dominance of the German historical school in the Finnish Economic Association, may be the reasons behind the minor attention to marginalist economics in the Finnish-speaking camp. In fact, it was only Nevanlinna who showed interest in the marginalist school before the Civil War. Clearly, the associations were not effective in presenting the new school of thought.

In the last decades of the 19th century, the theoretical influences in economics came increasingly from German-speaking Central Europe, where Finnish economists went to study. Because of their training as jurists or historians, the Finns undoubtedly avoided the mathematical language of the French and the English economists. This may be the reason why Knut Wicksell did not receive very much attention as an economic theoretician. The dominance of the German historical school directed the interest of the Finns towards non-mathematical theories such as Austrian economics.

How significant were the marginalists considered to be in Finland? The attitude towards the new economics seemed hesitant. The significance of the marginal utility theory as a new approach to the theory of value was recognised, but the Walrasian general equilibrium theory was not discussed at all despite some references to Wicksell. The French, English and Italian marginalists were named the "mathematical school", as distinct from the Austrian school.

Karl Willgren did not accept all the Austrian ideas as such, which is manifested in his articles on income distribution. He tried to find a transitional position in relation to the marginal utility theorists on the one hand, and to Tugan-Baranowsky and Stolzmann on the other. As stated before, Willgren confessed that he had been influenced by Russian economic thought, which was an unusual phenomenon in the Finnish context.

The articles that reflected the *Methodenstreit* between Austrian and German economics could be seen as efforts to understand the turning-point that was taking place in economic science. Nevanlinna himself, who had received his basic training in history, turned to advocate neoclassical economics, but not until after the Civil War. Uskali Mäki (1984) described the "Casselian turn" in Nevanlinna's thinking. In the 1920s, Nevanlinna abandoned relativistic and indeterministic German historicism in favour of the search for more general, abstract and theoretical Casselian neo-classical economics (Mäki 1984, 115–116). One of the reasons for the popularity of Cassel was his book *Theoretische Sozialökonomie* published in 1918 in German, which became one of the most influential books in economic theory all over the world in the 1920s. Methodenstreit as such does not seem to have affected the Finns.

The hegemony of German historical economics among Finnish economists was so strong that there are no signs of scholars with natural scientific training coming over to economics. As stated before, the only independent chair in economics at the University of Helsinki until the 1920s was held by Vennola, a strong supporter of historical economics. All the economists had the training of a historian or lawyer. The historical approach is clearly to be seen in academic dissertations written before 1920, and these were mainly empirical social studies (see Eriksson 1978, 41–64).

The textbooks, of course, had their own significance in the transmission of economic ideas to the periphery. Several textbooks were translated into Finnish at the turn of the century. These included *Principes d'Économie politique* by the Frenchman Charles Gide (1904), the part of the book *Socialøkonomik* by the Norwegian Professor Torkel H. Aschehoug (1904) dealing with the history of economic science, *Nationaløkonomien i Hovedtraek* by the Dane Harald Westergaard (1909)[80], *Volkswirtschaftspolitik* by the German Johannes Conrad (1913), and *Allgemeine Vokswirtschaftslehre* by the Austrian von Philippovich (1914).[81]

Marginalist economics was briefly presented in every book, but Aschehoug just mentioned Jevons' value theory when dealing with the Webbs and the Fabian Society (Aschehoug 1904, 164). Gide and Westergaard did not see marginalism as a radical uniform theory break. Gide divided marginalist economics into the "mathematical school" (for instance Jevons, Marshall, Walras, Pantaleoni, Pareto and Fisher) and the Austrian "psychological

[80] Compare with Niels Kærgaard's (1996) article. According to him, Westergaard's textbook, published in Denmark in 1891, "was the final establishing of marginalism as part of accepted economic science in Denmark" (Kærgaard 1996, 253).

[81] Adam Smith's, Friedrich List's and David Ricardo's famous main works originally published in 1776, 1841 and 1817 were translated into Finnish in the 1930s (Smith 1933, List 1935 and Ricardo 1937).

school" (Gide 1904, 20–21). Eugen von Philippovich was "one of the greatest teachers of the period", and due to his influence, "marginal utility theory filtered through to German students" (Schumpeter 1986, 853). He held a professorship in Vienna and sympathised with the historical method of the German historical school, and with German social policy.

5. ECONOMIC THOUGHT AND ECONOMIC POLICY

5.1 Ideas and Practices

As mentioned in the introduction of this book, we have given economic thought a very broad meaning. No strict distinction is made between economics as an academic discipline and other kinds of economic thought, primarily because there was no such distinction in 19th-century Finland either. Thus, after dealing mostly with academic economic thought in the previous chapter, we will now turn to the links between economic thought and economic policy. Our purpose is not to write a history of Finnish economic policy in the 19th century as such, but to examine, on the one hand, how economic thought shaped economic policy and, on the other hand, what kind of impetus the solving of the practical problems arising from the economic policy gave to more theoretical economic thinking. Our discussion therefore focuses only on the elements of economic policy that we meet on this two-way road between economic ideas and practices.

We could separate three kinds of links between the world of economic ideas and the world of economic policy in 19th-century Finland. First, there was the personal link: many academic "economists", introduced in the previous chapter, took part in debates on economic-policy issues. Further, there was an institutional link: economic associations, the press and, although perhaps to a lesser extent, committees, were among the forums where policy-makers and more theoretically orientated economic thinkers debated (see Chapters 2 and 3). Finally, and this is most relevant to our presentation, there was a thematic link: "pure" economic science was a very small part of Finnish economic thinking, in which a practically-orientated tendency was dominant. Thus, pol-

Lars Gabriel von Haartman (1789–1859)

Clas Herman Molander (1817–1897)

Leopold Stanislaus Mechelin (1839–1914)

iticians and "economists" were principally discussing the same themes. The link between academic economic science and economic policy was self-evident during "the cameralist bias" of the first half of the 19th century, when the main function of academic teaching concerning economic issues was to educate civil servants to take care of state finances. Later on, the relationship between economic thinking and economic policy changed somewhat: first, because economic science gradually gained more independence from other sciences as well as from its bureaucratic associations, and second, because the notion of economic policy changed, its domain widened outside the limits of state finances and it confronted new questions raised by the emerging market economy.

The economic policy discussion forum started to change during the latter half of the 1850s when the spreading of the "liberal" spirit gave more room to public discussion, and further in the 1860s, when Diet assemblies became regular. Although the actual power of the Diet on issues of economic policy remained quite limited, it became an important new forum for debate. Discussions in the Diet also strengthened other public discussion, especially in the press. However, along with this new public discussion, the old and less public economic policy forums, the Senate and the committees, maintained their influence.

Most of the academic economists involved in policy debates were introduced in the previous chapter, but there were also more practically-oriented shapers of economic policy. The most important among them was the director of the Financial Office of the Senate, the nineteenth-century equivalent of the Minister of Finance. Among the "theoreticians" examined in the previous chapter, two also held the post of Director of Finance: Johan Vilhelm Snellman in 1863–1868 and Leo Mechelin as deputy in 1882–1886. In terms of prominence, however, two figures rise above the rest: Lars Gabriel von Haartman in 1840–1858 and Clas Herman Molander in 1871–1897. Their combined careers add up to almost half a century (see Appendix 4).

These two long-term directors of finance were quite different in their administrative style, however. von Haartman, who acted simultaneously (1841–1858) as the head of the Economic Department of the Senate, as "Prime Minister" in modern terms, was undoubtedly the most powerful among the Finnish politician-bureaucrats of his era. He had close formal and informal relations with the governor-general, A. S. Menshikov, and he made use of these relations in matters concerning economic policy. However, apart from having good bureaucratic training and a talent for intrigue, von Haartman was obviously well-read in economic literature. This can be assumed from his library catalogue from the early 1840s,[1] and from the argumentations he presented in the various memorandums he wrote while preparing several important reforms of economic policy. Molander, on the other hand, was more of a grey bureaucrat, and so unobtrusive that he has been characterised as "the great unknown" of Finnish nineteenth-century history.[2]

In the following we will first describe the changes of economic policy régime, taking the conventional approach from the point of view of the mercantilism-liberalism dichotomy. Thereafter, four thematic bundles of economic policy which are considered the central ones are studied in detail: the monetary system, taxes, tariff policy and infrastructure.

5.2 Economic Policy Régimes

According to the conventional periodisation of Finnish economic policy during the period of autonomy, first came the mercantilism phase, lasting until the 1850s and 1860s, which was followed by the liberalism phase. This periodisation, although not without grounds, is somewhat misleading and is too much based on the changes in the institutional setting, mentioned above, and in the formal legal reforms. On the one hand, there was a great deal of continuity in economic policy over the breakthrough of liberalisation, and on the other hand, there were many "liberal" changes made in the field of economic policy during the decades before the 1860s. It therefore seems that the era of autonomy should rather be divided into four periods.[3]

During the first phase, from 1809 until the 1830s, the main economic policy concern was to carry out a smooth transition from Swedish to Russian rule. The second period, from the 1830s to the 1850s – especially during the rule of von Haartman (1840–1858) – saw reforms being carried out within the framework of the old bureaucratic system. The mercantilist system involved many kinds of privileges regulating economic activity. Some of

1 von Bonsdorff 1946, 441–443.

2 Kuusterä 1989a, 97–98.

3 Björkqvist 1986; Heikkinen 1994; Kuusterä 1989a; Peltonen 1989; Schybergson 1973.

these regulations, concerning trade and rural handicrafts for instance, were lifted. Moreover, the first steps were taken to develop the infrastructure: water transportation was improved by constructing channels, and occupational education was started. In the mid-1850s, several committees were established to prepare economic reforms, which were soon carried out in a liberalist way.[4] In this sense we could call this period protoliberalist.

The third period, then, would be the period of liberalist breakthrough from the late 1850s to the 1870s. Several reforms were carried out in order to create conditions for the development of the market economy. Restrictions preventing the mobility of factors of production were abolished and economic legislation was modernised to guarantee the predictability of economic activities.

Most of the mercatilist restrictions on economic activity were abolished between 1859 and 1868. The obligatory guild system was repealed, restrictions concerning trade (e.g. the prohibition of rural trade) were abolished, and the sawmill industry was liberalised. Modern employment relationships were created by reforming labour, vagrancy and poor-relief legislation. These reforms, carried out by the early 1880s, intensified the mobility of labour and transformed the employment relationship into a voluntary contract between free and judicially equal individuals. In the field of commercial legislation, the most important reforms were the Companies Act, the Bankruptcy Act, the Bank Act and the Bills of Exchange Act. These acts, all of which came into force in the 1860s, created a favourable environment for capitalist development.[5]

The "great breakthrough" of ideas of economic and political liberalism took place in the late 1850s and early 1860s, and gained legislative and practical momentum in the 1860s and 1870s. The liberalism of the 1850s, however, did not come out of thin air. The corporate economic system had been criticised in the preceding decades, for instance by A. H. Chydenius and J. V. Snellman. As mentioned earlier, Snellman saw liberal reforms as a possible means for solving the problem of pauperism. The same idea was elaborated by Johan Wilhelm Rosenborg, who in his dissertation on pauperism and poor relief (Rosenborg 1858) heavily criticised

[4] Björkqvist 1986, 299; Kekkonen 1987.

[5] However, freedom of trade was not absolute. For instance, capital movements were restricted by a 6 percent maximum interest rate. In agriculture, the rights to parcel land were seriously limited. Furthermore, the right to carry on a trade was granted only to Finnish nationals.

the system of "legal protection" for subordinating labourers, placing them under guardianship and thus "dividing the nation into masters...and slaves". He denounced paternalistic ideas and suggested that workers should be made "completely free", so that work would become "dependent on a sheer civil contract concluded by two equally free and sensible beings".[6]

Chydenius and Rosenborg belonged to the liberal Dagblad circle, as did Henrik Borgström Jr., Reinhold Frenckell, Leo Mechelin and Robert Montgomery. These intellectuals formed the core of Finnish economic liberalism. The most influential in economic policy was Mechelin. His field of activity was extremely wide-reaching, from practical banking to high posts in government. He was among the leading figures in the Diet, participating actively in economic policy discussion there. He was also a member of several committees, including those planning the Trade Act, the transition to the gold standard and tax reforms. (Nordenstreng 1936–1937)

Reactions to economic liberalism emerged after the 1870s. Yrjö-Koskinen and Th. Rein were the first to promote the German ideas of the *Kathedersozialismus* (see section 4.5). These anti-liberalist reactions started the fourth period of economic-policy discussion. The concrete results of this critique, however, were quite modest in the sense that the liberal fundamentals of the economic system were not shaken. The Labour Protection Act of 1889 was one of the few achievements in this field.

By the 1880s, the liberalist reform programme had been put into practice and there were then no big issues in public debate on economic policy. Following the example of the German historical school, the emphasis moved to questions of social policy. As far as the economic policy was concerned, tax reform was the most important issue.

5.3 Monetary Issues

Background

Debates on monetary issues illuminate the ways in which economic ideas are filtered into society. In the 19th century, monetary problems were at the centre of state economic policy measures, still narrow in their scope compared with their modern

[6] Bruun 1979: 57–60; Björkqvist, 1986: 178–180; Heikkinen 1997, 27.

counterparts. Those debates on monetary issues are thus interesting to us in the context of contemporary views of the role of the state in the economy, i.e. the limits of the government's responsibilities and the proper division of work between the private and the public sectors, as well as the proper design of the latter's intervention.

In their implementation of monetary reforms, the decision makers had to conceive of the economy as a whole, and ponder its reactions to reforms. These episodes may thus reveal, if only indirectly, such assumptions concerning economic behaviour which would otherwise have remained concealed. This interaction between theory and practice is made more accessible by the fact that monetary theory was relatively well developed in the 19th century, and discussion on monetary policy issues was normally based on a theoretical framework of some kind.

Interaction between theories and policies is made still more interesting by the fact that monetary issues typically become a problem during, or in the aftermath of, economic turbulence and instability. Policy makers thus face the problem of, first, how to apply theoretical insights largely assuming "normal", tranquil conditions to a situation that often could be described as a crisis. In this context they, second, have to make up their minds as to how to balance the immediate requirements of the crisis on the one hand and the long-run principles of well-organised monetary institutions on the other. Indeed, it is the difference in the relative emphasis given to these two often-conflicting considerations which has formed a perennial watershed in monetary thinking.

More recently, the schools of thought which find themselves in conflict on these issues have been called the "short-sighted", or pragmatist Keynesian approach on the one hand, and the Monetarist, or "fundamentalist" approach on the other, the latter laying more emphasis on the long-run stabilising forces of a market economy. Yet in the 19th century, this division had had its antecedent in the controversy between the Currency school and the Banking school as regards the stringency of control of currency issues. (Kindleberger 1986) This controversy was also reflected upon in the monetary policy debate in Finland at that time.

Finland, as a Grand Duchy of the Russian Empire, created its own currency, the Markka, during the course of the 19th century. Connected with this process towards monetary autonomy, Finland also became equipped with its own financial system – the central bank, i.e. the Bank of Finland, and gradually developed a proper central banking system in the course of the century (for the members of the board of directors, see Appendix 3). The banking system and, at least a rudimentary version of, other financial institutions also came into existence. Apart from eventual differences in theoretical views concerning the proper design of monetary institutions, the reforms in Finland were complicated by the political considerations connected to the fact that, as subjects of the Russian Empire, the Finns had to take into account Russian reactions. As a matter of fact, Finland acquired complete monetary autonomy vis-a-vis Russia in the course of the 19th century. This may have been one of the basic aims of the reformers, but it goes without saying that they had to proceed carefully so as not to evoke Russian counter-reactions.

In the 19th century, the development of a domestic financial system involved three major institutional rearrangements which raised public debate and engaged the attention of decision makers for a considerable period of time. The first of these reforms was the abolition of the two-currency system and the opting out from partial dependency on the Swedish currency, which happened in the first half of the century. This step towards stable monetary conditions was not possible until both Russia and Sweden had adopted a silver standard. However, the stability offered by the move turned out to be temporary, as Russia was compelled to leave the silver standard in the context of the Crimean War in the 1850s, and Finland had to follow suit. (Tallqvist 1900)

The second change was the transition from the Russian paper rouble to Finland's own currency, the Markka, convertible to silver, in the 1860s. This move, which produced the first form of Finland's own metallic currency, was taken under difficult economic circumstances and implied huge economic hardship during the transition. This made the balancing of the long-term gains of a stable currency against the short-run costs of adjustment particularly controversial. (Pipping 1928)

The third reform was the adoption of the gold standard in the 1870s. This completed the striving for a stable, metallic-based monetary framework in Finland. As a matter of fact, at a surprisingly early stage considering its overall degree of economic development, Finland became a member of the "élite" group of countries participating in the classical gold standard of the 19th century. The gold standard reform was planned in greater detail than the previous reform. Furthermore, although the economic conditions for the reform were somewhat unfavourable in the mid-1870s, the difficulties the transition imposed were minute compared with the hardships of the 1860s. By the same token, the degree of monetary stability provided by the classical gold standard turned out to be much higher than by the silver. (Björkqvist 1953)

Before going in further detail into these policy debates, an overview of classical monetary thinking is in order. Additionally, by way of an introduction to the monetary policy issues of the 19th century, a short account is given of Anders Chydenius' role in the lively monetary debate in Sweden in the late 18th century.

Classical Monetary Thought

The breakthrough of classical monetary thought in the 18th and early 19th centuries provided a central thrust for the contemporary critique of Mercantilist ideas of economic policy. According to the ideas behind classical monetary thought, first clearly stated in the writings of Richard Cantillon (1680–1734) and David Hume (1711–1776), the real wealth of the nation consists not of the amount of money in circulation, but of the commodities money can be exchanged for. The "classical dichotomy" compressed in the quantity theory of money elaborates this in a statement according to which the purchasing power of money varies in an inverse relationship to the amount in circulation; the higher the amount of notes and coins chasing the given amount of goods and services, the lower becomes their value in terms of commodities.

The classical dichotomy had, until those days, served as a source of ideas for organising the monetary institutions and drawing the outline of monetary policy. The basic aim was to establish monetary institutions that, through a well-functioning payments system and stable monetary value, would facilitate the continuous deepening of the division of labour in society and thus an increase in its wealth. A stable monetary value was also conceived of as providing a useful service to society by abolishing the uncertainty related to inflation and protecting property rights through a reliable basis for agreement. It was also thought to facilitate the development of a well-functioning banking system.

Early writings on classical monetary thought considered paper money and the reckless borrowing by the sovereign it easily gave rise to the greatest threats to monetary stability. Unconditional convertibility of notes to a precious metal, silver or gold, was recommended as the means to prevent such an excess in monetary expansion. In the "Bullionist Controversy" in England during the Napoleonic wars, representatives of classical monetary thought,

David Ricardo among them, accused the Bank of England of causing inflation by issuing notes and coins not backed by gold. To prevent this, full gold cover for the notes issued by the central bank was required. In 19th-century Britain, this requirement was met through the famous Peel Banking Act of 1844, following which, the representatives of the old bullionist ideas came to be called the "Currency School". (Kindleberger 1993)

There is an inherent problem in classical monetary thought in terms of monetary stability. The monetary system becomes a problem just when it is unstable. Under such conditions, the productive side of the economy is also typically disturbed, and there is reason to fear that the measures needed to restore monetary stability may harm production and employment in the short run. Critics of strict classical monetary thought put more emphasis on these short-term considerations of the linkages between the monetary and the productive aspects of the economy. In one way or another, they argued for a system of "managed money" in which the monetary authorities are expected to exercise discretion, based on the requirements of the real economy, in deciding the timing and the strength of the decisions affecting the amount of money in circulation. In the discussion of the Peel Banking Act, such views, represented by Thomas Tooke among others, came to be referred to as the "Banking School" which stressed the "needs of trade" as a criterion for note issue by the central bank. As Charles Kindleberger, for example, has observed, it is not too far-fetched to suggest that the Keynesian ideas of the 20th century represented the same general tradition of managed money (Kindleberger 1986).

The basic tenets of classical monetary thought were also reflected in Finland from the late 18th century onwards as the organisation of the monetary conditions of the country came on the agenda. Finnish authors followed discussions abroad, and lessons for domestic problems were drawn from those. Much of the inspiration came from French and Swedish authorities in the field, however, rather than from the British monetary debate.

Prelude to Monetary Reforms in the Late 18th Century: Anders Chydenius

During the "Age of Liberty" in 18th-century Sweden, unstable monetary conditions were a continuous cause of concern. The country had adopted a paper standard in 1745, when there was a war against Russia and the internal political system of the country was in a state of disarray. Later on, reflecting Mercantilist ideas, an increase in the amount of government debt certificates in circulation was motivated by the claim that this provided a stimulus to industry. This claim was denied by those who were familiar with the emergent ideas of classical monetary thought.

Anders Chydenius, the leading economic pamphleteer in Finland at that time, joined in this controversy on several occasions. It seems that his sympathies shifted somewhat over time, which clearly reflects the inherent tension between the long-term and short-term considerations referred to above.

Chydenius' first monetary policy statements presented ideas akin to those of Hume and Cantillon, blaming the issue of government debt certificates for the deterioration in the value of money. He called for a metallic standard, where circulating notes are fully backed by metallic reserves. Following the ideas of Anders Nordencrantz, a central figure in the contemporary monetary controversy in Sweden, he called for a return to the value of money that had prevailed before 1745, and for the drastic cut in the number of notes in circulation that the required decrease in price level would have called for. This was the recommendation he put forward in 1762 in his answer to the question posed by the Royal Academy of Sweden concerning the causes of emigration; according to Chydenius, the deteriorating value of money was largely responsible even for that. (Chydenius 1765c)

Chydenius soon came to revise his views. Through the writings of Pehr Nichlas Christiern, he became aware of the real disruption to the economy that might be caused by deflation.[7] This concern was reflected in the essay Chydenius wrote for the Banking Deputation to Parliament in 1766. He was now concerned about the devastating consequences for economic activity, both consumption and investment, that the anticipated deflation would have. Consequently, he now proposed stabilising the monetary conditions by moving to a metallic standard at the existing price level and thus avoiding harmful deflation. (Chydenius 1766)

Such an accommodative stance posed another problem to Chydenius. Accepting the earlier deterioration in the value of money would have implied that the interests of the old lenders who had lent out their money in times of a lower price level would be hurt. This could have been considered a violation against private property rights. To avoid this, Chydenius made his

7 In Sweden, the famous philosopher Emmanuel Swedenborg had given a similar warning in the 1720s, and Chydenius was aware of his work.

loan indexation suggestion: in the repayment of old loans, the purchasing power of money prevailing at the time the loan agreement was made would be observed.

In his brief comments on contemporary controversies, Chydenius pointed out an issue which was to become a recurrent cause of concern in the monetary debate in 19th-century Finland: given that stable money requires a metallic standard, should a transition to be made on the basis of the existing price level, or should the previous metallic value of money be aimed at, and, in that context, should the property rights of the lenders concerned in the original pay-back in real terms be observed regardless of later changes in the value of money? Interestingly, it was the latter "legalistic" concern with retaining the value function of money and the property rights of the holders of monetary assets which featured strongly in debates in 19th-century Finland.

Monetary Thinking and Monetary Reforms in the Early 19th Century

Not much changed in the monetary thinking in Finland in the early 19th century. Writers such as Daniel Myréen in his two-volume book on money (Myréen 1810–1811), submitted as a doctoral dissertation at Uppsala University, established the dominance of classical monetary thought in the country. He defended the government's exclusive right to print money. The negative consequences of deteriorating money for the economy were emphasised by Myréen who, like Chydenius before him and many of his successors in 19th-century Finland, linked the stability of the value of money to the property rights of the holders of monetary assets.

More changes took place in the monetary institutions of the country, brought about by the secession of Finland from Sweden and its submission to Russian rule in 1809. Russian money, the silver and paper rouble, had been made legal tender in Finland during the war, i.e. before the country was formally annexed to Russia. Finland's monetary system was discussed by representatives of the estates in Borgå in early 1809, when several forms of money were circulating in the country. The silver rouble was being replaced by Russian paper money, which was deteriorating in value, and Swedish paper money was also extensively used. One of the issues discussed by the estates was whether Swedish notes should be withdrawn from circulation, which was the official

Russian stance. Yet, representatives of the bourgeoisie, such as Peter Johan Bladh, emphasised the trade relations with Sweden and opposed the withdrawal of Swedish notes. They pointed out that Swedish money was flowing into the country because of Finland's positive trade balance with Sweden, which made the use of Swedish money convenient. Bishop Jacob Tengström, a central figure in the administrative reorganisation during the early phase of Russian rule in Finland, also defended a pragmatic approach to monetary re-arrangement. (Tengström 1809)

The formal decree by the Russian authorities in favour of the rouble notwithstanding, two forms of paper money, Russian and Swedish, were circulating in Finland for about three decades. The Bank of Finland, the future central bank, was established in 1811; yet the country lacked its own money and monetary policy, and the Bank of Finland acted rather like an ordinary credit institution. The banking system was highly rudimentary, and its development was not yet considered urgent.

The adoption of the silver standard by Russia and Sweden alike gave an impetus to a gradual change towards a more comprehensive national monetary system in Finland. The decision to remove Swedish notes from circulation was taken in 1840. Following the recommendations of L. G. von Haartman, a "soft" approach was taken: existing market rates of exchange were adopted as standards, and the Bank of Finland drew Swedish paper money from circulation by offering a favourable exchange rate. In the same context, the status of the Bank was changed more to that of a proper central bank by providing it with a mandate to issue notes tied to the silver rouble and backed by its own reserves. Reflecting views similar to those of the Currency School, a rigid relation (7:15) between reserves and circulating notes was imposed. Despite sometimes hefty criticism, this kind of partial, yet strict, cover requirement was maintained until the early 1870s.

The move to a metallic standard was favourably received by the representatives of the, still tiny, trading and industrial community who saw it as stable basis for expanding foreign trade and for gradually developing a system of private banking. These people, John Julin and Henrik Borgström Senior among the most outspoken of them, were influenced by French and British authors, although it was not until a little later, during the 1850s, that theoretically more advanced writings came out when Nordström, Borgström Jr and Snellman stepped in front of a public audience.

To sum up, by the 1850s, the narrow Finnish community of financiers and civil servants had, broadly speaking, a general understanding of contemporary monetary analysis. The importance of monetary stability for overall economic stability was well understood, and a metallic standard was regarded as a warranty for that. The need for a national banking system was also generally understood, yet it was still to be a couple of decades before the breakthrough. As elsewhere, there were different views as to how strictly the reserves of the central bank should dictate its note issue. Like the contrast between the contemporary Currency and Banking schools, this reflected the difference in the viewpoints of the "pragmatists" and the "fundamentalists" in monetary management. It was from such positions that the economic and monetary turmoil of the next decade was viewed.

The Monetary Reforms of the 1860s and 1870s

The Crimean War in the mid-1850s led Russia again to abandon the silver standard. The issue of paper roubles led to inflation in Russia, which had consequences for Finland when her central bank had to follow suit. The return to a paper currency and the dependence of domestic monetary conditions on the unstable Russian system evoked in Finland the idea of creating its own, metallic currency. Henrik Borgström, Jr. was one who suggested this (Borgström 1859). The reform itself was instigated by Fabian Langenskiöld, von Haartman's successor in charge of fiscal affairs in the Senate, and a close associate of Borgström Jr. After Langenskiöld's death in 1862, the currency reform was brought to a conclusion by his successor in the Senate, J.V. Snellman.

The creation of the silver Markka was a much more prolonged process than it was originally planned to be. Finland's own unit of currency, the Markka, defined as a quarter of a silver rouble, was created in the first phase in 1860. The original idea of Langenskiöld was that this should soon be followed by its convertibility to silver at this rate. Deteriorating economic circumstances and ongoing Russian inflation, however, delayed this until it was finally imposed, still at the old parity, in late 1865. Due to the intervening inflation imported from Russia, the decision implied a revaluation of the currency by almost 20 per cent which harmed exports, necessitated tight monetary policies to maintain the currency reserves, and imposed a need to decrease the price level in the midst of a deep slump in the international economy and a sequence of bad harvests at home. (Pipping 1928)

The difficulties of monetary reforms under unfavourable economic circumstances were repeated, on a smaller scale, in the late 1870s. This was when Finland, following Germany, the Scandinavian countries and France, which was chosen as the model to be followed, moved to the gold standard in 1877–78 as a reaction to the deteriorating value of silver. Even then, a revaluation, this time by about 10 per cent, was imposed in the midst of an international recession. Yet, there was no contraction in credit volume at that time, and the recession was consequently milder than during the previous reform. (Björkqvist 1953)

Controversies Surrounding the Late 19th- Century Monetary Reforms

The introduction of the silver Markka under difficult economic circumstances evoked criticism. However, the ensuing debate was restrained because the civil society was still poorly organised and the reform was planned and executed by a small group of leading civil servants and members of the business élite. The reform of the 1870s was more open, prepared by a high-level committee set up by the Senate under the chairmanship of Robert Montgomery (1832–1898), who had served as Liljenstrand's deputy as Professor of Economic Law and Economic Studies.

The reforms of both the 1860s and 1870s were made under unfavourable economic circumstances. This is not surprising as such: monetary reforms are motivated by the need for more stable monetary conditions, and this stability is typically undermined by a sharp destabilisation in the economic environment. At the same time, however, instability in the underlying economic conditions complicates the execution of reforms. Typically, reformers are faced with the difficult task of compromising between flexibility and pragmatism, and a rigorous sticking to simplified fundamental theoretical principles. The transition could be made easier by flexibly adjusting the terms of the reform, but, as a rigorist would argue, this would take place at the cost of undermining the credibility of the new system. It is in such a context that the conflict between monetary pragmatists and fundamentalists, referred to at the outset of this section, has typically spelled itself out in monetary controversies.

The monetary reformers in 19th-century Finland mainly followed a rigorist approach. While it was the sharp weakening of the prevailing monetary standard, i.e. the Russian paper rouble, in the 1860s, and silver in the following decade, which prompted the reforms, in both cases the decision was made to undo the depreciation by adopting the previous metallic parity as unchanged: in the currency reforms of the 1860s, the new monetary unitMarkka, created in 1862, first depreciated along with the paper Rouble. In the next phase, before and in the aftermath of the imposition of the convertibility of the Markka to silver in 1865, deflationary monetary policies were pursued. These were needed in order to undo the depreciation and to support the old parity of the silver Rouble to Finnish authorities were determined to restore. The amount of money in circulation decreased from 1864 to 1866 by one quarter, and the curtailment of credit volumes followed the same pattern. (Pipping 1961, 542–545)

The reforms were aimed at stabilising the monetary conditions which, at the same time, were disrupted by deflationary tendencies in the international economy. Under these conditions, maintaining the parity, and apparent monetary stability, necessitated deflationary policies which, in turn, disrupted the real economy by severing the deflationary tendencies already going on. Tight monetary conditions led to a wave of bankruptcies; in the second half of the 1860s, on average about one quarter of the lending of the Bank of Finland was submitted to insolvency procedures while, according to some estimates, as many as 10 of the 30 biggest enterprises in the country went into bankruptcy. The wave of bankruptcies almost destroyed the emerging export industries, especially in the areas of metal and clothing in which were heavily dependent on their competitiveness in the Russian markets. (Kuusterä 1987, 53)

The impact of the monetary contraction following the silver exchange constraint was made more devastating by the fact that it coincided with a series of bad harvests at home, which resulted in a severe famine and an excess death toll of almost 10 per cent of the population (Pitkänen 1991, 283–298). Although bad harvests were the immediate reason for the famine, it was also partly a consequence of policies: there was a shortage of currency reserves immediately after the monetary reform in autumn 1865. Even during the worst year, 1867, imports were delayed until the very late autumn, and the famine had already made its worst impact. (Soininen 1975, 402–410)

The move to the gold standard in 1877–78 also imposed revaluation under difficult external economic circumstances. The economic hardships were repeated, although on a much smaller scale. Again, while the preparations for the reform were being made in 1876, the ongoing sharp depreciation of the silver Markka was overlooked and its old gold parity was adopted as the gold exchange from the beginning of 1878. A period of deflationary policies followed, once again coinciding with an international recession, the deflationary impact of which was clearly felt, although it remained milder than in the case of the reform of the 1860s. There was no collapse of credit this time, and the halt in output growth remained short-lived.

Furthermore, the working of the gold standard was made more flexible in practice by certain changes in the institutional arrangements. Thus the rigid cover rule of 7:15 for note issue, which had been heavily criticised in the context of the silver standard reform, and by Borgstrom Jr. before that, was finally removed in 1872 and replaced by a fixed, but adjustable ceiling (Pipping 1969, 84–86). This concession towards the principles of the Banking School was made even more significant by the fact that, among the participants of the classical gold standard, Finland was one of the few countries which included foreign currencies as well as gold in the cover for the issue.

These qualifications notwithstanding, the similarities between the monetary reforms in the second half of the 19th century in Finland are strong enough to enable the following question to be asked. Why did the authorities stick to their original plans which, as a consequence of adverse changes in the external economic environment, necessitated imposing more restrictive policies than originally conceived? How did they argue for their standpoint? What criticism did they face?

One explanation that has been suggested emphasised the political context of the monetary reforms. They were conceived of as, and also resulted in, an enhancement of Finnish autonomy in the period in which the means of directly strengthening the political independence of the country had been destroyed. It has also been maintained that the civil servants initiating the reforms thus took charge of extending the country's autonomy in times when political life still remained subdued.

This interpretation may not hold under close scrutiny. Finnish monetary reformers were generally loyal to Russian interests and tried to take them carefully into account. When the reforms of both the 1860s and 1870s were started, it was believed that Russia would follow suit with similar measures. Since, due to Russia's own difficulties, this expectation did not materialise as rapidly as was originally thought, the Finns had to move on their own. Increasing monetary and economic autonomy thus turned out to be a side product of the reforms of which the original intention had not been primarily political. (Pipping 1928; Björkqvist 1953)

Yet it remains true that the political constraints, especially relations with Russia, played a crucial role in the execution of the reforms and pushed pure economic arguments into the background. In gauging their reactions, the Finnish authorities had to take into account Russian counter-measures. This was most clearly evident in the case of the 1860s reform. The Emperor had accepted the reform plan in 1862, and in this context the silver parity of the Markka was also fixed. When the reform then had to be postponed mainly due to unforeseen economic difficulties, and Russian inflation eroded the value of the Markka, Snellman feared that changing the silver value of the Markka – a decision which should have been submitted to the Russians for approval – would have given the Emperor an excuse to reject the whole reform, which was no longer in the Russian interest since it had become evident that the Russians were not able to stabilise the Rouble.

These political constraints do not diminish interest in the economic viewpoints on which the reforms were assessed. On the contrary, they suggest even more exacting demands on the economic policy skills of the reformers.

As is evident from the above, the debate around the monetary reforms in 19th-century Finland was dominated by a view which stressed the importance of stable monetary conditions for the overall stability of the economy. A metallic standard was generally considered the best system to provide this inherent stability. The striving for stable monetary conditions was in turn motivated by a need to remove the obstacles from developments considered important for increasing economic well-being: 1) expanding foreign trade and providing stable conditions for exports conceived of as the main source of an increase in economic well-being; 2) the creation of a domestic banking system; 3) a stable currency was also taken as a prerequisite for establishing unviolated and well-defined property rights. From the point of view of money as a valuable stock item, this emphasis on property rights in the context of monetary reforms had already played a crucial role in monetary debates in Finland in the late 18th century.

The tight monetary policies imposed by the cover requirement led to devastating economic consequences. This evoked criticism. Consequently, a proposal for lifting the 7:15 requirement was discussed by the Estates in 1867, which was not accepted at that time, however. The old cover rule was finally replaced by a fixed, but adjustable quota on note issue in the 1872 session of the Estates. This relaxation of the monetary policy rule played a role in weakening the recessionary impact of the revaluation in the context of the gold standard reform .

As far as foreign theoretical influences were concerned, the authorities on monetary theory referred to by Borgström Jr and Nordström remained standard references in the Finnish debate in the latter part of the century. They mainly represented contemporary liberal economic thought. The second edition of Chevalier's work (Chevalier 1846) was translated into Swedish in 1867, and was cited by Snellman in his writings on monetary issues. Another French liberal monetary theoretician often cited in Finland was Coquelin, whose book (Coquelin 1850) had been translated into Swedish in 1855 and cited by Snellman in his first published writing on money and banking issues (SA VII, 165–181).

Generally speaking, extensive references to foreign theoretical authorities in the domestic policy debate remained few. In most cases, only second-hand references were made, often included in some older texts published in either Finland or Sweden. It was not until in the context of the gold standard reform of the 1870s that more explicit reliance on foreign experiences was evident. The secretary of the committee set up by the Senate to prepare the reform, Robert Castrén, had undertaken economic studies in Paris under Professor Paul Leroy-Beaulieu, and reported on the contemporary monetary debate in France in a series of articles in Helsingfors Dagblad. Furthermore, through Mechelin's international contacts, a plan for Finnish monetary reform was requested from the Swedish banker, A. O. Wallenberg. (Committee Report 1876).[8]

The planners of the reforms typically represented state-centred, cameralist views which emphasised the consequences of different policy options for the state's finances. This was partly true for Snellman in the 1860s. More characteristically prominent civil servants such as Herman Molander in the context of the reform of the 1870s, and before him Lars Gabriel von Haartman in the context of the first reform of the 19th century, motivated the reforms as a means to relieve the burden of foreign borrowing on the government. From this point of view, it was indeed the preceding monetary volatility and the deterioration of the external value of money which increased the cost of foreign borrowing in domes-

[8] Reliance on Swedish expertise was, in fact, also evident when Finland returned to gold in the 1920s. Eli F. Heckscher was asked to write an extensive memorandum which had a great influence on the Finnish decision in 1925 to return to gold, albeit with changed parities. Finally, in the context of the post-war settlements in the 1950s, the expertise of Erik Dahmén was used.

tic money, which in turn prompted the reforms and, at least implicitly, targeted them at revaluation.

Such a state-centred view on revaluation easily overlooked the wider economic consequences of a higher external value of the currency for exports and imports, as well as for domestic purchasing power. As these repercussions led to unforeseen economic difficulties in the currency reform of the 1860s in particular, fiscal-cameralist and broader economic considerations clashed with one another, in turn giving impetus to a renewal in thinking.

Concentration on the state's finances exemplified a more general feature, a de-emphasis on the transitional problems connected with the changing monetary institutions. These problems, extending over several years, largely came as a surprise to the decision makers, who had to revise their plans. The way this was done provides further evidence of the development of contemporary economic thinking. This necessity to adjust measures to changing circumstances in turn motivated further developments in economic argumentation.

One example of the transitional problems concerned the implementation of monetary policies during the reform phase. This was commented on above in the discussion on the contrast between the Currency School and the Banking School in the Finnish debate on the rules covering note issue. Another example was the relationship between exchange rate changes and the domestic price level. The reforms of both the 1860s and 1870s, which were preceded by currency volatility and loss in the external value of the domestic currency, imposed a revaluation of the currency, and the authorities were faced with two related questions. The first concerned the relation between the internal and external price levels; did the revaluation create the need to adjust the domestic price and cost level downwards? Second, how quickly would this domestic price adjustment take place, and how serious would the transitional difficulties be, in terms of cost crisis, industrial slack and bankruptcies?

As far as the first question was concerned, the poor quality of the available statistics on prices meant that the relationship between the external and internal price levels was unclear, even statistically. In the context of the reform of the 1860s, no attempt was made to collect relevant price information – although the need for such information was stressed. In fact, the first rough attempt was made by Borgström Jr. in his book cited above.

The time needed for domestic price adjustment was hardly

mentioned in the debate. There was an interesting exception, however. In an obscure Pro Memorium from 1865 (Pipping 1928, Appendix), J. V. Snellman showed his skills in conceptual economic analysis. The PM was written before the reform was in fact announced, to a committee dealing with the increased costs of the maintenance of the Russian military in Finland – an issue raised by the Russians themselves and presented as an argument against the planned monetary reform.

In his paper, Snellman relied heavily on a doctrine which later became known as the purchasing power parity theory for the internal value of money. According to this theory, labelled by the Swedish economist Gustav Cassel in the early 20th century, the internal price level is related to foreign prices through the exchange rate, the changes in which are passed on through proportional changes in domestic prices.

Dealing equally with cases of both depreciating and appreciating currency, Snellman argued for an extreme version of the purchasing power parity view according to which exchange rate changes would be fully passed on through domestic prices in a time span of weeks, or a few months, rather than years, as was generally assumed later on. On this basis, Snellman denied that exchange rate changes had any effect on export and import volumes, for example, since rapid domestic price adjustments neutralised any changes in the relative profitability of foreign and domestic goods.

Indirect evidence bearing on the relevance of this theoretical standpoint to Snellman's view on how the reform should be planned and executed was provided in his short remarks after the reform explaining the roots of some of the actual difficulties met. He regretted that the issue of silver in 1865 had had to be postponed until very late autumn, which meant that the winter break in sea traffic had already begun, and the absence of imports delayed the inevitable fall in domestic prices for several months until spring. Perhaps it was this doctrinal standpoint, natural to a philosopher, that made Snellman so resistant to various pragmatist critics of the reform, and this is discussed more closely below.

Snellman's view of the transmission process was more explicit than the views of most of his contemporaries. Thus the committee planning the gold standard reform, under the heavy influence of Leo Mechelin, took the view that the depreciation of the currency which, for several years, most notably from late 1874 to 1876, preceded the reform imposed in 1877–78 did not have any noteworthy influence on domestic prices. Either there was no impact, or if there was, it would take a long time to take effect. On this basis, it was maintained that the recent decrease in the price of silver had not yet had any effect on the domestic price level; consequently, a revaluation in the context of the reform did not have any deflationary impact. Mechelin himself was most outspoken on this latter view. (Committee Report 1876)

This view, at least to the extent that it totally ignored the link between the external and the internal value of the currency, made the transitional problems look easy, as there was no pressure to push the domestic price level downwards.[9] It met resistance, however. It was criticised in the debate in the Diet, and the chairman Robert Montgomery included his own reservations in the resolution of the committee, maintaining that although the price consequence of the fall in the value of silver in 1876 could be overlooked, earlier depreciation had already been reflected as domestic price increases in the previous 3 to 4 years. (Committee Report 1876)

An intermediate view was also represented in the committee, most explicitly put forward by W. Hackman, a businessman from Vyborg in Eastern Finland, and representing the interests of foreign trade. According to him, the impact of the exchange rate changes was concentrated on export and import prices (as well as on the burden of foreign debt) (Committee Report 1876). It is interesting that this view was fiercely attacked by old Snellman himself in parliamentary debates, when he expressed his astonishment that such views were still maintained:

"How can one doubt that a domestic purchaser of an export commodity would also have to pay ten per cent more... But as the price of the produced commodity increases, the price increases move over to raw materials and wages." (SA XII, 339–342)

Interestingly enough, Snellman was fiercely critical of the deflationary impact of the gold standard reform. He now repudiated his own views of the 1860s, and indeed admitted that his own critics had had a point in calling for devaluation. His changed attitude may also have reflected the fact that he had moved to the

[9] This issue is more complicated if the claim is based on the view which Mechelin seemed to advocate in his PM, according to which the passing on of exchange rate changes to domestic prices is very slow, extending over several years. In that case, the Committee should have considered the claim that, due to the depreciation of the Silver Mark, cost and price increases were still in the pipeline, which, if burdened by inflation, would incur losses to traders and manufacturers.

Mortgage Association, the viable interests of which were damaged by deflation and bankruptcies.

In the absence of any structured theoretical controversy over the reforms, critical views were mainly voiced by groups in society whose economic interests were directly affected by them, especially by the deflationary policies they necessitated. The reforms of both the 1860s and 1870s, implying changes in real exchange rates, had, at least in the short run, different consequences for different segments of society. In 19th-century Finland, however, the organisation of interest groups of exporters, merchants, bankers and farmers was rudimentary and uneven, although the coverage increased towards the end of the century.

This patchy organisation of economic interests was reflected in monetary reforms in several ways. On the one hand, initial reform plans typically paid closest attention to the interests which were most effectively represented in the planning process. On the other hand, the impact of the reforms gave the impetus to develop more efficient organisation of interests in the segments of the society which were affected.

It seems that two groups, partly overlapping, were best represented in preparation for the monetary reforms, civil servants and merchant houses. The influence of the new industrialists, exporters and farmers was not as effective, and they had to put more thrust on external pressure, such as press and Parliamentary procedures.

The critics of the 1860s reform represented groups of exporters and farmers who were heavily dependent on the Russian markets, including iron manufacturers, as well as sawmill and estate owners in Eastern Finland selling their products to Russia. Their most active spokesman was G. S. Schatelowitz, an estate owner and entrepreneur from Eastern Finland with a landed-gentry background. His opposition to the reform lasted for most of the decade, and the group around him was often referred to as the "Elimäki Party", after the place where Schatelowitz himself was living. (Pipping 1928, 298)

Schatelowitz' critique took different forms on different occasions. Its main thrust remained the same, however: the devastating consequences of the deflation necessitated by the reforms on vital economic interests in the country. During the first stage in the early 1860s, as the Russian paper Rouble started to fall, he called for devaluation as a precondition. This was rejected, and he and his allies suggested that the reform should be postponed. Thus a group of industrialists and estate owners from Eastern Finland signed a petition demanding that the reform should either be abandoned or redesigned, because:

"The whole indebted part of the population, mostly comprising the country's producers and farmers, would realise that their production capacity remains depressed, in many cases destroyed, for a long period by the significant increase in the real value of their debt." (Pipping 1928, 284–285)

At this stage, Schatelowitz made a proposal which provoked a lively debate and made the decision makers, even Snellman, hesitant, at least for a while. The proposal was to reduce the nominal value of old loans in order to avoid the capital losses debtors would otherwise have incurred as a result of the fall in price level. This possibility was considered by Langenskiöld, for example, in his early plans for reform.

The reactions of the reformers, especially Snellman, to these proposals were negative, and did not influence the way the reforms were carried out. It should be noted, however, that devaluation across the board was rejected much more firmly than the proposal for debt realisation. To Snellman himself this was natural, as he was convinced that the reform was only a change in the nominal unit of account to which the domestic price level would rapidly adjust. Thus the profitability of exports or imports would only change temporarily. This explains Snellman's aggressive reactions later on to reports of bankruptcies in different parts of the country. He felt that these failures had nothing to do with the monetary reform, and that unprofitable business should not be kept alive by "artificial" measures: "What is rotten should be let fall down", is a well-known statement attributed to him by his biographer (Rein II 1981, 434). This harsh attitude may also have reflected Snellman's critical attitude towards the open-handed policies of the 1850s and early 1860s (see below). In the same vein, he insisted that business failures were, to a large extent, a consequence of harvest failure, i.e. a natural catastrophe for which the monetary reform should not be blamed.

Assuming the need for almost immediate price adjustment, Snellman was more in favour of downscaling old debts. He explicitly pondered this possibility in a private letter to his cousin J. W. G:son Snellman (Pipping 1928, 293–294). Upon closer investigation, however, the conclusion was reached that it would injure the property rights of creditors. This ethical standpoint was a key concern to Snellman, too, and was reflected in monetary controversies in Finland from the late 18th century onwards, when Anders Chydenius called for the indexation of old loan agreements.

By the time of the gold standard reform, the interest groups were already more effectively organised. On the other hand, this reform was less controversial, and the transition phase attached to it less painful. The preparations for the gold standard were much more open and systematic than in the context of the adoption of the silver Markka that preceded it (Björkqvist 1986, 418). The reform was based on the proposal of a high-level committee which took different viewpoints into account. Its work was discussed in the press, and foreign expertise was systematically used. All these features represented a gradual increase in the standard of economic argumentation in the country.

The above observations on the discussion of the monetary reforms in Finland in the second half of the 19th century suggest two general conclusions. First, the authorities in charge were primarily not adherents to hard money, but rather took a rigid administrative approach, paying only sporadic attention to the wider economic context. They understood the importance of the reform mainly in a political and administrative context. Deterioration in the economic environment, which came as a surprise, seemed to endanger the originally-conceived framework, which made the authorities think it was necessary to harden their stand in order to keep their plan intact and not to undermine its credibility or political feasibility. This was further complicated by the suspicions of the Russians. It was in such a situation that the authorities made tactical use of the maxims of sound monetary policy supplied by classical monetary thought, generally known by the late 19th century. In other words, it was for tactical convenience that monetary fundamentalism served the authorities whose basic approach to economic management was pragmatist.

Second, the authorities were not much pressured to change their plans by the public, which saw their economic hardships as largely independent of the actions taken by the authorities. The pressure on them was also diminished by the fact that the institutional preconditions for economic policy debate prevailing in 19th-century Finland were rather sporadic: professional economics, as exercised at the university, for example, was next to non-existent. The domestic press was still in its infancy, and economic interest groups were only just becoming mobilised. The most influential representatives of business interests, the merchant houses, combined the roles of industrialist and exporter, who had reason to oppose revaluation, and of importer and money lender who rather saw advantages in it. On balance, they found themselves among the supporters of the reform. The owners of the newly-established iron processing factories, as well as the big farmers, were more unequivocally opposed to revaluation, yet they were too weak to get their voice through.

The above propositions suggest that the standard of economic discourse, assessed on the basis of monetary debate, was still rather rudimentary in 19th-century Finland. The basic theoretical standpoints were well known, however, and there were significant advances between the silver standard reform of the 1860s and the gold standard reform of the 1870s.

Later Developments

The gold standard brought the Finnish monetary system some stability which lasted until the First World War. Its peripheral economic position notwithstanding, Finland became a member of the élite group of countries which participated in the classical gold standard, generally considered a success. This increased the credibility of the country, facilitated its access to foreign credit, and provided the impetus for rapid growth in foreign trade and the further development of the financial sector. Apart from an adjustable cover requirement, monetary management in Finland was made more flexible by the fact that foreign currencies (tied to gold) were included in the reserves of the central bank.

Under these conditions, inflation was low, interest rates stable, and the average rate of economic growth relatively high, a few recessionary periods notwithstanding. The settled conditions under the gold standard were also reflected in the fact that monetary issues were pushed into the background in the economic policy debate. Nor was there much interest in monetary and banking theory.

Mention should be made, however, of the work of Paavo Korpisaari on the theory of banking which came out during the war (Korpisaari 1915). This book gives a systematic survey of the history of banking theory, mainly from the point of view of the historical school with which Korpisaari had become acquainted through his participation in Adolph Wagner's seminars in banking theory in Berlin in 1909 and 1912. Of special interest are the accounts of the recurrent liquidity crises in the banking systems of different countries, and the fact that the subsequent restrictions on credit lead to disruptions on the real side of the economy. Korpisaari criticised late 19th-century banking theory for overlooking the factors giving rise to such crises and, faithful to his roots in the historical school, regarded this as a consequece of its exclusive concentration on the British deposit banking system. To avoid further crises, Korpisaari recommended the adoption of cash reserve requirements and tighter banking supervision.

5.4 Tax Issues

Tax Policy Traditions

The public finances of the Grand Duchy of Finland were based on the self-taxation traditions of the Swedish era, i.e. on the principle that taxes had to be approved by the assembly of estates. During the Age of Liberty (1719–1772) the assembly of estates had even ruled over the use of state finances. The 1772 constitution, however, emphasised again the role of the King, giving him the right to decide on the use of public finances for the benefit of the country. The constitution also gave the King the right to prescribe customs duties, which were decided by the assembly of estates during the Age of Liberty.[10] This situation remained after Finland was incorporated into Russia. Customs duties were decided by the Emperor on the basis of proposals made by the Finnish Senate, whereas all other changes in taxes had to be approved by the Diet. Old taxes were, of course, collected as before.

Nineteenth-century Finland thus inherited the traditions of the Gustavian era. The Gustavian revolution of 1772 was a reaction to developments during the Age of Liberty when the assembly of estates became very powerful, even in matters concerning public finances. The 1772 constitution increased the power of the Monarch and the situation resembled that in the eighteenth century. This kind of system emphasising the power of the sovereign was well suited to the autocratic Russian Emperor, the highest authority in the Grand Duchy since 1809. In the field of public finances, the Emperor approved the annual budget, within the limits of which the Finnish Senate decided on the use of state revenue. Therefore, as long as traditional "ordinary" taxes, as they were called, and customs revenues, decided by the Emperor, were sufficient, the consent of the estates was not needed. Thus Finland was run for more than a half a century (1809–1863) without asking the opinion of the estates, which would have been obligatory if a new tax had been imposed. (Rauhala 1915; 1921)

[10] HM 1772 § 45; YVK 1789 § 1.

This distribution of power in matters of taxation greatly affected public finance practice during the period of autonomy, and also influenced discussion about it. A further factor, which was also part of the Swedish tradition, was the principle of estate privilege. Exemption from taxes, for instance, was a privilege that could not be repealed without the consent of the group in question, which was a hindrance to the development of the tax system. Because it was difficult to change old taxes, or to impose new ones, customs duties became a more and more important source of state revenue – just because they could be decided by the Emperor and the Senate alone. Customs duties are discussed in more detail in the next section.

"Ordinary" direct taxes largely comprised the land tax, i.e. a tax on farmland. It could almost be called an immemorial tax form, which could be interpreted as ground rent paid to the King – the ultimate owner of the land. Land tax was very static; it was a fixed sum on each and every farm, not dependent on its actual income. Therefore, land-tax income hardly changed during the nineteenth and early twentieth centuries. Moreover, the burden of this tax, which was regarded as heavy during the first part of the nineteenth century, was alleviated greatly during the second part.

Tax Reforms

In principle, the potential for tax reform improved in the 1860s when the Finnish Diet started to assemble regularly. In practice, however, any changes were minor. Because customs duties were decided by the Emperor alone on the basis of proposals made by the Finnish Senate, they increased in significance. Other indirect taxes – especially on alcohol – were introduced too, and taxes requiring the consent of the estates lost their importance as state revenue. However, although indirect taxes became the dominant tax form, some new taxes requiring the consent of the Diet were also imposed, which gave impetus to discussions on tax issues. Committee reports and other material produced during the tax-reform preparation phase – including what was not put into practice – make it possible to analyse Finnish economic thinking on taxation.

A clear demand for the total reform of the tax system was presented in the January Committee, which assembled in 1862 to prepare the call for the Estates assembly (which materialised in 1863). August Armfelt, a member of the committee, spoke for the introduction of a general income tax. His idea was that a tax system based on land tax was not suitable for the new economic realities. Similar proposals were also made later, at the 1872 Diet, for example, by Ernst Linder, a liberal member of the nobility. J. V. Snellman supported direct taxation for various reasons. On the one hand, he wanted to increase state tax income, and on the other, he saw the possibility of taxing people according to their wealth, as he stated in his article on state income and expenditure published in Litteraturblad in 1863 (SA XI.1, 90–98).[11]

The fact that the Diet had assembled regularly since 1863 made economic and social reform possible. The material infrastructure and the educational system were developed, and these and other reforms had to be financed from state revenue. It was not very difficult to find support for these reforms in the Diet, or for the taxes necessary for financing them, which implies that the reforms were judged beneficial for the development of the Finnish economy and society at large.

There were four basic elements in the tax reforms carried out during the latter half of the nineteenth century. The first was the standardisation of the poll tax. Old personal taxes were an incoherent collection of different taxes, but now a new system was created, in which privilege based on estate or birth was abolished, and the equality of citizens was emphasised. At first, the plan was to make poll tax progressive and to take into account the differences in the tax-paying abilities of the citizens, but this proposal was not put into practice because of the opposition of the nobility. As a substitute for tax progression, the poor were exempted from paying tax. Following the imposition of one unified poll tax, several older personal taxes, collected on varying grounds, were repealed.

The second element of the tax reforms consisted of measures intended to reduce transaction and contract costs, and involved stamp duty and a tax on credit, for example. According to the new philosophy that was adopted, emerging business was not to be burdened with any unnecessary costs, and this meant, for instance, that the stamp duty levied on share certificates and estate inventories was reduced substantially. The same applied to the stamp duty on bills of exchange and debentures. These reforms were liberal in spirit in aiming to keep transaction costs low for the evolving capitalist business activity.

Thirdly, there was the introduction of income and property tax.

11 The first experimental income taxation system in Finland was the so-called suostuntavero (approval tax) in 1865–1885.

It was a crucial development in the field of taxation that the estates agreed to impose a universal tax – at least in principle – on income and property. The new tax might be characterised as the first serious step towards a horizontally just taxation system. The tax was levied on wages and salaries, as well as on income derived from real property. According to the original plan, the tax on real property should have been related to the real value of the property. This plan did not materialise, however, and so the tax on property was determined on the basis of the estimated value derived from it. (Nevanlinna 1907; Wikström 1985)

The new income and property tax was also justified on a vertical basis. It was progressive, albeit very weakly. More important in this respect was the argument that indirect taxes, such as customs duties, were consumer taxes and so they burdened the economically disadvantaged part of the population most. Income and property taxation, which was direct personal taxation, could much more easily take into account differences in the ability to pay than consumer taxes, which were object taxation. This crucial difference was also pointed out in discussions on Finnish income and property tax in the 1860s.

The new income and property tax was an important innovation in principle, but in practice it was a disappointment. It generated only 4 to 5 per cent of the annual sum of all state taxes. Consequently, the Diet did not renew the tax after 1885. One reason for the modest yield was the fact that the use of exchange and money was still limited in the Finnish economy, and production for private use, payments in kind and barter still had a significant role. Economic activity which could most easily have been taxed – income and revenue paid in money – were thus of limited significance. Agriculture would, of course, have offered the best potential basis for taxation, but in practice income and property tax did not apply to it. In the late nineteenth century, the transition towards animal husbandry, together with income from forestry and wages paid in money, had all increased the monetary flow in the agricultural sector, but they were not taken into account in the new income and property tax. (Kuusterä 1989b)

A simple way to increase the sum collected through the income and property tax would have been to raise the tax rate. The Diet, however, was not ready for this, and so the necessary new state revenues were collected in the form of new excise taxes. This was the fourth new element in the nineteenth-century Finnish tax system, although it was admitted that these taxes burdened the poor more heavily than the rich. This meant that the items to be taxed were those that were judged as unnecessary or even harmful and immoral. Thus, new taxes on beer, alcohol and tobacco were imposed. In spite of the moral justification of these taxes, their aim was purely fiscal, not a reduction in consumption.

Cameralism or Liberalism?

A clearer picture of the conflicting economic ideas on taxation emerges from closer analysis of the thinking of two prominent figures in the field of public finances: Herman Molander and Leo Mechelin. Molander, who was the Head of State Finances in 1871–1897, belonged to the cameralist tradition. The old system, divided into multiple separate funds, posed no problem to him, and he emphasised the importance of strong state finances. The difficulties of the 1860s, among other things, led him to believe that the state must be prepared for bad times, caused mainly by crop failures, by having good reserves, and collecting savings in separate funds. State finances, also divided among several separate funds, could be administered and accumulated by civil servants without keen supervision by the Diet. This fund system was finally settled upon in 1883, when a special reserve fund was established with only one purpose – to accumulate mainly international government bonds, which could be easily cashed in case of a national crisis. (Kuusterä 1989a, 97–104)

Mechelin, who also worked closely with Molander, supported a classical liberal view. He insisted that a systematic budget system should be created instead of a system consisting of several separate funds, so that outsiders – especially members of the Diet – could have a good overall view of state finances. The aim of his proposal was to make the management of public finances "transparent". He emphasised that the Diet should have the right to control public finances in general, and not only the taxes that especially required its consent. In line with his liberal ideas, he wanted to delimit the tasks of the government mainly to the activities which were necessary for taking care of internal and external security, or which could not be run by the private sector in an economically rational way. He therefore supported the view that the tax rate should be kept to a minimum. He emphasised the role of citizens, and therefore large public reserves were not needed. Mechelin's views on taxation might be characterised as Ricardian, although he did not refer to Ricardo directly. Ricardo thought that taxes, whether they were levied on capital or labour, could diminish profits. This, again, could prevent the growth of national wealth, or even diminish it. (Ricardo 1978 [1821], 94–95) This was also the general standpoint held by Mechelin. (Nordenstreng 1936–1937)

Towards a Modern Tax System

The Finnish discussion on taxation, the main forums of which were the Diet and governmental committees, was concentrated in two distinct periods: the first was in the 1860s–1880s, and the second from the 1890s until the First World War. During the first period, ca. 1865–1885, the main theme of the discussion was income and property tax. The dominant ideas belonged to the tradition of classical political economy. In line with the taxation principles presented by Adam Smith, the starting point in the Finnish discussion was that every citizen must pay for the services provided by the government, such as general protection for business, and that this payment, i.e. tax, must be in just relation to the extent of services enjoyed (Smith 1931 [1776], 306–309). This involved abolishing old tax privileges such as those enjoyed by the nobility. Neither were the old principles of domain and regal taxation compatible with the classical view. The tax-paying ability of citizens should be taken into account, which meant in practice that the poorest citizens could be exempted from taxes.

There were doubts about imposing an extensive income and property tax, because it was feared that it would hamper economic activity. The discussion highlighted an interesting division between consolidated and nonconsolidated income. Income from property was defined as consolidated, because it was seen as relatively stable, whereas income from (manual) labour was seen as unconsolidated, because it could fluctuate very sharply. The implication of this division was that consolidated income could be taxed more heavily than unconsolidated income. However, in practice, this distinction did not greatly affect the tax system. It should also be noted that this division was somewhat contradictory to the classical view, according to which tax on capital could be a harmful burden on production. (Wikström 1985)

The reforms of the 1860s and 1870s, which were intended to decrease taxes on transaction and contract costs, could be regarded as Ricardian. According to Ricardo, taxes levied on transactions were harmful because they hampered the optimal allocation of wealth (Ricardo 1978 [1821], 96–97). In fiscal terms, the most important taxes were consumption taxes: customs duties and excises. However, customs duties should not hinder economic growth, and should therefore not be imposed on exports or on the import of raw materials and machinery (on tariff policy, see the next section). It was admitted in discussion that indirect consumption taxes could be unjust because they hit the low-income population hardest. On the other hand, supporters of consumption taxes emphasised that most of the taxes were imposed on goods that were not necessities.

The second active period of the Finnish tax discussion was at the turn of the century. A large comparative research project on tax systems in European countries was started in 1892. This research, carried out mostly by Karl Willgren, was finished in 1897. In 1907–1908, immediately after the parliamentary reform, the necessity for tax reforms was the subject of lively parliamentary discussion, and in 1908 a committee was appointed to plan the reform. The work of the committee, however, was interrupted because of internal disagreements and difficulties in Finnish-Russian relations (Wikström 1985).

The committee did agree that land tax was an inappropriate basis for direct taxation. Because it was paid only by members of one social class, it was not horizontally just. Furthermore, it was a fixed tax and therefore it was not vertically just either, because it did not take into account differences in tax-paying ability. For these reasons it could be harmful for the whole economy (Committee Report 1911:12a, 272–273). The dominant consumption taxes were criticised heavily in the discussions that took place during the first decade of the twentieth century. The representatives of the labour movement, who had entered Parliament after the 1906 reform, particularly criticised indirect taxation for being socially unjust, and in principle, the unjustness of consumption taxes was admitted by all the parties. For the 1907 parliamentary session, August Hjelt made a detailed statistical calculation of the social incidence of customs taxation.

The tax-reform goal of the 1908 committee was transition towards a system in which the dominant direct tax was a universal, subjective income tax added to a property tax. The subjective income-taxation model was taken from Prussia, where a new tax system was introduced in 1891. The committee also considered the indirect taxation alternative, but its deficiencies were too many. As already mentioned, the worst of these was the unjustness of consumption taxes. Another problem was fiscal. The amount collected through indirect consumption taxes could fluctuate considerably from year to year, making it difficult to predict the development of state finances. (Committee Report 1911: 12b)

According to the proposal made by the committee, tax liability was universal, i.e. all individuals and all companies should pay it. Income was defined as "the increase in the pure wealth which the taxpayer received during the tax year, and which he could consume or otherwise use without diminishing his former wealth, i.e. without causing deterioration in his economic state". Income was defined in net terms: costs were deducted from gross income.

The legal basis for paying income tax was a person's citizenship and his tax-paying ability. It was thought that the state did not have the right to impose tax on those who were not able to pay it. In practice, this meant that a certain minimum income was defined and tax was payable only on income exceeding that minimum. A new idea was that the tax rate should be set in relation to tax-paying ability, so that the real tax burden should be equal for all taxpayers. This would be achieved by introducing progressive taxation, and this was considered thoroughly in the report of the 1908 tax committee. However, there was also the principle of moderation to be followed. Progression should be limited so that the majority of income was left for personal use, and the tax rate should thus not rise over a just maximum level.

In order to guarantee the justice of taxation it was necessary to introduce the declaration principle, and to impose sanctions to make sure that declarations were accurate. Furthermore, taxpayers should be able to have taxation mistakes corrected. An interesting practical comment on the planned tax reform was given by J. K. Paasikivi in Parliament in 1908. He saw the influence of German theories behind the reform proposals, citing Wagner, who suggested that a good tax system was only an ideal which would never be achieved in practice, and that reform could be put into practice only when there was no need to increase state revenues. (Kuusterä 1989b)

Paasikivi was right in his scepticism: the proposals of the committee were not accepted in Parliament. However, profound changes in the Finnish taxation system were made soon after, but not by Parliament. They were imposed as an administrative act in the exceptional situation of the First World War. The situation of Finnish state finances became desperate as foreign trade diminished and customs duties, which had produced almost 90 per cent of state revenues, diminished also. A quick decision had to be made in order to keep the state machinery rolling. The solution to this problem was the introduction of income and property taxes. They were imposed without the consent of Parliament, at a time when there was deep conflict between Finland and Russia. (Wikström 1985)

The first of the new "war taxes" included tax on capital and "high income". The aim of the tax on "high income increases" was to put a squeeze on wartime speculation profits. New forms of indirect taxes were introduced as well, including taxes on train tickets, phone calls and entertainment. The introduction of income and property taxes was technically relatively easy, since such reforms had been on the agenda since the 1890s. These reforms brought the dawn of a new era in Finnish taxation. Income and property tax was imposed and it was progressive. Tax rates were far above the income and property tax of the 1860s–1880s. Direct taxes became the dominant tax form, and although the proportion of indirect taxes grew again after the World War, it did not reach the pre-war level.

5.5 Tariff policy

The Double Role of the Tariff Policy

Customs duties had a double role in Finnish nineteenth-century economic policy: on the one hand they were a trade-policy tool, and on the other a central tax-policy instrument. They were readily used as consumption taxes because, as mentioned in the previous section, they fell outside the authority of the Diet and, unlike other tax, could be decided by the Emperor alone. This was of crucial importance especially during the decades (1809–1863) when the Diet did not assemble. Even after 1863, customs duties could be, and were, altered without the consent of the Diet. This constitutional fact obviously diminished the fervour and relevance of parliamentary discussion on customs policy, although it did not completely prevent it. Customs policy was discussed in the press and in economic societies and journals, but the actual policy was shaped by the Senate, which usually established a committee to prepare the necessary tariff changes.

The constitutional setting affecting Finnish customs policy and discussion on tariffs was not purely an internal affair, however, and we have to remember Finland's position within the Russian Empire. Finland was not a sovereign state and was not independent in her trade policy either. According to international law, she could not conclude trade agreements of her own, and the special agreements concerning trade between Finland and Sweden (until the 1840s), for instance, were agreements between Russia and Sweden. These agreements were special in the sense that there were representatives of Finland in the Russian negotiating delegation. Finnish opinions were also heard when the trade agreement between Russia and Spain was concluded in 1887, Leo Mechelin being the advocate of Finnish interests. In most cases, however, Finland had no way of influencing Russian trade agreements, which were also applicable in Finland. The second restriction affecting the independence of Finnish customs policy was that it did not concern her trade relations with Russia. The original intention of Russia after the occupation of 1808 was to annexe Finland onto her customs area. This aim was not realised for various reasons, but neither did Finland become a customs area totally independent of Russia. The general principle was that Russian products were duty-free in Finland and vice versa, although some exceptions were made to this rule, especially in 1859 and 1885. On the other hand, however, Finland's customs tariffs towards foreign countries, excluding Russia, were only occasionally the same as Russia's. All this meant that, during her Grand-Duchy period, Finland was not in the same position in her trade policy as non-sovereign countries with a single uniform customs border. She was not free to decide on her tariff policy either. Because the trade between her and Russia was almost free, changes in tariffs concerning foreign countries did not directly affect Finnish-Russian trade. (Heikkinen 1994)

From a Swedish to a Russian Tariff Policy

The aim of Russia in 1808–1809 was, as already mentioned, to annexe occupied Finland onto her customs area. In March 1808, while war was still being waged, the old customs border between "Russian and Swedish Finland" was ordered to be abolished, "and trade to be made free, as is customary between subjects of one Empire".[12] Although this plan remained the target of Russia, it was never completely realised, and Finland gradually gained a semi-independent position in her customs policy.

In 1809, after the War, customs policy issues were first discussed at the Diet in Porvoo. Because no special committee dealing with foreign trade and other economic issues had been established, which was in accordance with the wishes of the estates, these

[12] Heikkinen 1994, 133.

matters were taken up in petitions submitted by each of the four estates. The main purpose of these petitions was to maintain the old trade and customs systems as far as possible in the new situations. Some interesting changes were also proposed.

Trade policy was dealt with most thoroughly, as one might expect, within the burgher estate. The proposals dealt with customs tariffs, trade with Sweden, "peasant shipping" (bondeseglation), the staple town (stapelstad) system, and the Swedish Navigation Act, the produktplakat of 1724. The burgher estate emphasised the importance of the produktplakat, characterising it as an "absolutely necessary foundation of our foreign trade".[13] The other three estates did not question its rationale, according to which foreign (including Finnish) ships could bring only their own products or products from their colonies to Sweden. The burgher estate suggested that the practice of favouring domestic ships should be continued as well. These cornerstones of Swedish mercantilism were thus also supported by Finnish merchants in the new political situation. In tariff policy, however, the burgher estate offered modest criticism of the import prohibitions and excessively high customs duties which were characteristic of eighteenth-century Swedish tariffs. It also considered lower tariffs to be a wiser solution, since Finland needed a tariff of her own because her import needs differed from those of Russia.

At the Diet of Porvoo, the burgher estate continued the mercantilist line of the eighteenth century in the debate on "peasant shipping", too. It opposed the freedom, just as it had done in the eighteenth-century Swedish Diets. It argued that, "according to the principle dividing society into different trades and industries, the refining and distribution of domestic products as well as the purchase of the commodities farmers need from foreign countries belong to urban industry". The estate strongly defended the townsmen's monopoly on trade and shipping, and the separation between urban and rural industries.[14] The peasant estate, of course, argued for freedom in "peasant shipping", and also received support from the nobility.[15]

One urgent issue of trade policy discussed in the Porvoo Diet involved trade relations with Sweden. The nobility, the burghers and the peasant estate were all of the opinion that Sweden

[13] Borgare ståndets protokoller 1809, 191.
[14] Borgare ståndets protokoller, 222–223.
[15] Lindström 1905, 63.

should not be treated like other foreign countries. The nobility was especially interested in the freedom of iron ore imports from Sweden, because Finnish iron mills, most of which were owned by members of the nobility, were totally dependent on imported Swedish raw material. The peasants, again, wanted exports of Finnish agricultural products to Sweden to continue as before. These hopes were fulfilled by the peace treaty signed in Hamina in September 1809. This guaranteed that free trade between Sweden and Finland would continue for two years, but the period of validity of the order was extended to 1815. After that, Sweden had a more limited but still special position among Finland's trade partners until 1845, when she was finally regarded as equal with other foreign countries (Schybergson 1973, 188–197).

Finnish trade policy was also discussed in the committee appointed in autumn 1809 to plan the reorganisation of Finnish customs administration. The three-member committee was headed by Eric Tulindberg, the head of finance, and the other two members were former customs officials. The committee was expressly forbidden to present proposals on customs duties, because – according to the constitution – they came under the jurisdiction of the Emperor alone. Yet, the committee was asked if the right to conduct foreign trade, the "staple right", should be given to all towns. In its response, it was allowed to state its opinion on trade policy in general, which it did in its report completed in February 1810 and discussed by the Council in March. They were quite radically in favour of free trade, and against the mercantilist arguments presented by the burgher estate at the Diet of Porvoo. The committee wrote in its report that it was

> not necessary to repeat those numerous and well-known reasons, which have confirmed the common opinion stated both in foreign and domestic writings and proven by indisputable experience that privileged corporations usually misuse monopoly rights granted to them, and that the freedom of trade is the best way to promote their success and, at the same time, the common good.[16]

Furthermore the committee referred to the lessons of Finnish commercial history and the fact that the towns that had received staple rights had prospered. It also took an egalitarian stand by

[16] National Archives, Senaatin arkisto, Hallituskonseljin talousosaston ptk 27.–28.3.1810.

claiming that "it is reasonable that all taxable citizens should enjoy the same freedom of trade protected by law", and proposed that produktplakat should be abolished, that the staple town system should be repealed and all towns be made equal, and that it should be legal for all citizens to engage in foreign trade, in other words that "peasant shipping" should be permitted. In short, the committee was against all the basic elements of mercantilist trade policy that the burgher estate had strongly defended in the Porvoo Diet. This proposal was quite radical, and it is no wonder that it did not receive support in the Council, which was of the opinion that it would have violated "the rights and privileges which different towns, estates and corporations had had for a long time". Thus this early attempt to reform the mercantilist trade policy did not succeed.

From the 1810s to the 1830s, Finnish tariff policy towards "totally" foreign countries, i.e. Russia and Sweden excluded, followed the fluctuations of the Russian policy. Finland set her first tariffs in 1812, and any changes were made following what Russia did. Thus, when the Russian policy eased in the 1810s, Finland followed suit, and when it became more protectionist in the 1820s Finland went along with that, too. There was no public discussion on the actual tariff, which was up to the Emperor, and to him alone, to decide.

Liberalism Before Liberalism?

This protectionist, or even prohibitive, trend in tariff policy did not get support from the Finnish customs administration. In the 1830s, the Customs Board often criticised the high tariffs in the annual report it gave to the Senate, and proposed that they should be lowered. The 1830 annual report is a good example, in which the Board claimed that "the so-called protective tariffs do not serve a purpose".[17] This led to a Board proposal for lower tariffs in 1833, and this concentrated mostly on the lowering of tariffs on different consumer goods formerly regarded as luxury items: rum, wines, coffee, sugar, tobacco, cotton, linen, silk and woollen cloth. However, the proposal had not been put into practice before tariff policy was discussed again in a committee established in 1834. This committee proposed lowering the tariff rate to an average level of 20 per cent or less, but this again was not realised because of Russian government opposition because

[17] National Archives, STO KD 15/273 1831.

they feared that it would encourage smuggling in Russia, where the tariffs would have been higher than in Finland. Some of the suggested reductions were made in 1840, for financial reasons. A committee had been established in 1838 to find ways to increase state income. Raising taxes would have required the consent of the estates, which had not assembled since 1809, whereas tariffs could be changed simply by decision of the Emperor. The committee rightly calculated that lowering the tariffs on some consumer goods – luxuries turned into necessities – would increase tariff income by diminishing smuggling and increasing consumption. Thus, both the financial interests of the state and the welfare of the citizens were promoted. (Heikkinen 1994)

The motivations and arguments presented by the Customs Board and several committees in the 1830s were also the basis of Lars Gabriel von Haartman's tariff reform of 1841. This was an exceptional manoeuvre by which customs duties on the most important consumer goods were lowered significantly from the sky-high percentages of the official tariff by an average of two thirds, to the level of ca. 20 per cent. This system was first applied only for one year, 1841, but it was continued until 1859, although after the 1852 tariff reform, von Haartman's exceptional tariff was applied to fewer items than before. This tariff is usually called "von Haartman's secret tariff" in Finnish historical literature, but this name is misleading because it was not secret, although it was not published in the code of statutes. It should rather be called an "exceptional tariff" or "modification", which were the terms von Haartman himself used. It was, simply, a temporary exception from the basic tariff that was otherwise still in force. Whatever the name, it is significant that von Haartman's tariff started the move towards freer trade, almost two decades before the start of "official" liberalism. It might, therefore, be called liberalism before liberalism. The emergence of a more liberal tariff policy was also manifested in the lowering or abolishing of export duties, which had been a central element of mercantilist customs policy (Schybergson 1973, 50–51, 191; Heikkinen 1994).

Between Free Trade and Protectionism

Finnish customs policy became officially more liberal in the late 1850s. In this, Finland followed the example of Russia, where customs duties were lowered first in 1850 and again in 1857. Some of the 1857 changes were immediately adopted in Finland too, and an entirely new tariff was adopted in 1859. Corn duty was abolished in 1864. This signified the beginning of the era of free corn trade that lasted until 1914 (Rasila 1966, 299). Finnish customs tariffs were adjusted several times during the 1860s, and export duties were abolished almost totally. New general tariffs were agreed in 1869, again following the Russian pattern of 1868 (Harmaja 1933, 85–86). The new tariff applied to almost 70 duty-free items and export duty was almost non-existent. The 1869 tariff was valid, with minor adjustments, until 1919.

It should be borne in mind in any discussion of Finnish tariff policy that there was imposed free trade between Russia and Finland, which narrowed the scope of policy choice. This was clearly reflected in the discussion of the corn trade issue, for example. The free inflow of Russian cereals made any protectionism measures against third partners irrelevant, and the internationally current controversy between free-traders and protectionists had no voice in Finland.

The only time corn duty was discussed was in the so-called January Committee in 1862. Most of those involved supported the liberalisation of the corn trade (Harmaja 1922, 278–283), and it was only K. M. Creutz, Ph. D. who demanded unbiased treatment of both agriculture and industry in customs policy. He thought that corn duty should be abolished only in the case of total trade liberalisation, otherwise industry, which was protected, would benefit at the expense of agriculture (Heinonen 1987, 58). He claimed that agriculture remained the most important source of income for the Finns, thereby expressing an agrarian protectionist stand. Creutz himself was an estate owner. However, all the other members of the committee voted for the liberalisation of the corn trade, which was then implemented two years later in 1864.

Wilhelm Lavonius published his doctoral dissertation on tariff legislation in Finland (1873). This was the first accomplished academic presentation on customs policy and theory seen from the point of view of tariff legislation, and should thus be considered one of the most important works in this field.

According to Lavonius, agriculture had had worse treatment than industry in the Finnish tariff system. He referred to the fact that farmers had been forced to pay a price for industrial goods that had been raised by the amount of the tariff imposed on imports, and thus agricultural capital had been used to protect industry and manufacturing. His conclusion was that tariff protection should be abolished totally (Lavonius 1873, 164), and the only duties that were acceptable were revenue duties. He wrote:

> Customs duties are payments that the state imposes on the goods which are brought over its border. They are paid over and above the price of the merchandise, and it is therefore a *protective duty*. As state income, it is a *revenue duty*.
>
> We have spoken against the preservation of protective duties, not of financial duties. These must be preserved as an appropriate form of indirect taxation, although the Finnish customs tariff needs adjustments to benefit the financial duty system in view of the removal of the protective duty. (Lavonius 1873, 168; italics original.)

The supporters of protectionism had maintained that the abolition of protective customs duties would be detrimental to the development of industrial production. Lavonius (Lavonius 1873, 165) denied this argument by pointing out that the removal of protective duties would force industry to develop increasingly on a domestic basis. He emphasised the fact that the supporters had not been able to prove the advantages of a protective customs policy, and in particular that the alleged welfare gain based on protective measures had not been proved.

Lavonius opposed the taxation of exports, although he accepted the use of customs as an instrument of indirect taxation: he thought imported alcoholic drinks, coffee and spices should be subject to customs duty. Referring to the financial effects on the state of customs duties, he mentioned the existence of many unprofitable duties that did not benefit the public treasury, that disturbed commerce and burdened the administration (Lavonius 1873, 169). Thus, it is indisputable that Lavonius was a firm opponent of protectionism.

Protectionist views were mainly presented in the context of the Listian infant-industry argument. Among the few promoters of protectionism should first be mentioned Agathon Meurman, who presented his Listian views in an article (Meurman 1866) and a booklet (Meurman 1878). The Fennoman movement saw the importance of establishing a domestic industry, and as a leading Fennoman, Meurman consistently supported domestic industry and manufacture. He wrote on issues of customs policy in his booklet on taxes, published in 1878. Although he admitted that protective duties taxed consumers for the benefit of industry, he mentioned the difficulties of a young nation's industry in competing with developed industrial countries equipped with large supplies of capital and know-how (Meurman 1878, 28). He thought that, because a national industry benefited all countries, current advantages could be sacrificed to gain larger benefits in the future. This is an indisputable Listian infant-industry argument, which Meurman softened by referring to the matter as “delicate”.

Another leading figure of the Fennoman movement, Professor Karl Gabriel Thiodolf Rein, also presented Listian views concerning customs policy in his article *Kansantalouden uusi oppikunta* (Rein 1879a). This article was connected to the controversy on liberalism discussed earlier in Chapter 4.4.

Although Rein did not distinguish between infant-industry customs and protective duty, he wrote on the issue in an indisputably Listian spirit:

> A nation can act wisely by agreeing on sacrifices for a certain time period, if, with the help of protective duties, it helps industrial branches which, in the future, will profit by more than the amount of the present loss. A nation is an association not only of the people living in a certain period, but also of past and future generations, and the state naturally must watch over the interests of the latter. Secondly, a nation’s civilisation and independence benefit if its own production extends to a variety of industries so that it need not pay for other countries’ industrial goods with only agricultural products. This frees it from the effects of business cycles, wars, port taxes, etc. (Rein 1879a, 31.)

Thus, Rein emphasised the importance of protectionism as a provisional measure to give a domestic industry the chance to grow and diversify. He thought that present sacrifices would turn to future gains when domestic industry was capable of competing. However, he warned his readers that the artificial maintenance of industries which were not capable of surviving, such as the cultivation of silk in a cold climate, could result in unnecessary sacrifices.

Both Meurman and Rein expressed their Listian infant-industry arguments during a time when there were no big changes in Finnish customs policy. They took Listian stands on the grounds of principle rather than as a reaction to some concrete adjustments or plans concerning customs tariffs.

The Waning of Liberalism

The ideas of free trade were introduced to Finnish customs policy in the 1860s and 1870s, but the movement stopped, and even slightly reversed, in the 1880s. However, Finnish developments in tariff policy did not turn protectionist as they did in many other European countries, and only a few staunch supporters of protectionism can be found in the Finnish customs policy discussion. This may be explained by Finland's precarious position as a Grand Duchy of the Russian Empire.

The actual customs policy line was discussed when a committee was appointed in 1881 to plan a new customs tariff. The head of the Financial Office of the Senate, Herman Molander, outlined the general picture of planned reform in his memorandum to the committee.[18] The dual character of customs duties as a form of tax and as an instrument of economic policy was clearly noted in his memorandum. The importance of customs revenues was pointed out in the first paragraphs: "As an indirect tax, customs duties are intended to obtain revenue for the government in the least burdonsome way and, thus, to diminish the need for imposing direct taxes." However, Molander wrote that customs duties should be "reasonable" as consumption taxes, allowing both consumption to grow and state revenues to increase. Here he made the conventional distinction between luxuries and necessities. He also acknowledged the protective aspect of customs duties, suggesting that if there was the chance for a fairly large manufacturing industry to use domestic raw material, this should be protected by a "reasonable duty". Furthermore, he also stated that if industry used customs-free foreign raw materials, while at the same time a duty was levied on the corresponding finished goods, the protective measures were in fact a reward for industrialists at the expense of consumers and public finances. He did admit, however, that the "reasonable interests" of existing factories should be taken into account in the planning of customs reforms.

The situation was changing as Russia took a more protectionist course in her tariff policy, and because the special position of the Grand Duchy was causing more discontent in Russia. Finland's special position was criticised in the conservative Russian press. A committee was set up in 1884 under the leadership of the Minister of Finance, Bunge, and one of its aims was to check the position on duty-free Finnish exports (Pihkala 1970, 36). Russian customs tariffs were raised in 1886–1887, and Finnish import duties on metal and engineering products were raised a little to protect domestic production (Harmaja 1933, 86–87). The tariffs on stimulants were raised in the spring of 1888.

[18] National Archives, STO KD 39/339 1882.

A committee was appointed at the end of the 1880s to assess the need for corn duties, but no measures against free corn trade were actually taken. The corn trade was also discussed in the Diet in 1888. The peasantry and the clergy submitted proposals asking for reconsideration of the corn duties, but they came too late. Plans to revive the corn duties were caught up in the machinery of bureaucracy partly because of the delicate nature of the issue. It seems indisputable that many Finns did not want to turn the Russians' attention to issues of customs policy. Fears of the Russian reaction to autonomy were on the increase.

Russian industrialists had very strong interest groups to help to further their aims. A new committee was set up in 1890 to consider the customs policy and plans to unify Finnish and Russian customs duties, as well as the monetary and postal institutions, under the Governor General von Heiden (Rasila 1966, 307). The Finnish and the Russian Post Offices were merged. Because of its privileged position, the City of Tampere was able to postpone the implementation of the Finnish-Russian Customs plan until 1905, and in fact it never materialised. However, the general increase of protectionism in international trade and in Russia resulted in an increase in some Finnish customs tariffs in 1897.

When Russia adopted the gold standard in 1900, it signified a rise in customs duties for some Finnish products being exported to Russia. In the same year, another committee was set up to conclude the unification of monetary and customs institutions, but the privileges enjoyed by Tampere prevented this from happening. The 1910s saw rises in only a few tariffs, and corn duty returned only in 1914 on the recommendation of two committees and following heated discussions in the Diet (Heinonen 1987, 110–133, and 1989). This is the background to the discussion on customs policy that follows.

Ekonomiska Samfundet i Finland, the Society for Swedish-speaking Economists founded in 1894, has been characterised as a society in which economic liberalism was predominant. The society gave a statement to the Finnish-Russian customs committee in 1900. Although the aim of the statement was the preservation of the status quo, its tone was not protectionist, but rather the contrary. The Society (Ekonomiska Samfundet 1901, 27–31) pointed out that food prices had risen because of the increase in customs duties, and that high duties encouraged smuggling. It was also suggested that Russia had suffered widely because of her protectionist customs policy. The following facts were given to justify maintaining independent Finnish customs tariffs (Ekonomiska Samfundet 1901, 39–40): 1) both Finland and Russia had separate financial administration; 2) alcoholic beverages were exported to Russia duty-free via Finland; 3) the unification of customs tariffs would damage Finland; and 4) unification would harm the financial administration of the Finnish state. Efforts to induce The Finnish Economic Association to back the statement failed.

The leader of the Society Leo Mechelin, presented his views on customs policy at a conference of economists in France in 1900. He was known as a supporter of economic liberalism and freedom of trade. He said openly in his lecture (1904) that Finland had no reason to make demands for the reform of the existing "rather liberal" customs tariff, and advised the Finns to avoid calling the Russians' attention to the issue. He accepted the use of pure revenue duties, and referred to the problems inherent in protective customs duty: a rise in prices in the importing country. Thus, according to Mechelin, customs duties were best imposed exclusively on products not produced domestically.

Customs Duties and Interest Groups

Export duties imposed on forestry products were a perennial controversial issue in Finland reflecting, apart from obvious fiscal interests, concern with the devastation of the forests and the safeguarding of fuel material for the domestic iron industry. Understandably, these duties had been fiercely opposed by exporters of sawn goods since the 1860s, with some success. This debate continued well into the 20th century.

Hugo Gröndahl (1905) gave a lecture at a meeting of the Finnish Economic Association, which was published in Yhteiskuntataloudellinen Aikakauskirja, in which he supported temporary customs duties on the export of wood products to prevent the wasteful utilisation of the forests and to guarantee the supply of raw materials for domestic industry. He admitted the problems in determining the level of customs duties so as not to violate the economic rights of forest owners on the one hand, and not to encourage excessive consumption on the other.

At the same time as Gröndahl was supporting the interests of the Finnish forest industry, Anders Benjamin Helander, a trained forester, was defending the interests of forest owners. He wrote an article (Helander 1909) in which he resisted proposals to increase export duties on wood products, although he accepted the need for revenue duties. He referred to the German and Austrian writers Johannes Conrad, Richard Schüller and Wilhelm Lexis, who had listed the following exceptions to the general principle of free trade: 1) when the exporting country has an absolute or local natural monopoly, 2) when export duty is imposed on merchandise that can be processed, 3) when export duty is used as a weapon in war, or 4) when the exporting country has a relatively low population and large natural resources which can be profitably exploited (Helander 1909, 64). He emphasised the need to restrict export duties in cases of extreme need.

Heikki Renvall briefly commented on the principles of customs policy in his book on the export of Finnish forest products (1910). He mentioned Finland's lacking real autonomy in customs policy as a Grand Duchy of the Russian Empire, and suggested that the goals of the economic policy concerning forestry should be the protection of the forests from wasteful utilisation, an increase in profitable activities, and an increase in the degree of forest product processing (Renvall 1910, 313).

One interesting feature concerning the discussion on customs policy was the consumer's viewpoint that was accentuated by Verner Malin (since 1906 Malinen). Malin raised the problem of the incidence of taxation through customs tariffs in his booklet Veroista (On Taxes), published in 1890. He was concerned about the justice of using customs tariffs as indirect taxes. Because poor people spent most of their income buying necessities, and especially food, they were paying relatively more taxes than wealthier people (Malin 1890, 37–38). The defenders of customs duties maintained that workers could demand higher wages when prices rose, which would mean that the tax burden would be transferred to the producers. Malin refuted this argument by pointing out that only a rise in the demand for labour could lead to a rise in wages.

He also referred to the harmful effect that customs duties had on the flow of trade when goods could not be acquired easily. They also affected small firms more than larger ones or wholesalers, and the collecting of duties was very costly to the state. Malin ended his piece by admitting the need for revenue from duties to bolster state finances (Malin 1890, 50). As a solution, he proposed that all customs duties which were not remunerative to the state should be abolished, and that in any case, salt, as a necessity, should be freed from duties. He was also against corn duties because they put the tax burden on poor people rather than the wealthy. Thus, his emphasis was on the unfavourable effects of customs duties on the distribution of income in society, particularly from the consumer's viewpoint.

Yrjö Jahnsson (1908) also called attention to customs duties as a form of taxation in his book on the principles of Finnish taxation policy. However, he gave credit to the Finnish tax system which imposed very few customs duties on food materials (Jahnsson 1908, 80). As a strong supporter of temperance he proposed an increase in taxes on beer, coffee and tobacco, although he was positive on the whole about the principles of the Finnish customs duty system.

The corn trade issue was much discussed in many countries during the second half of the 19th century. The lower costs of transportation enabled a massive flow of cheap American and Russian corn onto the world market, which raised protective claims among peasants in many European countries. Only a few farmers supported the imposition of customs duties on imported corn in the 1880s (Rasila 1966, 300–302), and in the next decade, some flour-mill representatives demanded protection against the rise in imports of German flour. All in all, these discussions did not affect policymaking.

The Finnish autonomous position in customs policy was a source of dissatisfaction in Russia. Russian exporters applied to the Russian Ministry of Trade to impose customs duty on corn imported to Finland from outside Russia. The Russian corn traders wanted to improve their position against the Germans on the Finnish corn market. The proposal was strongly opposed in the Finnish press in the summer of 1911, and this was the beginning of what can be called the most heated debate on customs policy.

The Social Democrats were most passionately opposed to the plan to restore customs duty on imported corn, and submitted a proposal to keep it duty-free. The Standing Committee for Taxation at the Diet asked ex-senator Lennart Gripenberg for advice, and his response (1913, 17–21) was that customs duty would only benefit the Russians, that it would raise the cost of living in Finland, and that the Finnish economy would suffer. However, the Social Democrats'proposal was not passed until the end of the Diet session and the general election in August 1913. The Social Democrats won the election, together with the Agrarian Party.

Two motions concerning customs were submitted to the Diet. The Social Democrats proposed that imported corn should be left duty-free, emphasising the tax burden and the negative effect on the wellbeing of the labour class and poor people. They also pointed out possible changes in domestic market competition as well (Heinonen 1989, 162). The Swedish Party requested that the independence of Finnish customs should be guaranteed.

The Committee for Customs Issues gave its report to the Diet and proposed that the Diet should ask the Russian Czar to reject the corn duty plan. The report was discussed in the Diet on 24 March 1914. The Social Democrats were opposed to the corn duty and the discussion culminated in a controversy between K. H. Wiik and J. R. Danielson-Kalmari.[19] K. H. Wiik strongly resisted the corn duty plan and put forward a few interesting ideas involving wage rigidity and the possibility of a lack of demand or underconsumption (Valtiopäivät 1914 Pk 1, 489–490). The former was related to Keynesianism, and the latter to the underconsumptionist tradition of Thomas Malthus, Simonde de Sismondi, Rosa Luxemburg and, later, John Maynard Keynes. Danielson-Kalmari defended corn duties as a provisory measure of structural policy (Valtiopäivät 1914 Pk1, 511–13), and appealed to the authority of the German economist Johannes Conrad.[20] He considered them a social policy tool to prevent unemployment, and in this he was clearly influenced by the German *Kathedersozialisten*.

Wiik reacted to Danielson-Kalmari's defence of corn duties by referring to the writings of Conrad as well. He pointed out that Conrad saw the problem of rising prices related to corn duties, and had emphasised that there could be a tendency towards the monopolisation of the corn trade, and that this would be an economic and social drawback (Valtiopäivät 1914 Pk1, 517). Conrad himself did not totally exclude the possibility of using customs duties in trade policy, although he emphasised the need for prudence, especially concerning agricultural duties (Conrad 1913, 681). The use of Conrad's writings in parliamentary discussion was an interesting phenomenon: one and the same authority was used to defend opposing views in economic political debate.

[19] Both were members of the Committee for Customs Issues. Karl Harald Wiik (1883–1946) was a member of the Social Democratic Party and a journalist. He was a student of literature and became one of the most important figures in the Swedish-speaking labour movement in Finland. Johan Richard Danielson-Kalmari (1853–1933) was one of the leaders of the Old Finnish Party, and a professor of history.

[20] Johannes Conrad (1854–1915) was Bruno Hildebrand's disciple and a representative of the Younger historical school in German economics. Lindenlaub (1967, 191) pointed out that Conrad was a supporter of free trade. The second part of his work *Grundriss zum Studium der politischen Oekonomie* (Conrad 1913) had recently been translated into Finnish by Leo and Laura Harmaja.

The report of the Committee of Customs Issues was approved in the Diet session without adjustment. Despite the cautious Finnish protest, the Russian duma and privy council approved the legislative proposal concerning Finnish corn duties in the summer of 1914. Those duties were political customs duties that had almost no immediate effect on the quantity or the direction of corn imports. Their effect on inflation during the First World War is very difficult to estimate because the immediate effect of the outbreak of the war was extensive (Rasila 1966, 390–393, 398).

There was lively academic discussion concerning the corn trade. Kaarle Väinö Hoppu (1913), Juho Heikki Vennola (1913) and Tor von Wright (1916) mentioned the problems caused by possible monopolisation, and Hoppu also referred to the heavy burden on poor citizens caused by the rising costs of living. Rolf Thesleff (1915) emphasised the fact that corn duties benefited Russian agriculture, corn trade and the milling industry most. He also pointed out that, from the viewpoint of state finance and tax policy, corn duties did not fulfil the requirements of a good taxation system. Those academic writings were empirical statistical examinations following the strong tradition of Finnish empirical social research described earlier in Chapter 4.5.

5.6 Government and Infrastructure

In the 19th century, a central forum for debate on the role of the government in the economy developed in the context of developing the infrastructure to meet the needs of an industrialising nation: how far should the government's responsibility be extended here; which areas of infrastructure investment should be especially promoted by the government and, especially, what should be the relative importance of investment in the physical infrastructure and human capital.

This section examines these issues in the Finnish context. Particular attention is paid to how the Listian perspective on the development of national productive forces was reflected in Finnish perceptions of the responsibility of the government in various infrastructure investment projects. It comes out clearly that the positive economic and social externalities related to the development of the physical infrastructure, communications in particular, were given particular attention by the Finnish élite. They also took a pragmatic stance as far as the division of labour between public and private, presumably subsidised, initiatives was concerned; incidentally, it soon turned out that the scope for profitable private initiatives among the railway, road and waterway development projects was bound to be limited in the Finnish conditions.

The Listian vantage point also implied an inherent tendency to emphasise the role of education in the development of the nation. Yet, investment in human capital remained subdued during the period. The Finnish authorities consistently gave priority to the physical infrastructure. Moreover, the cameralist ethos long dominated the allocation of sparse educational investments, the education of civil servants retaining an overwhelming share of the total. It was not until the end of the century that resources were allocated to vocational training in various institutes of technical education. In the same period, opportunities in basic education at the secondary level were extended, with private initiatives occupying an important role in the establishment of new educational institutions. Throughout the period, the sparseness of resources devoted to primary education remained a salient feature of the Finnish educational system in spite of the frequent public debates on primary education reforms.

The Listian Model

The evolving infrastructure reflects the concrete ideas behind the economic policy of nineteenth-century Finland. However, the highest civil servants and politicians only exceptionally wrote about the economic arguments behind the decisions recorded in the documents related to the decision making of the senate. These decisions give some indication of the kind of targets the decision makers had, and how these targets changed.

The striking feature in the planning and constructing of the infrastructure was the dominant role of the state, which is not surprising. Infrastructure investments have large positive externalities, and the social returns are higher than the private returns, so these kinds of investments could not be executed by market mechanisms alone. This argument was especially relevant concerning the construction of the communication network in Finland. In such a thinly-populated country, the number of users was bound to stay small, and private capitalists were obviously not willing to direct resources to communications investments. However, the need to develop the communications network was urgent because Finland was split into economically isolated regions and good communications were essential in the integration of the country into an economic unity.

The problem was demonstrated for example in the senator von Haartman's report in the Senate on economic conditions in Finland in 1812 and 1816[21]. His contemporaries were well aware of them, too. By way of an example, von Haartman mentioned the sparse settlement, the poor demand for agricultural products, and the resulting poor performance of the economy as a whole. (Senate 1812–1816)

In Finland, the evolution of the infrastructure followed the Listian model of retarded development in many ways, for example, how a peripheral country can compete with more advanced countries. According to List, the most important way to ensure development was to maximise the productive powers of the society. At the same time, he criticised the classical school for their emphasis on exchange value and neglect of productive power. The task of the state was to provide a good environment for the economy. In order to accomplish this, the government needed to make fundamental institutional reforms, organise a stable monetary system, manage the construction of the communications network and education system, and secure good administration free of corruption for the whole society. The common denominator in these reforms was the integration of the society into an economic unity. However, it was not enough to build up an operating framework for the economy but the state also had to support industry in its first phases of development. This meant imposing protective tariffs to curb imports from more advanced countries.

List's background was early nineteenth-century Germany, a society that was characteristically agrarian and state-ruled. Such German ideas suited Finnish bureaucrats. In the Finnish mental climate, the government was easily able to persuade its citizens to concentrate their efforts on developing the productive powers of the society and abstaining from consumption in the short term. The nation was ready to make sacrifices for the future.

The Communications Network and Positive Externalities

The first important decisions concerning the development of the communications network were made by the Tariff Committee which began its work in 1834. Members of the committee included L. G. von Haartman, C. A. Ramsay, Nils Nordenskiöld, J. C.

[21] G.E. von Haartman was father to Lars G. von Haartman.

von Bonsdorff and A. Avellan. The Committee's main task was to decide on a new customs tariff, but its members also aired their views about how to encourage domestic trade, agriculture and other industries. Their report particularly emphasised the regional imbalance between the eastern and western parts of the country. The only way to eliminate this imbalance was to establish transport connections from the Saima watercourse to the sea. Thus the building of the Saima canal was first suggested, although the motion was preliminary and there was no further discussion on how to tackle such a big investment.[22]

Ten years later, the time was ripe and the question of building the Saima canal was seriously taken up. The most reasonable arguments outlining the importance of the new canal were put up by Snellman. He pointed out the positive effects of the new waterway, and predicted that the canal would generate much more income than the simple canal dues, as the following paragraphs show.

1. The canal will encourage new industrial enterprises and new farms, which will mean more tax income.
2. This new activity will bring in its train more imports end exports, which will also mean more tariff income and benefit for the whole society.
3. Government expenditure will decrease because less will be paid out in poor relief, and there will be less tax arrears
4. Compared to the above, the canal dues are only a minor aspect of the public benefits. (SA IV, 123–132)

Ideas about positive externalities, or the distinction between social and private benefits, are clear in Snellman's argumentation. The canal generated such large indirect government revenue that it did not make sense to base decisions only on anticipated income from direct canal dues. The dues were insignificant compared to the public revenue generated by the canal.

However, Snellman's vision was of no account at that time because the new Head of the Senate Financial Department, von Haartman, had the last word. He also understood the economic significance of the new transport connection, but he could not start the building process until the state finances were stabilised, and this was not possible as long as the monetary conditions

[22] National Archives, VSV 38/1935

were unsettled. This was accomplished at the beginning of the 1840s when monetary realisation solved the problem.

After the canal-building period of 1845 – 1855, there arose the question of railway building, and the first public debate about economic matters in Finland took place around this theme. The decisive factor behind this new phase was the relaxation of censorship. Nevertheless, discussion was focused on economic matters because political discussion was still out of the question. It is interesting to note that behind the economic arguments lurked arguments related to power and private interests.

In this public debate, one pressure group consisted of people emphasising the superiority of the canals, the most influential being J. G. von Bonsdorff and von Haartman. They had very good connections to the Senate, and they considered the railways useless because Finland already had a communications network based on canals. Thus, the railways would only encourage unhealthy competition with the canals. They may even diminish the value of the investments put into the canals and thus be harmful to the state. There was a clear cameralist emphasis behind these arguments.

Another pressure group was centred around the Wiborg newspaper. Its members fiercely resisted the railways because they saw them as a threat to the Saima canal, and to the economic hegemony of the city of Vyborg, the largest import and export centre in the country. This opposition directly reflected the economic interests of the Vyborgian merchant class, but it also had supporters among the estate owners in the Kymi river region. They were afraid that the beginning of the railway era would signal the end of the Kymi river development, and so threaten their own economic interests.

The third, quite heterogeneous, group supported the building of railways. It included both representatives of the Russian central government and native Finns. Railways were important to the Russians for two reasons. First, they were seen as a stimulus to the entire Finnish economy. Second, it was thought that they would provide more efficient connections between Finland and the mother country, Russia. The native Finns in this pro-railway group emphasised the economic factors. Again, the best arguments for the railways were put forward by Snellman. He sent a long article to the Wiborg newspaper, in which he maintained his position against the earlier anti-railway articles that had appeared (Suomen Valtionrautatiet 1912, 10–32).

Snellman's view was the same as ten years earlier when he had fought for the Saima canal. He again stressed the positive externalities of the railways. The Listian influence in his argumentation was seen even more clearly than earlier, as he pointed out the importance of productive powers for the future development of society, instead of the Smithian emphasis on exchange value. He felt that an efficient communications network was essential for the integration of society, and that railways would speed up the mobility of goods, knowledge and people. In order to maximise the use of this mobility, the country should have as extensive a railway network as possible. The importance of the railways was not limited only to economic matters; they would help to raise the intellectual level of society. They were not only a substitute for waterways, but would be the very core of a national communications system. They would play a crucial role not only in taking care of the needs of export industries, but also in integrating society into an economic unity and providing channels for intellectual stimulus.

Public Contra Private Enterprise

In spite of the very authoritative opposition the supporters of the railways rapidly succeeded in establishing a strong foothold, and after the beginning of the 1860s there was no more debate about the relative merits of the railways and the canals. Instead, there arose a new topic of public discussion, and this concerned the form of control over the railways, whether they should be based on public or private ownership. This controversy first arose in the Diet in 1863. The estates wanted to discuss extending the railway network after the completion of the first line between Helsinki and Hämeenlinna. Members of the Diet discussed it and came down on the side of state ownership. They felt that railway investments were so expensive that private national companies could not be expected to have enough resources to cover the costs. The domestic capital markets could not finance such large investments either. The only way to cover the financing would be to turn to foreign lenders. The majority were of the opinion that both the building and running costs of the railways would be cheaper if the system were managed by the state, although the minority emphasised the advantages of private enterprise. In their opinion, the sole function of the state should be to guarantee the foreign loans (Suomen Valtionrautatiet 1912, 37–51).

The following year, 1867, the private alternative received more support in the Diet. Under the proposal put forward by the estates, the senate was given the mandate to decide what alternative – public or private – to use in the extension of the railways. The resolution that granted private enterprises state guarantees for foreign loans already indicated that opinion was turning towards the private alternative. This support for private enterprise was not only in rhetorical speech, since the senate had given three private enterprises concessions to build and operate private railway lines. Among these enterprises were foreign companies which were trying to penetrate Russian markets via Finland (Suomen Valtionrautatiet 1912, 68–72).

The most significant resolutions were passed in the 1872 Diet. Now the Senate asked the estates about selling all of the railway lines to private companies. The response was resoundingly negative, the arguments behind it being based on the concept of positive externalities. The main task of the railway system was to take care of the communication needs of the whole society, and private companies were only willing to operate the commercially profitable lines. Thus it was felt that the least that could be done was to hold the main trunk lines under state ownership. Furthermore, the private companies would be dependent on foreign investors, and this could have lead to the solution in which national interests might be passed over.

The vision of the estates turned out to be quite right. All the private railway companies ran into trouble, and the unfinished railway lines went bankrupt. The only operative solution was the state-owned railway system, and the controversy between public and private enterprise faded away. Practical experience showed that the natural monopoly dominated in this area, and as a result, the preconditions for the operation of private companies were minimal. The idea of a natural monopoly, however, was not expressed during the contemporary debate on railways.

Finnish society suffered from a very severe famine and a deep economic crisis during the first phases of the railway building. In this context the link between this kind of big infrastructure project and the economy was established, and the importance of expectations regarding the economy was mentioned for the first time. Some members of the estates were of the opinion that large investment decisions might change the pessimistic atmosphere and engender positive expectations (Suomen Valtionrautatiet 1912, 72–82).

The National Communication Strategy takes Shape

The national communication strategy began to take on a definite shape in the middle of the 1870s. The starting point was a state-owned railway system, the building of which would be financed by foreign debenture loans. Because of the active involvement of the state, the mandate concerning the planning of the railway lines was held by the government, and so it was possible to adhere to its all-inclusive targets. In practice this meant that the railway network evenly covered the whole country. It was not only the needs of the export sector of the economy, but also the needs of the domestic sectors that influenced the planning decisions. The railways benefited the whole of society, and not only a small enclave, and the positive forward and backward linkages could be maximised.

As mentioned above, the financing of the railway building was based on foreign loans, which was a conscious policy of the government, motivated by two separate factors. Firstly, the investments needed were so huge that domestic savings would not have been large enough, and secondly, the government was willing to keep the domestic capital markets open and available for the private sector. However the use of foreign loans was not a foregone conclusion because, according to the prevailing economic policy, attitudes to public borrowing – especially foreign borrowing – were negative. The starting point was that the government was allowed to take loans only for productive purposes. The railways had large positive externalities, and so it was acceptable to use foreign loans for the building even though repayment might take many decades. It turned out that the railways produced quite good revenue for the state, and the investments turned out to be sound. However, in the last decades of the nineteenth century, the government had been emphasising the public benefits of the railways and was not so interested in the commercial results. In practice, this meant that the owner, in other words the government, allowed the profitability to decline.

The national communications system consisted not only of the railways, but also included sea transport. A competitive and reliable sea transport network was vital for Finland's commercial connections to Western Europe. The first phase was the rebuilding of the Finnish merchant fleet after the Crimean war, during which it had been almost totally destroyed. This was financed through big state subsidies. In the second phase, the state financed the development of the town of Hanko to become the seafaring centre of the whole country. It was particularly suitable for winter use, which was why the state invested so heavily in the town and its harbour. At first, winter seafaring was managed by private icebreaker companies subsidised by the state, but later the state assumed the whole responsibility for the icebreakers. (Kuusterä 1989a, 338–340)

The government also began to subsidise private domestic merchant fleet companies by offering them cheap loans. The new private steamship companies took the majority of their loans from the government, without which they would not have been ready to make the transition from sail to steam in the face of hard international competition. Because sea transport was an integral part of the Finnish national communications system, the government view was that the only way to develope a competitive merchant fleet was to strongly subsidise the private companies. (Kuusterä 1989a, 338–340)

The term national communications strategy was even more relevant because the government used the railway tariffs as a means of directing its economic policy, the main target of which was to increase exports and decrease imports. Thus, tariffs on the most important export items, such as forest-sector and agriculture products, were lower than the tariffs on imported goods. Moreover the state tried to improve the degree of refining in the export industry, and so the tariffs on unprocessed wood were higher than those on the more processed forest-industry products. (Vanamo 1936, 225–286)

The privileged position of the communications sector was evident not only from the rhetorical outpourings of the highest politicians, but also, more concretely, in the attitude to public finances. Systematic data collection concerning annual state expenditure began in 1860, and this data indicates the level of priority given to the maintenance of the communications network in public policy in the latter half of the 19th century. The proportion of communications expenditure was about ten percent in 1860, but this rapidly rose to nearly one third after the beginning of the railway building era. The total amount of public money invested in the railways between 1860 and 1900 rose to 263 million marks. Comparison with the total state expenditure gives some idea of what this amount meant; in 1900 this was three times the amount. (Pihkala 1977)

Finally, we would like briefly to take up the relationship between infrastructure investments and social-policy questions. Generally speaking, the central government's role in social policy was modest. Matters concerning poor relief were the concern of the local authorities at the community level, not of central government. Furthermore, after the 1879 poor-relief decree, the ideology behind the social policy was liberal-oriented. The starting point was that every man had to feed himself, and only children, the physically or mentally handicapped and the elderly could obtain assistance. Moreover, there were more constraints on its distribution. According to the poor-relief decree of 1852, all destitute people were entitled to assistance, but this had led to untenable high costs for the communes during the famine years of the 1860s, and as a result the whole system was changed. (van Aerschot 1996, 56–129)

This liberal atmosphere meant that the state did not systematically utilise the infrastructure investments to level out the trade cycles, although the attitudes of the government changed during the 19th century. The famine years of the 1860s had been so hard that the state gave generous relief loans to the communes during the subsequent depression in the first years of the 1890s. These loans enabled the communes to finance various minor infrastructure investments such as local road building and the drying up of lakes or marshes, which thus provided job opportunities.

Large public works were foreign to the prevailing economic ideology after the second half of the 19th century, however, and the state emphasised the importance of private economic life. This ideological attitude is clearly seen in the pay policy for the public railway building, according to which wages were kept considerably below the prevailing level. It was stressed that these public works must not lead to demands for higher wages in the private sector.

A Narrow View on Human Capital

The evolution of the intellectual infrastructure had a dualistic position in public policy. On the one hand, the estates and the most senior civil servants actively discussed the importance of education, and these positive attitudes were still further reinforced in the latter half of the 19th century. On the other hand, the public resources directed to education remained very modest. Only four percent of all state expenditure was allocated to education in 1860. This proportion rose slightly in the following years, but it was not more than ten percent in 1900. Thus, the government preferred to make investments in physical infrastructure such as the communications network rather than in the intellectual infrastructure.

Table 2. The structure of educational expenditure according to the state balance, 1860–1900 (% and 1 000 mk).

Sector	1860	1870	1880	1890	1900
Primary education	–	2	9	14	22
Secondary education	68	49	39	45	39
Universities	21	35	29	20	14
Vocational training inst.	11	14	22	21	25
Totals, 1 000 mk	1 069	2 093	3 691	6 700	11 515

Source: Pihkala 1977.

The crucial factor behind this inferior position of the intellectual infrastructure was the prevailing economic policy doctrine which adhered to the requirement of a balanced budget and was unfavourably inclined towards public borrowing. Foreign loans could only be used to finance physical infrastructure investments, where the repayment periods were short and the gains were concretely seen. Gains from better education facilities are realised only slowly, and are in a way incalculable, so the government was not willing to use foreign loans for educational investments. As a result, educational expenditure grew only slowly within the framework of the growth of public finances, and no sudden increase in the proportion of educational investments was to be expected.

Moreover, the benefits of better educational facilities were spread very unevenly in society, so there were no homogenous interest groups to fight for more investment. As a result, there was a lot of discussion about education but no one was really ready to make economic sacrifices for it. This is a well-known issue in modern public choice theory, one aspect of which supports the popular hypothesis that the small and homogenous interest group is better able to get its targets through the state apparatus than the larger and more heterogeneous group.

The Finnish education policy was an integral part of the general economic policy which was dominated by the cameralist tradition, according to which the first and most important function of the education system was to produce enough civil servants. This cameralist focus was particularly striking until the 1860s and 70s, when the proportion of expenditure on secondary education and universities rose to 80–90 percent of the total expenditure on education.

As a result of the good coverage of secondary schools, the number of university students was high in Finland, especially in view of her economically-retarded position. For instance, there were 3 200 students in Finland in 1910, compared with 7 600 students in Sweden and 1 500 students in Norway (Mitchell 1975). In international comparisons, Finland's position was surprisingly high, and this should be pointed out in any discussion of the development potential of Finnish society. It was also an important factor behind the country's efficient administrative system.

The second focus of the education policy was on vocational training, reflecting utilitarian or liberal attitudes towards education. Society gave priority to vocational training because this kind of education was of direct use in commercial and industrial life. The first time this argument arose was in the 1830s when the Manufacturing Directorate was established. One of the main tasks of this new central office was to organise and supervise technical education and its development. In reality, its achievements in the field of technical training were very modest.

The question of the development of vocational training arose again in the 1855–56 proposal of the industrial committee, but concrete results were minor (Kekkonen 1987). It took three decades to transform the old-fashioned "Sunday schools" into handicraft schools.

The most significant change was in attitudes towards the status of technology. Finnish society was going through a modernisation process during which theoretical technological education and vocational training were being separated into independent fields. Technology was given new status as an independent scientific subject which had an important role in economic development. Part of this transformation process was the establishment of the Polytechnic Department at the Technical University of Helsinki. This department was the base on which engineering education developed, and at the end of the nineteenth century, Finland could educate both engineers and architects at home without using foreign, mainly German, help. Like university education, this technological education was organised by the state. (Konttinen 1991)

The strongest supporters of vocational education were found among the representatives of business circles. Through the medium of the liberals in power they were able to convince the highest officials and decision makers of the immediate benefits of vocational education. This small and homogenous pressure group was able to advocate the reform of vocational training very effectively.

Public debate focused on primary education; how to extend the school network over the whole country, and especially over the countryside. The arguments used in this debate were based on Listian views about education, and were finalised during the latter half of the 1850s. An improvement in general educational standards was seen as a prerequisite for economic development as a whole. Moreover, it was essential for education to penetrate into all classes of society. Well-organised primary education was considered an efficient way to increase the productive powers of society, and as a good springboard for further development.

Moreover, Mikael Soininen (up to 1906 Johnsson), who was an active debater on educational issues and the first Minister of Education in independent Finland, put forward a new view on the role of public primary education in society. He believed that higher levels of general knowledge in all classes of society would lessen disagreements among people, and thus make it easier to resolve societal conflicts (Johnsson 1892, 682). This kind of thinking was typical of the liberally-oriented people who were ready to reject paternalistic attitudes.

The Primary School Act of 1866 was based on Listian views. This meant that education was no longer the responsibility of the church, and the state tried to bring about a unified primary education system which would cover the whole country. The object of primary education was to give citizens universal tools to educate themselves instead of relying on the old religion-centred education of which the objective was to pass the confirmation class.

Although the communes had the responsibility for giving school-aged children the opportunity to attend school, there was no decree to compel parents to send their children to school, or to ensure that, in one way or another, their children would receive comparable education. This reflects the dispute over the right of the state to interfere in the private matters of individuals. In other words, did the state have the right to oblige parents to send their children to school? The "father" of the Finnish primary education system, Uno Cygneaeus, still emphasised the voluntary nature of school attendance, but the concept of compulsory education gained a strong foothold after the 1870s. The leading persons in educational matters understood that it was only by insisting on compulsory school attendance that it would be possible to get all children to school, but it was not until 1920 that the law on compulsory education came into force.

Attitudes towards compulsory primary education being organised by the secular state instead of the church were quite divided.

Many divergent factions aired their views – the liberals contra the Fennomans, the clergy contra young pedagogues and urbanites, contra the rural population. This meant that the supporters of educational reform did not form one powerful interest group. The benefits of better education were also very widely spread, and they were difficult to account for concretely. All this resulted in a situation in which it was very difficult to accomplish any reforms. In many ways, the Listian demands for educational reform were primarily rhetorical.

All in all, the primary school system based on voluntary attendance did not succeed in attracting school-aged children, and the proportion of school pupils in Finland was much lower than in her western neighbours, as can be seen in the following table.

Table 3. Children in primary school in Finland, Sweden and Norway, 1880–1915.

Year	Finland	Sweden	Norway
	%	%	%
1880	7	72	56
1900	19	69	67
1915	28	70	69

(The figures refer to the age groups 5–14 years, which poses some problems because the actual school ages were 9–12. Thus the figures give unrealistically low values. However the distortion is the same for all three countries.)
Sources: Mitchell 1975; Statistical Yearbook of Finland 1910.

As a consequence, the proportion of literate people remained low in Finland. The country is normally ranked quite highly in international comparisons in the latter part of the 19th century, but this is misleading. Such comparisons counted all Finns who had completed the primary education given by the church among the literate. In fact, this education only guaranteed the ability to read, and not necessarily to both read and write. Thus, a better indicator was the ability to write. In 1880, only 11 percent of Finns could write. Four decades later, this proportion had risen to 65 percent.

The peripheral situation of Finland was thus clearly perceptible in her intellectual infrastructure; especially in primary education. Many people in the thinly-populated Finnish countryside were content with the inadequate primary education given by the church in the primitive schools, and children were not sent to public primary schools. Moreover, the rural communes were not willing to build and run primary schools. As a consequence, the actual educational standard of the lower classes remained quite low.

On the other hand, any backwardness was compensated by the high proportion of people who had attended secondary school and who went on to university. Thus, the real significance of education in Finnish economic and social development is difficult to evaluate because of the simultaneous strikingly high and low levels of education.

6. Conclusions

6.1 Economic Thought in a Country without Economics

The focus of this study differs from that of conventional doctrinal histories of economic thought. Most of them are accounts of the gradual progression of economic theory in a more or less established form. Had we chosen this "high road of progress and theoretical innovation"[1], this book would have been very thin indeed, because there was not much originality, or even self-determination, in Finnish economic thought in the nineteenth and early twentieth centuries. Finland remained on the periphery of the economic discipline. The intellectual infrastructure of the subject was poorly developed; academic chairs were few, as were experts in the field outside university; publication channels were weakly developed. In these conditions, Finnish economic thought did not possess its own internal dynamics: genuine scientific discoveries were non-existent. Nor can one distinguish a major tradition of, or continuity in, domestic economic discourse. Finnish contributions were rather made up of isolated comments on, or introductions to, various aspects of the subject as developed in the outside world; they did not form a coherent continuum.

The peripheral status of Finnish 19th-century economic thought alone makes the high-road approach of doctrinal history unsuitable. Therefore we have rather written a story of adaptation and application: we have looked at the foreign sources of influence early Finnish economists turned to, and for what reasons; and we have traced the use of economic thought in the country in the

[1] This formulation is Keith Tribe's (1988, 7), whose study on German economic discourse in 1750–1840 follows "instead the rather more mundane course of development taken by economic pedagogy".

age of the early modernisation of the economic structure as well as in her more general efforts at nation building.

We might, however, consider whether a virtue could be made of this necessity to apply a "low-road approach". One obvious problem with the high-road approach of doctrinal history is its inherent teleology: the goal of historical development is modern economics as we know it. This means that the past currents of economic thought that do not end up in modern economics, especially in its "mainstream" version, are ignored. As a consequence, the teleological histories of economics, while emphasising the unity and continuity of the discipline, do not do justice to the actual diversity and discontinuity in the development of economic thought. To illustrate this diversity in the light of the Finnish case, as well as the existence of a number of dead traditions, each considered full of promise in its own day, has been one of our aims.

As a consequence of this, our view of the development of economic science highlights the elusiveness of the disciplinary borders separating it from other intellectual activities, as well as the heterogeneity of economic thought and the discontinuity, even inconsistency, of its development. Our book is an account of the somewhat uneasy birth of the economic discipline in Finland. We noticed a gradual maturation taking place in the course of the century. The academic infrastructure of chairs, curricula and publication forums was established, although still in a rather rudimentary form, by the end of the period of the autonomous Grand Duchy of Finland in 1917. The discipline also lent itself in an increasingly consistent way to certain sources of foreign influence; and it was through this process that a distinguishable domestic tradition with its own internal continuity was finally developed over time.

We have departed from the standard approach of doctrinal history in another respect, too, by studying rather extensively the use of economic arguments in economic policies as well as in general political and ideological debate. Thus our study is an account of development on the periphery – a description of the use of economic arguments in the economic policy of a peripheral country lagging behind in development. Under these conditions, the state often assumes a central role in fostering economic modernisation. This was especially the case in Finland – a fact that makes the policy applications of economic theory the more interesting. The low standard of the domestic economic discipline notwithstanding, the economic policy makers had to rely on a certain conceptual structure for organising their thinking about the economic policy as well as about the chains of influence various measures might have on it. The search for the intellectual roots of such an economic policy "model" is a novel feature of our study. As a matter of fact, it appears that such a policy model may possess a high degree of continuity and coherence over time, and be capable of reproducing itself quite independently of the state of the domestic scientific discourse; conversely, it may have a strong impact on the orientation of the domestic economic discipline.

In what follows, we will first summarise our views of the maturation process of Finnish economics, and then we will conclude our findings on the relationship between economic thought and economic policy in nineteenth-century Finland by tracing the roots of the Finnish economic policy model.

6.2 The Tardy Birth of Finnish Economics

The history of economic thought in the nineteenth century can be understood as a process of gradual specialisation and professionalisation. In this process, economics separated itself from natural history, jurisprudence, philosophy and history, and emerged as an autonomous discipline with its own, quite well-defined research community and contacts with users of economic knowledge in the civil service, politics, business and culture. The maturation process was unfinished at the end of the period and the economic discipline remained somewhat peripheral in comparison to many other subjects. By this time, however, it was ready for a final breakthrough. The necessary prerequisite for this was set at the beginning of the 20th century when a new economics chair was founded in the Faculty of Philosophy at the University of Helsinki, and new chairs were founded, first in the Institutes of Technology and Commerce. The number of economic dissertations grew rapidly. Books, both domestic and translated, were published on the subject more frequently, and scientific journals, both Finnish and Swedish, were started.

Until the late eighteenth century the dominating concept of economic science was that it was assimilated with natural history and technology, in the tradition of Linné. Following a very old European tradition stemming from ancient Greece, the economy was primarily conceptualised as household economy, for which science was to provide practical advice. It should be mentioned, however, that Swedish intellectual life was well aware of the predecessors of Smithian ideas, where economic issues were understood as a part of moral philosophy and the study of society. Samuel Pufendorf was the foremost name in this line of thinking, and his ideas were further developed in Finland by Anders Chydenius.

Another concept of the economy, already prevalent in the 18th century, was that of state finances. This cameralist tradition, adapted from Germany, became dominant in Finland in the early 19th century. As a manifestation of this change in orientation, a chair in economic science was transferred from the Faculty of Philosophy, from the sphere of natural history, to the Faculty of Law. The main task of economic teaching was to provide civil servants with a basic knowledge of public finances and administration. This thrust prevailed for the rest of the century. Mathias Calonius, Daniel Myréen, Wilhelm Gabriel Lagus and Johan Jakob Nordström were representatives of this tradition. An interesting exception was Michaël Tjeder, who showed keen interest in classical political economy in early 19th-century Finland.

A new concept of economic science was connected with the rise of the national movement from the 1840s onwards. Parallel intellectual currents in Germany again formed the main source of ideas for Finnish thinkers. Apart from his many other activities, Johan Vilhelm Snellman, a major intellectual figure in 19th-century Finland, gave the main impetus to economic thought and policy. He was the first proponent of Listian ideas in Finland. These ideas emphasised the role of productive forces, material as well as intellectual, in economic development at the national level. According to List, the main challenge of economic development for young nations was how to evoke the dynamism inherent in these broad productive forces. This message was adapted and moulded to suit Finnish circumstances by Snellman, and this was the economic part of Snellman's Hegelian national philosophy. In this view of the economy, the state kept its central role, but now as a promoter of broader national interests, not only of state finances.

The next phase in Finnish economic thought, the 1850s–1870s, was combined with political liberalisation and accelerating economic modernisation. Regular meetings by the Diet were started, which increased the demand for economic expertise. The number of newspapers increased. The expansion of industry and foreign and domestic trade, as well as of the banking sector, created a class of businessmen interested in economic issues. This increasing demand was met by cautious reform in the education system, as the teaching of economic issues in the Faculty of Law was reorganised.

Economic liberalism was mainly adopted as a political programme in Finland. Its impact on economic thought remained rather low-profile, not amounting to much more than references to French liberal writers such as Frédéric Bastiat, Michel Chevalier and Joseph Garnier. Among the businessmen, intellectually active persons who were oriented towards these foreign sources of influence included Henrik Borgström Jr. and Otto Reinhold Frenckell. In university circles, Axel Liljenstrand supported liberal ideas, perhaps a bit half-heartedly. He wrote the first proper economic textbook in Finland.

The German influence on Finnish economic thought stayed alive during this liberal intermezzo. Again parallel to intellectual developments in Germany, the Listian inheritance was transformed into the historical school. The younger generation of this school, including Gustav von Schmoller and Adolph Wagner, became the dominating source of influence in Finland. Now the young generation of Finnish scholars travelled in numbers to German universities to study under the leading authorities of the historical school. This scientific tourism remained one-directional, as none of these idols visited Finland.

The Historical School was adopted in Finland as a programme of concrete historical and statistical research. This furthered the development of statistical administration and gave rise to a wave of empirical social studies, but its impact on the economic discipline remained weak. Scientific associations and professional economic journals were also established. Apart from this progress, attachment to the historical school, which turned out be a decaying tradition, delayed the development of Finnish economics up until the Second World War, in other words, beyond the period covered in our study, and this represented a deviation from the contemporary progress of economic thought in the other Scandinavian countries.

It was not until towards the end of the period under study that the analytical school of economics began to exercise noteworthy influence. Although the liberals of the 1870s and 1880s were mainly confined to the sphere of politics, the liberal tradition did not die out during the dominance of the historical school. At the turn of the century, marginalist ideas were first introduced to the Finnish audience by Karl Willgren, who showed an exceptional analytical interest in neo-classical economics in the Finnish context.

A salient feature of the community of economists in Finland, as elsewhere, was the almost total absence of women in the profession. Exceptions to the rule were Vera Hjelt and Laura Harmaja, who both concentrated on questions of consumption and household economy, as was expected of females at that time.

In terms of the methodological division lines in 19th-century economic thought in general, Finnish economists quite consistently reflected the approach that was most forcefully put forward in the German intellectual tradition. In contrast to the mainstream classical/neo-classical tradition in economics, this approach was characterised by its empirical and inductive methodology, with emphasis on collecting statistical material. This was in turn backed by an emphasis on the practical relevance of economic analysis for nation building and solving concrete economic problems. This approach represented a consistently collective rather than a rational individual viewpoint.

This basic methodology in turn anchored Finnish economic thought firmly to certain foreign influences. Continental, primarily German, influence was dominant rather than the "mother" of modern economics, i.e. the British classical tradition. In the first phase, the disciplinary influences from Germany and France were transmitted via Sweden, but in the course of the 19th century, the focus moved to Germany, and the import of ideas from there became direct, i.e. the mediating role of Sweden diminished.

Late 19th-century developments in economic thought in Finland differed from those in neighbouring Sweden, where an independent and very powerful tradition of analytical economics developed. This was largely due to a few creative thinkers, including Knut Wicksell, Gustav Cassel and David Davidsson, and may have been partly accidental: Finnish economics was not enriched with such strong individuals. More systematic differences in the intellectual traditions of the two countries also played a role, however. Nation building and a collective ethos inspired economists in Finland, and economic thought remained firmly in the sphere of the historical school. In contrast to Ricardo and Mill, Hegel and List remained a source of inspiration. This very broad approach, where economic issues played a subordinate role, was adopted by Snellman and it remained an obstacle to specialisation in economic science *per se* throughout the period.

On the whole, developments in Finland showed some general features of the history of economic thought on a scientific periphery, as was also found in the United States and Japan (Carlson

1995; Herbst 1965; Matsuura 1972). The German intellectual heritage was evident in North American economic thought during the nineteenth century. List was despatched to America in 1825–30, and his book *Outlines of American Political Economy* (1827) was keenly read by scholars such as Henry Carey and Daniel Raymond. During the second half of the century German universities attracted thousands of young Americans, who were impressed by the way nation building and the consequences of rapid industrialisation were being managed in their host country. Almost 9,000 Americans studied at German universities between 1820 and 1920. At the beginning of the period, most of them studied natural sciences, but the balance turned towards social sciences and humanities after the 1870s.

These young scholars gave the ideas of the German historical school quite a strong foothold in many American universities, including Johns Hopkins and MIT. Representatives of the historical school founded the American Economic Association in 1885 as an equivalent of the Verein für Sozialpolitik. The new society operated upon the following principles: a) the state is an inevitable organ of social development; b) economic studies must be founded on historical and statistical research rather than on speculation; c) representatives of the church, the state and the academic world must unite to solve the many social problems brought about by the conflict between capital and labour.

Japan, like Finland, and because of its language, was in a very unfavourable position in relation to the development of economic theory that took place in Europe. There, too, the German historical school was highly esteemed and imitated (Matsuura 1972, 534). We can sympathise with Matsuura's view that scientific and other ideas arise from the intellectual soil of the country in question. Because economics was imported into Japan from the European intellectual environment and scientific atmosphere, it has kept aloof from Japan's traditional intellectual history. As far as economics is concerned, the same type of isolation is characteristic of Finland, notwithstanding the fact that the country lies geographically relatively close to Central Europe, and in general has close intellectual relations with it.

Thus, it is easy to establish many common features in the development of economic thinking in these three countries. However, the small size of Finnish society made our economic thinking much more one-sided than in the United States.

6.3 Theory and Practice: Ideas Backing Economic Policy

Finland inherited a relatively well-developed civil bureaucracy and juridical framework from Swedish rule. Thanks to the broad degree of autonomy in economic and social affairs granted by the Russian Czar after annexation in 1809, the inherited administrative system was ready to work. However, while the civil service and the inherited legal framework were rather well developed, the representative part of the political system remained at a standstill for most of the period. The Diet did not convene between 1809 and 1863, and decision making in economic policy remained in the hands of the bureaucracy, the Senate included, with the Emperor performing the task of the legislator in the last resort. The role of this bureaucratic structure remained dominant even in the latter part of the period of Autonomy, including the first decade of a democratically elected Parliament from 1906 onwards. The bureaucracy represented continuity in economic policy-making in the country, and it determined how the issues were conceived of and tackled.

The bureaucratic view of the basic economic policy problem consistently emphasised the peripheral economic, social and indeed political position of the country. Finland was seen as poor, perhaps even permanently doomed to poverty, and badly lacking in essential materials, and in the social and human resources needed for rapid development and catching up with its more advanced neighbours. Against this background, the bureaucracy consistently took on the central role of overcoming obstacles to economic development and modernisation.

A combination of a relatively well-developed administrative structure and the admission of the peripheral status of the country in turn gave the state structure a pivotal role in advancing economic development and change. This role, given under such conditions of relative backwardness, cannot be conceived of in terms of the classical dichotomy between a liberal "nightwatch" state and an active, interventionist or regulative state. It is rather more akin to the concept of a strong state, described as characteristic of peripheries by Alexander Gerschenkron and many of his predecessors and successors. Such a strong state sees its tasks as both fostering liberal reforms in order to boost the free market, as well as using the state machinery for direct intervention in the economy. The choice between these two forms of state regulation depends on the circumstances and the problem at hand; the point is that the bureaucracy makes the choice, and both market-oriented reforms and intervention are seen as alternative instruments for overcoming various aspects of backwardness.

The economic policies of 19th-century Finland provides examples of both these forms of regulation by a strong state on an economic periphery. From the 1850s onwards, Finnish bureaucracy was active in removing the remaining obstacles to market development. A stable monetary system, attempted at in several stages, was conceived for this purpose, as was the reform of economic legislation in the latter part of the century, in order to provide a stable institutional framework in which the markets could function. On the other hand, it is clear that the bureaucracy did not hesitate to take a direct state initiative to enhance or diversify the productive structure of the economy. The building up of the infrastructure, especially communications, was a good example of this. Finally, it is of some interest to realise that the state was ready to give up its direct intervention in production if the bureaucratic forces felt that the market system was well enough developed to take care of the activity in question. The prompt withdrawal of the state from the financial market as private banking was finally established in the country is an example of this.

The flexible and pragmatic attitude towards the economic role of the state shown by the economic bureaucracy in 19th-century Finland goes well with the fact that the élite of the higher bureaucracy and the rising business classes overlapped to a large extent. People at the top changed their roles, and it was not rare for them to take on both at the same time. The basic viewpoint was thought to be the same in any case; the antagonism characteristic of the distinction between liberal and interventionist views of the role of the state was absent. In one way, in its economic role, the state was like a single company on open world markets; its task was to facilitate adjustment to given external circumstances, not to regulate them.

Realisation of the need to overcome economic backwardness, and of the usefulness of a strong state for this purpose may, in turn, provides a natural "material" explanation for the fact that economic thought in Finland turned to the German historical school as its main source of inspiration in the latter part of the 19th century. In fact, it is interesting to note that even before that, Friedrich List was an important source of inspiration for Finnish civil servants. Given that both List and the representatives of the historical school were preoccupied with similar types of problems of being on the periphery as the Finnish bureaucrats, it is no wonder that the latter found their ideas interesting.

In one sense, economic policy thinking in 19th-century Finland remained closer to List's thinking than to the later historical school. The basic function of economic policy was conceived of as fostering production and its competitiveness on world markets. Social cohesion and integration were not seen as related issues. Labour was basically regarded as an input in production, not as an economic and social class to be entitled to its own rights and integrated into society. This was reflected in the neglect of mass education that persisted up until the 20th century. The emphasis by the proponents of the historical school, such as Yrjö-Koskinen, on social integration was given attention in theory, but did not produce significant practical results. These ideas of social reformism did not gain a foothold in the Senate, and did not change the traditional economic-policy model.

This view of society reflected in economic policies was also criticised by the liberals. They saw certain social and institutional reforms, such as the modernisation of industrial relations, as a necessary follow-up to the basic market reforms of the 1860s and 1870s. Their aim was a well-functioning market economy, in which capital and labour were organised and in which the state did not play an active role. This was reflected in their approach to property rights. While the Fennomans were ready to give the government the right to organise the leasing arrangements between landowners and crofters, the Liberals considered this a private contract not in need of public intervention or regulation.

From their own points of view, both wings of reformers – the proponents of the historical school and the liberals – saw the need for change in Finnish society at the turn of the century, but neither camp succeeded in bringing it about to any great extent. In retrospect, it has to be said that derogation of social reforms and the consequent lack of social cohesion, together with situational factors, pushed the nation to the tragedy of the civil war in 1918.

Appendix 1: Table 1. Doctoral Dissertations in Economic Science (1809–1917).

Year of publication	Writer	Title of the dissertation
(1) 1810–1811	Daniel Myréen	Academisk afhandling om penningar och mynt I–II. Upsala.
2) 1813	Wilhelm Lagus	Akademisk afhandling om vexlar I. Åbo.
(3) 1820	Bergbom, Carl Gustaf	Om Ränte-Persedle Undervisningen för Salo Härad uti Uleåborgs Län. Åbo
(4) 1826	Michael Tjeder	Tankar om Frihet i Handel. Åbo.
(5) 1832	Johan J. Nordström	Skildring af bevisningsmethoderne i brottmål efter de gamla Landskapslagarne. Åbo.
(6) 1837–1838	Gabriel Rein	Kejsardömet Rysslands statistik i sammandrag. Helsingfors.
(7) 1853	Axel Liljenstrand	Historisk teckning af den i Finland tillämpade lagstiftningens grundsatser för näringarnes och det allmänna väståndets befrämjande. Helsingfors.
(8) 1858	Johan Wilhelm Rosenborg	Om fattigdomen och allmänna fattigvården i Finland. Helsingfors
(9) 1859	Paavo Tikkanen	Väki-luvun ja asukasvaiheiden rakenteita Suomessa. Helsinki. (The first doctoral dissertation written in Finnish language.)
(10) 1873	Wilhelm Lavonius	Om tull-lagstiftning i Finland. Helsingfors.
(11) 1882	Axel J. Lille	Om försäkringsväsendet. Dess historiska utveckling och nationalekonomiska betydelse. Helsingfors.
(12) 1882	Joel N. Lang	Den nationalekonomiska teorin för jordkreditföreningars organisation med ett bedrag till dessa ansstalters historie. Helsingfors.
(13) 1886	Josef V. Tallqvist	Recherches statistiques sur la Tendance à une Moindre fécondité des mariages. Helsingfors.
(14) 1886	Karl Langenskiöld	Om öfverflyttning af skatt. Helsingfors.
(15) 1887	August Hjelt	Sveriges ställning till utlandet närmast efter 1772 års statshvälfning. Bidrag till kännedom af Finlands natur och folk 45. Helsingfors.

(16) 1889	Hannes Gebhard	Savonlinnan läänin oloista vuoteen 1571. Bidrag till kännedom af Finlands natur och folk 49. Helsinki.
(1) 1899	Ernst Neovius (Nevanlinna)	Suomen raha-asiain järjestämisestä Porvoon valtiopäiviä lähinnä seuranneina vuosina.I. Helsinki.
(18) 1899	Heikki Renvall	Fysiokratian vaikutus Ruotsi-Suomen kansantaloudelliseen kirjallisuuteen XVIII vuosisadan loppupuoliskolla. Helsinki.
(19) 1900	Juho H. Vennola	Pohjois-Suomen maalaisvarallisuus 16:lla ja 17:llä vuosisadalla. Tutkimuksia Suomen taloudellisesta historiasta II. Helsinki.
(20) 1907	Leo Harmaja	Gööteporin järjestelmä Suomessa. Taloustieteellisiä tutkimuksia IV. Helsinki.
(21) 1907	Yrjö Jahnsson	Tutkimuksia Suomen kansantaloustieteen historiasta vuosina 1810–1860. Erityisesti silmälläpitäen yleisen kansantaloudellisten suuntien kehitystä. I. Helsinki.
(22) 1907	Rolf Thesleff	Studier i aktiv sparbankspolitik. Helsingfors.
(23) 1908	Frans M. Pitkäniemi	Yhtymät (renkaat, kartellit, trustit) suurteollisuuden alalla, 1 osa. Teoreettinen tarkastus. Kotka.
(24) 1909	Martti Kovero	Valtion uutisasutus Ruotsin-Suomessa jälkeen Ison-vihan. Asutuspoliittinen tutkimus. Taloustieteellisiä tutkimuksia X. Helsinki.
(25) 1909	Edvard Gylling	Suomen torpparilaitoksen kehityksen pääpiirteet Ruotsinvallan aikana. Taloustieteellisiä tutkimuksia IX. Helsinki.
(26) 1910	Georg C. Schauman	Studier i Frihetstidens nationalekonomiska litteratur. Idéer och strömningar 1718–1740. Bidrag till kännedom af Finlands natur och folk 73:1. Helsingfors.
(27) 1911	Nathanael von Stackelberg	Der bankmässig organisierte Agrarkredit in Estland. Helsingfors.
(28) 1911	Paavo Korpisaari	Suomen ulkomaankaupasta vuosina 1812–1825. Kauppahistoriallinen tutkimus. Kotka.
(29) 1911	Ilmari Kovero	Die Bewertung der Vermögensgegenstände in den Jahresbilanzen der privaten Unternehmungen mit besonderer Berücksichtigung der nicht realisierten Gewinne und Verluste. Berlin.

(30) 1911	Ola Castrén	De sociala strömningar i Frankrike på Ludvig XIV:s tid. Helsingfors.
(31) 1912	Viljo Hytönen	Suomen valtion paloviinapolitiikka vv. 1826–1886. Helsinki.
(32) 1912	Kaarlo Mannelin	Finlands smörexport. En statistisk-ekonomisk studie. Helsingfors.
(33) 1913	Oskar K. Kilpi	Suomen ammatissa toimiva väestö ja sen yhteiskunnalliset luokat vuosina 1815/75. I, Maaseutu. Väestötilastollinen tutkimus papiston väkilukutaulujen tiedoista. Taloustieteellisiä tutkimuksia XII. Helsinki.
(34) 1913	Oskar Lundell	Bidrag till den finska befolknings-statistikens historia. Helsingfors.
(35) 1913	Topi Kallio	Palvelijapolitiikasta Suomessa 18. vuosisadalla. Taloustieteellisiä tutkimuksia XI. Helsinki.
(36) 1914	Alf E. Tudeer	Hämeen läänin väestön lisääntyminen vuosina 1811–1910. Tutkimus eri paikkakuntien väenlisäysilmiöiden erilaisuudesta. Taloustieteellisiä tutkimuksia XVI. Helsinki.
(37) 1914	Eino Kuusi	Talvityöttömyys, sen esiintyminen, syyt ja ehkäisytoimenpiteet Suomen suurimmissa kaupungeissa. Taloustieteellisiä tutkimuksia XV. Tampere.
(38) 1914	Torsten Kaila	Europan Venäjän väestösiirroista XIX vuosisadan lopulla. Taloustieteellisiä tutkimuksia XIV. Helsinki.
(39) 1914	Åke Dalberg	Brandförsäkringsrisken. Grunderna för dess sammansättning och värdesättning inom den finska brandförsäkringen i deras utveckling till närvarande tid. Åbo.
(40) 1915	J. T. Hanho	Tutkimuksia Suomen metsätalouden historiasta 19. vuosisadalla. 1. Sahateollisuudesta ja sahantuotteiden viennistä 1840- ja 1850-luvuilla. Suomen metsänhoitoyhdistyksen julkaisuja. Erikoistutkimuksia 3. Helsinki.
(41) 1915	Östen Elfving	Vermögensbildung kleinbäuerlicher Ansiedler in Finnland. Helsingfors.
(42) 1915	Oskari W. Louhivuori	Kunnallinen köyhäinhoitorasitus Suomen suurimmissa kaupungeissa ennen nykyistä kunnallishallitusta. Taloustieteellisiä tutkimuksia XVIII. Helsinki.

Sources: Björkqvist 1986, Eriksson 1978, Heinonen 1987, and Kuitunen, T. & Sullström, R. 1984.

Appendix 1: Table 2. A Classification of Economic Dissertations according the Branch of Economic Research (1809–1917).

Branch of Economic Research	Dissertations	Number
History (economic and social history)	(16), (17), (18), (24), (25), (30), (35), (40)	8
Legal and administrative history	(3), (5), (6), (15)	4
History of economic thought	(18), (21), (26)	3
Public finance and taxation	(10), (14)	2
Trade, industry and business	(4), (23), (28), (29), (32)	5
Money, credit and insurance	(1), (2), (11), (12), (22), (27), (39)	7
Statistical population studies and statistics	(6), (9), (13), (33), (34), (36), (38)	7
Social policy (empirical social research)	(8), (20), (31), (37), (41), (42)	6
Total		42

Appendix 2: The chairmen of Kansantaloudellinen Yhdistys and Ekonomiska Samfundet i Finland, 1892–1918.

	Chairman	
Years	Kansantaloudellinen Yhdistys	Ekonomiska Samfundet i Finland
1892–1893	Yrjö S. Yrjö-Koskinen	–
1893–1894	Kaarlo F. Ignatius	–
1894–1895	Agathon Meurman	Leo Mechelin
1895–1896	Joel N. Lang	Leo Mechelin
1896–1897	Ernst G. Palmén	Emil Schybergson
1897–1898	Ossian Bergbom	Leo Mechelin
1898–1899	Ossian Donner	L. von Pfaler
1899–1900	Yrjö S. Yrjö-Koskinen	Leo Mechelin
1900–1901	Hannes Gebhard	Th. Wegelius
1901–1902	E. G. Palmén	A. Ramsay
1902–1903	Otto Stenroth	L. von Pfaler
1903–1904	J. R. Danielson	Leo Mechelin
1904–1905	K. A. Brander	A. Ramsay
1905–1906	Ernst Nevanlinna	J. J. Sederholm
1906–1907	August Hjelt	Ossian Donner
1907–1908	Juho H. Vennola	J. J. Sederholm
1908–1909	Juho K. Paasikivi	G. Granfelt
1909–1910	Onni Hallstén	A. E. Alfthan
1910–1911	Kyösti Järvinen	Leo Ehrnrooth
1911–1912	A. Listo	G. R. Snellman
1912–1913	J. J. Karvonen	G. Granfelt
1913–1914	Jaakko Forsman	J. O. Wasastjerna
1914–1915	S. Gripenberg	K. A. Moring
1915–1916	P. W. Hannikainen	A. Frey
1916–1917	Juho H. Vennola	J. O. Wasastjerna
1917–1918	G. Komppa	A. Neovius

Sources: Harmaja 1934, pp. 153–154 and Pipping 1944, p. 137.

Appendix 3: Members of the board of directors of the Bank of Finland during the period of autonomy, 1809–1917.

Years	
1812–1816	Claes J. Sacklén (Edelsköld), temporary chairman
1812–1817	Gustaf Gadolin
1812–1816	Johan J. Dreilick
1815–1820	Carl J. Idman (Idestam), chairman 1817–1820
1816–1827	Otto H. Lode, chairman 1820–1827
1817–1841	Johan G. Winter, chairman 1827–1841
1820–1822	Erik Wallenius (Wallensköld)
1822–1837	Claes J. Gripenberg
1826–1840	Axel E. Boije
1827–1834	Alexander Armfelt
1834–1840	Curt G. Stjernvall
1837–1840	Samuel Werner von Troil
1840–1853	Carl W. Trapp, chairman 1841–1853, free from office 1845–1853
1840–1854	Axel Federley, acting chairman 1853–1854
1841–1861	Wilhelm Blidberg, chairman 1858–1861
1845–1866	August E. Mannerheim
1845–1856	Axel L. Born, acting chairman 1845–1853, chairman 1853–1856, but free from office
1854–1856	Robert (von) Trapp, acting chairman
1856–1858	Frans I. Edelheim, chairman
1856–1858	Johan H. Nordenswan
1858–1865	Per A. Törnqvist
1858–1861	Lars H. Langenskiöld
1862–1866	Carl I. Björkman, chairman
1862–1875	August W. Florin, chairman 1870–1875

1865–1870	Victor G. von Haartman, chairman 1866–1870
1866–1875	Otto R. Frenckell
1867–1871	Albert W. Nykopp
1871–1872	Johan Cronstedt (Galindo)
1871–1872	Anders J. Rudbäck
1873–1882	Emil Lindebäck
1875–1884	Gustaf A. von Troil, chairman
1876–1879	Paul F. von Hausen
1879–1894	Alexander E. Wallenius
1883–1891	Waldermar Eneberg
1884–1897	Gustaf R. Charpentier, chairman
1893–1894	Erik A. Wallén
1894–1903	Karl Zachris Bergbom
1894–1913	Karl F. Stenius
1895–1918	Clas H. von Collan, extraordinary 1895–1907, chairman 1907–1918
1898–1906	Karl T. Wegelius, chairman
1904–1920	Jalo W. Järnefelt
1907–1923	Kaarlo A. Basilier, extraordinary 1907–1914
1914–1922	Uno A. Broberg, extraordinary

Sources: Pipping 1961, pp. 572–573 and Pipping 1969, p. 469.

Appendix 4: The Heads of the Office of Financial Matters in the Senate during the period of autonomy, 1809–1917.

Years	
1809–1812	Erik E. Tulindberg
1812–1815	Gabriel E. von Haartman
1816–1820	Claes J. Sacklén (Edelsköld)
1820–1833	Anders H. Falck
1833–1840	Lars Sacklén
1840–1858	Lars G. von Haartman
1858–1863	Carl Fabian Th. Langenskiöld
1863–1868	Johan V. Snellman
1868–1871	Robert von Trapp
1871–1897	Clas Herman Molander
1897–1900	Gustaf R. Charpentier
1900	Henrik W. Åkerman
1900–1905	Edvard R. Neovius
1905	Ernst Neovius (Nevanlinna)
1905–1906	Per K. Antell
1906–1908	Karl Th. Wegelius
1908–1909	Juho K. Paasikivi
1909–1917	Viktor B. Hedlund

Sources: Pipping 1961, p. 572, Pipping 1969, p. 469 and Kuusterä 1989, p. 88.

BIBLIOGRAPHY OF WORKS BY SCHOLARS FROM THE PERIOD STUDIED

Aschehoug, Torkel H. ([1903–1908]1904): *Yhteiskunnallisen taloustieteen historia [Socialøkonomik; transl. V. Malin]*. Helsinki, Otava.

Bastiat, Frédéric (1830): *Les Harmonies Économiques*. Paris.

Becker, Thorald (1905): J. V. Snellmanin kansantaloudellisista kirjoituksista [On J. V. Snellman's Economic Writings]. *Yhteiskuntataloudellinen Aikakauskirja [The Finnish Economic Journal]* 1, 97–116, 149–156 and 197–210.

Berch, Anders (1747): *Indelning til Almänna Hushålningen, innefattande grunden til Politie, Oeconomie och Cameral Wetenskaperne [Introduction to General Economy and Cameral Sciences]*. Stockholm.

Bergbom, Carl Gustaf (1820): *Om Ränte-Persedle Undervisningen för Salo Härad uti Uleåborgs Län [On Land Taxes]*. Åbo.

Betänkande från Komiten för uppgörande af förslag om guldmyntfots införande i Finland [The Report of the Gold Standard Committee] (1876). The Archives of the Financial Office of the Senate, The Finnish National Archives.

Bonsdorff, J. G. von (1833), *Stor-furstendömet Finlands kameral-lagfarenhet, systematiskt framställd [The Tax and Finance Legislation of Grand Duchy Finland]*. Helsingfors.

Borgström, Henrik, Jr. (1858): *Om Hypoteks-Föreningar [On Mortgage Associations]*. Helsingfors.

Borgström, Henrik, Jr. (1859): *Penningställningen år 1859 och privatbanker [Monetary Conditions in 1859 and the Private Banks]*. Helsingfors.

Böhm-Bawerk, Eugen von (1909): *Kapital und Kapitalzins II: Positive Theorie des Kapitales*. Innsbruck, Verlag der Wagnerschen Universitätsbuchhandlung.

Carey, Henry C. (1849–51): *Det Förflutna, Närvarande och Tillkommande, I–III [Past, Present and Future, I–III; transl. C. V. Bergman & S. J. Callerholm].* Stockholm, S. Magnus förlag.

Cassel, Gustav (1903): *Nature and Necessity of Interest.* London.

Chevalier, Michel (1846): *Cours d'Économie politique fait au Collège de France.* Paris.

Chydenius, Anders (1765a): *Källan till Rikets Vanmakt [The Source of the Nation's Weakness].* Stockholm. (Palmén 1880)

Chydenius, Anders (1765b): *Den Nationnale Winsten [The National Gain]. Wördsamast öfwerlemnad Til Riksens Höglofliga Ständer, Af En Deras Ledamot.* Stockholm. (Palmén 1880)

Chydenius, A. (1765c), *Svar på den af Kunglika Vetenskaps Akademien förstälta Frågor: Hvad kan vara orskane, att nådan myckenhet Svenskt folk årligen flytter utur Landet? Och genom hvad Författningar det kan bäst förekommas? [What areReasons for Emigration?].* Stockholm (Palmén 1880).

Chydenius, A. (1766), *Rikets hjelp, genom en Naturlig Finans-System [For a Natural Finance System*]. Stockholm (Palmén 1880)

Committee Report 1911: 12b. Willgren, Karl, Silmäys nykyaikaiseen valtiolliseen tulo- ja varallisuusverotukseen Euroopassa [A Review of Modern Income and Wealth Taxation in Europe]. V*erokomitean julkaisuja [Publications of the Tax Committee]*, II.

Committee Report 1911: 12c. Lakeja ja lakiehdotuksia tulo- ja varallisuusverosta muutamissa Euroopan maissa [Laws and Law Proposals on Income and Wealth Tax in some European Countries]. *Verokomitean julkaisuja [Publications of the Tax Committee]*, III.

Conrad, Johannes ([1897]1913): *Kansantalouspolitiikka II [Volkswirtschaftspolitik; transl. Laura and Leo Harmaja].* Porvoo.

Coquelin, Charles (1850): *Du Crédit et des Banques.* Paris.

Ekonomiska Samfundet i Finland (1904): Utlåtande i tullfrågan [A Statement concerning the Customs Tariff Question]. *Ekonomiska Samfundets i Finland Föredrag och Förhandlingar* II:4, 1–40. Helsingfors.

Forsman, Jaakko (1912): *Mistä syystä sosialismi levisi Suomen maalaisväestön keskuuteen [Why Did Socialism Spread Among the Finnish rural population?].* Helsinki.

Frenckell, Otto Reinhold (1858): *Börsen i Paris [The Stock Exchange in Paris]*. Helsingfors.

Frenckell, Otto Reinhold (1860): *Om det industriella arbetet i förhållande till nationalförmögenheten [Industrial Labour and National Wealth]*. Helsingfors.

Garnier, Joseph (1846): *Élements de l'Économie politique*. Paris.

Gebhard, Hannes (1889): *Savonlinnan läänin oloista vuoteen 1571 [On Conditions in the County of Savo up until 1571]*. Helsinki.

Gide, Charles ([1883]1904): *Taloustieteen pääpiirteet [Principes d'économie politique; transl. Jaakko Forsman]*. Helsinki, Otava.

Granfelt, Axel F. (1873): Om vår tids sociala rörelser [On Social Movements in our Times]. *Morgonbladet*, nrs. 188, 190, 191, 196 and 197.

Gripenberg, Lennart (1913): *Lausunto viljatullikysymyksestä valtiovarainvaliokunnalle valtiopäivillä vuonna 1913 [A Statement to the Public Finance Committee on Corn Duty Issue on Parliamentary Session 1913]*. Helsinki.

Groundstroem, Oskar (1897): Helsingin työväen taloudellisista oloista [On the Economic Conditions of the Workers of Helsinki]. Esitelmä Kansantaloudellisen Yhdistyksen kokouksessa 1894. *Esitelmiä Kansantaloudellisessa Yhdistyksessä* 2. Porvoo.

Groundstroem, Oskar (1903): Några drag ur v. Böhm-Bawerks produktionsteori [Some Points concerning v. Böhm-Bawerk's Theory of Production]. *Ekonomiska Samfundets i Finland Föredrag och Förhandlingar 1903*, III:3, 32–46.

Gröndahl, Hugo (1905): Pienemmän sahaamattoman puutavaran maastaviennistä [On the Export of Small Unsawn Timber]. *Yhteiskuntataloudellinen Aikakauskirja* 1, 179–187.

Gylling, Edvard (1909): *Suomen torpparilaitoksen kehityksen pääpiirteet Ruotsinvallan aikana [The Main Characteristics of the Development of Finnish Crofter System under Swedish Rule]. Taloudellisia tutkimuksia 9*. Helsinki.

Harmaja, Laura & Leo Harmaja (1914): *Kansantaloustieteen oppikirja [Textbook of Economics]*. Helsinki, Otava.

Hegel, Georg W. F. ([1821]1981): *Grundlinien der Philosophie des Rechts oder Naturrecht und Staatswissenschaft im Grundrisse*. Berlin, Akademie-Verlag.

Helander, Anders B. (1909): Pienemmän puutavaran vientitulleista [On Export Duties on Smaller Timber]. *In Suomen Metsänhoitoyhdistys Tapion I vuosijulkaisu v. 1908*. Hämeenlinna.

Hjelt, Vera (1912): *Tutkimus ammattityöläisten toimeentuloehdoista Suomessa 1908–1909 [A Study on Workers' Living Conditions in Finland 1908–1909]. Työtilasto* XIII. Helsinki.

Hoppu, Kaarle V. (1913): *Viljatulli, miten arvosteltava [How to judge the Corn Customs Tariff].* Yhteiskuntataloudellisia kirjoituksia VIII. Helsinki.

Häusser, Ludwig (1850): Friedrich List's Leben. In *Friedrich List's gesammelte Schriften, I–III (ed. Ludwig Häusser)*, erster Theil. Stuttgart und Tübingen, Gottascher Verlag.

Häusser, Ludwig, ed. (1850–51): *Friedrich List's gesammelte Schriften,* I–III. Stuttgart und Tübingen, Gottascher Verlag.

Jahnsson, Yrjö (1907–08): *Tutkimuksia Suomen kansantaloustieteen historiasta [Studies concerning the History of Finnish Economics].* Helsinki.

Jahnsson, Yrjö (1908): *Suomen verotuspolitiikan periaatteista [On the Principles of the Finnish Tax Policy].* Helsinki.

Johnsson, Mikael (1892), Koulu- ja opetusvelvollisuudesta [On Compulsory Training and School Attendance], *Valvoja* 1892.

Järnefelt, Arvid ([1907]1980): *Maa kuuluu kaikille [The land belongs to everybody].* Keuruu, Otava.

Järnefelt, Arvid ([1893]1983): *Isänmaa [The Fatherland].* Juva, WSOY.

Keynes, John N. (1891): *The Scope and Method of Political Economy.* London & New York.

Kilpi, Oskar K. (1915): Talous- ja sosiaalipoliittiset ideaalit nykyajan kansantaloustieteessä ja niiden kritiikki [Ideals and Critiques of Contemporary Economic and Social Policy]. *Yhteiskuntataloudellinen aikakauskirja* 11, 229–257.

Kilpi, Oskar K. (1917): *Suomen siirtolaisuus ja 19. vuosisadan kansantalous [Finnish Emigration and the Economy of the 19th Century].* Taloustieteellisiä tutkimuksia 22. Helsinki.

K[oskinen], Y[rjö] (1874): Työväenseikka [The Workers' Question]. *Kirjallinen Kuukauslehti*, nrs. 1874:1, 4, 8 and 9, 1–9, 91–97, 195–199 and 219–227.

Kovero, Martti (1909): *Valtion uutisasutus Ruotsin-Suomessa jälkeen ison-vihan [Public Settlement in Sweden-Finland after the Great War at the beginning of the 18th Century]. Asutuspoliittinen tutkimus.* Taloustieteellisiä tutkimuksia 10. Helsinki.

Korpisaari, Paavo (1915), *Talletuspankkien likviditeettiperiaate. Pankkiteoreettinen tutkimus [The Liquidity Principle of Deposit Banks. A Study on the Theory of Banking].* Taloustieteellisiä tutkimuksia 19. Helsinki.

Kuusi, Eino (1914), *Talvityöttömyys, sen esiintyminen, syyt ja ehkäisytoimenpiteet Suomen suurimmissa kaupungeissa [Winter Unemployment, its Occurance, Causes and Prevention in the Largest Finnish Towns]*. Tampere.

Lagus, Wilhelm G. (1813): *Academisk Afhandling om Wäxlar [Academic Study on Bills]*. Åbo.

Lang, Joel N. (1882): *Den nationalekonomiska teorin för jordkreditföreningars organisation med et bidrag till dessa ansstalters historie [An Economic Theory for the Organization of Land Credit Associations, and a Supplement to the History of those Associations]*. Helsingfors.

Lang, Joel N. (1893): Kansallisen taloustieteen merkitys opetusaineena [The Meaning of National Economic Science as a Subject]. *Esitelmiä Kansantaloudellisessa Yhdistyksessä* I. Porvoo, WSOY.

Lavonius, Wilhelm (1873): *Om tull-lagstiftning i Finland [On Customs Tariff Legislation in Finland]*. Helsingfors, J. C. Frenckell & Son.

Lavonius, Wilhelm (1874): *Kateder-socialisterna. Tidskrift utgifven af Juridiska Föreningen i Finland* X, 197–212 and 293–309.

Leffler, Johan (1894): *Det Ekonomiska Samhällslifvet. Handbok i nationalekonomi I [The Economic Life of Society. Handbook of National Economy]*. Stockholm.

Liljenstrand, Axel (1853): *Historisk teckning af den i Finland tillämpade lagstiftningens grundsatser för näringarnes och det allmänna välståndets befrämjande [A Historical Description of the Principles of Legislation for the Promotion of Industries and Common Welfare applied in Finland]*. Helsingfors, J. C. Frenckell & Son.

Liljenstrand, Axel (1857): *Om skifte af jord [On the Shift of Landed Property]*. Helsingfors.

Liljenstrand, Axel (1860): *System af samfundsekonomins läror. Ett försök. Första häftet [A System of Theories of Political Economy. An Attempt. The First Notebook]*. Helsingfors.

Liljenstrand, Axel (1873): Den politiska ekonomin i förhållande till själfviskheten och materialismen i vår tid [The Political Economy in Relationship to Egoism and Materialism in our Times]. *Tidskrift utgifven af Juridiska Föreningen i Finland* IX, 142–152.

Liljenstrand, Axel (1875): Om förhållandet mellan näringsfrihet och skattskyldighet [On the Relationship between Freedom of Trade and Tax Liability]. *Tidskrift utgifven af Juridiska Föreningen i Finland* XI, 250–273.

Liljenstrand, Axel (1878–79): Reflexioner om den politiska ekonomins framtid [Reflections on the Future of Political Economy]. *Tidskrift utgifven af Juridiska Föreningen i Finland* XIV–XV, 301–313.

Liljenstrand, Axel (1880): *Om Kredit och Vexlar [On Credit and Bills]*. Helsingfors.

List, Friedrich (1840): *Om vigten och betydelsen af slöjder och manufakturer för ett samhälle [On the Weight and Importance of Home Industries and Manufacturing for a Society; transl. Johan Johansson]*. Stockholm, Högbergska Boktryckeriet.

List, Friedrich ([1841]1950): *Das nationale System der Politischen Oekonomie*. Jena, Verlag von Gustav Fischer.

List, Friedrich ([1841]1935): *Kansantaloustieteen kansallinen järjestelmä [Das nationale System der Politischen Oekonomie; transl. Ilmari Teijula]*. Porvoo, WSOY.

List, Friedrich (1850a): Die Freiheit und die Beschränkungen des auswärtigen Handels, aus den historischen Gesichtspunkt beleuchtet. In *Friedrich List's gesammelte Schriften, I–III (ed. L. Häusser)*, zweiter Theil, 63–100. Stuttgart und Tübingen, Gottascher Verlag.

List, Friedrich (1850b): Das Wesen und Werth einer nationalen Gewerbsproduktivkraft. In *Friedrich List's gesammelte Schriften, I–III (ed. L. Häusser)*, zweiter Theil, 101–149. Stuttgart und Tübingen, Gottascher Verlag.

Lotz, Johan Friedrich (1821–1822): H*andbuch der Staatswirtschaftslehre, I–III*. Erlangen.

Malin, Werner (1890): *Veroista [On Taxes]*. Oulu, K. Kivekäs.

Mechelin, Leo (1879): De politiska partierna [The Political Parties]. *Finsk Tidskrift* IV, 116–147.

Mechelin, Leo (1901), Är det till gagn för vårt land, att de finska statslånen upptagas företrädesvis i utlandet? [Is it Good for the Country to Take Up Loans Mostly from Abroad?] *Ekonomiska Samfundet i Finland. Föredrag o. Förhandlingar*, 1., 1901

Mechelin, Leo (1904): Några drag ur nutidens handelspolitik [Some Features of Contemporary Trade Policy]. *Ekonomiska Samfundets i Finland Föredrag och Förhandlingar* III:3, 67–85. Helsingfors.

Menger, Carl (1883): *Untersuchungen über die Methoden der Sozialwissenschaften und der politischen Ökonomie insbesondere*. Leipzig.

Menger, Carl (1884): *Die Irrthümer des Historismus in der deutschen Nationalökonomie*. Wien.

Meurman, Agathon (1878): *Veroista Suomessa [On Taxes in Finland]*. Helsinki, Suomalaisen Kirjallisuuden Seuran kirjapaino.

Meurman, Agathon (1897): Näkökohtia kansantaloustieteen alalta [Economic Considerations]. *Esitelmiä Kansantaloudellisessa Yhdistyksessä* II. Porvoo, WSOY.

Meurman, Agathon (1866): Varallisuus ja yleinen talous Suomessa [Wealth and the General Economy in Finland]. *Kirjallinen Kuukauslehti* 1:10, 224–227.

Myréen, Daniel (1810–1811): *Academisk afhandling om penningar och mynt [An Academic Study of Money and Credit]* I–II. Upsala.

Myréen, Daniel (1812): *Afhandling om jords taxering [A Study of Land Taxation]*. Åbo.

Nevanlinna (Neovius), Ernst (1899): *Suomen raha-asiain järjestämisestä Porvoon valtiopäiviä seuranneina vuosina [On Arrangements concerning Finnish State Finances in the Years after the Porvoo Diet Session]*. Helsinki.

Nevanlinna, Ernst (1913): *Kaksi kansantalouden tutkimuksen merkkimiestä [Two Prominent Men in Economics]*. Helsinki, kustannusosakeyhtiö Kirja.

Nevanlinna, Ernst (1914): Wilhelm Lexis – Eugen von Böhm-Bawerk. *Yhteiskuntataloudellinen Aikakauskirja* 10, 252–278.

Nordström, Johan Jakob (1832): *Skildring af bevisningsmethoderne i brottmål efter de gamla Landskapslagarne [A Description of Municipal Legislation in Finland]*. Åbo.

Nordström, Johan Jakob (1839–1840): *Bidrag till den svenska samhälls-författningens historia I–II [A Contribution to the History of Swedish Constitutions]*. Helsingfors.

Nordström, Johan Jakob (1853): *Afhandlingar rörande Läran om Crediten, I. Credit- och Bankväsendet [Studies on the Theory of Credit, I. Credit and Banking Business]*. Stockholm.

Philippovich, Eugen von ([1893]1914): *Yleinen kansantaloustiede [Allgemeine Volkswirtschaftslehre; transl. Lauri Rosendahl]*. Helsinki, Otava.

Rabenius, Lars Georg (1829): *Lärobok i National-Ekonomien [Textbook of National Economy]*. Försök. Upsala.

Rantakari, K. N. (1910): J. W. Snellmanin kansantaloudellisista mielipiteistä [On J. W. Snellman's Economic Views]. *Aika* 4, 402–408.

Rau, Karl Heinrich (1826–1837): *Lehrbuch der politischen Oekonomie. I–III*. Heidelberg.

Rein, Karl G. Th. (1878): Liberalismi ja socialismi [Liberalism and Socialism]. *Kirjallinen Kuukauslehti,* nrs. 1878:4 and 8, 73–79 and 169–179.

Rein, Karl G. Th. (1879a): Kansantalouden uusi oppikunta [A New School of Thought in Economics]. *Kirjallinen Kuukauslehti,* nrs. 1879:1 and 2, 1–10 and 31–37.

Rein, Karl G. Th. (1879b): Ännu några ord om 'liberalismen' [Still some Words on 'Liberalism']. *Morgonbladet,* nrs. 106, 116, 117 and 123.

Rein, Karl G. Th. (1895): *Juhana Vilhelm Snellmanin elämä, I osa [The Life of Juhana Vilhelm Snellman, part I].* Helsinki, Otava.

Rein, Karl G. Th. (1899): *Juhana Vilhelm Snellmanin elämä, II osa [The Life of Juhana Vilhelm Snellman, part II].* Helsinki, Otava.

Rein, Th. (1915): *Leo Mechelin.* Helsingfors.

Renvall, Heikki (1910): *Suomen metsäntuotteiden vienti. Kansantaloudelliselta kannalta [The Export of Finnish Forest Products. The Economic Point of View].* Helsinki.

Ricardo, David ([1817]1937): *Kansantalouden ja verotuksen periaatteet [Principles of Political Economy and Taxation; transl. B. Tuunanen].* WSOY, Porvoo.

Roscher, Wilhelm (1874): *Geschichte der National-Oekonomik in Deutschland.* München, R. Oldenburg.

Rosenborg, J. W. (1858): *Om fattigdomen och allmänna fattigvården i Finland [On Poverty and Poor Relief in Finland].* Helsingfors.

Rossi, Pellegrino Luigi (1840–1854): *Cours d'Économie politique, I–IV.* Paris.

Say, Jean-Baptiste ([1803]1823): *Afhandling uti Statshushållningsläran, eller Enkel framställning om sättet, huru förmögenhet uppkommer, fördelar sig och förbrukas Första delen. [Traité d'économie politique ou simple exposition de la manière dont se forment se distribuent et se consomment les richesses I, transl. Carl David Skogman).* Stockholm.

Schulze-Gävernitz, Gerhart von (1899): *Volkswirtschaftliche Studien aus Russland.* Leipzig, Verlag von Duncker & Humblot.

Schumpeter, Joseph (1911): *Theorie der wirtschaftlichen Entwicklung.* Leipzig.

Schüller, Richard (1899): *Die Wirtschaftspolitik der Historischen Schule.* Berlin, Carl Heymanns Verlag.

Senate 1812–1816, *Suomen hallituskonseljin ja senaatin alamai-*

set kertomukset vuosilta 1812–1816. Suomen taloudellisesta tilasta, hallinnosta ja lainkäytöstä [The Senate's Report on Economic Conditions and the Administration of Finland in 1812–1816]. Todistuskappaleita Suomen historiaan VII. Helsinki 1915.

Sidgwick, Henry (1883): *The Principles of Political Economy.* London.

Smith, Adam ([1776]1974): *The Wealth of Nations.* Harmondsworth, Penguin Books.

Smith, Adam ([1776]1931): *An Inquiry into the Nature and Causes of the Wealth of Nations.* Volume II. London, J.M. Dent & Sons LTD.

Snellman, J. V. (1855): Om privatbanker [On Private Banks]. *Litteraturbladet.*

Snellman, Johan V. (1860): Review of Axel Liljenstrand's 'System af samfundsekonomins läror'. *Litteraturblad för allmän medborgerlig bildning* 1860:5, 193–198.

Snellman, Johan V. (1992–1998), *Samlade Arbeten [Collected Works].* Helsingfors.

Snellman, Johan V. ([1840]1976): Kauppapolitiikan kysymyksiä [Issues of Trade Policy; transl. J. Manninen]. *Politiikka* 18:3, 276–279.

Soden, Friedrich von (1805–1806): *Die National-Oekonomie. Ein philosophischer Versuch über die Quellen des National-Reichthums und über die Mittel zu dessen Beförderung I–II.* Leipzig.

Steffen, Gustaf (1890): Den nya riktningen inom Englands nationalekonomi [VH1][A new Direction in English Economics]. *Finsk Tidskrift* 29, 3–18.

Steuart, James (1767): *An Inquiry into the Principles of Political Oeconomy* I–II. London.

Suomen Valtionrautatiet 1862–1912. Historiallis-teknillis-taloudellinen kertomus I [The Finnish State Railways 1862–1912] (1912) Helsinki.

Tallqvist, J. V. (1900): *Bidrag till belysande af det svenska myntets historia i Finland sedan år 1808 [On the History of Swedish Currency in Finland after 1808].* Helsingfors.

Tengström, J. ([1809] 1892): Om Finlands penningeställning vid grundandet af Finlands Bank. [On Finland's Monetary Conditions at the Time of the Founding of the Bank of Finland] Ett uttalande af biskop J. Tengström. Meddelande af Aug. Hjelt. *Historiallinen Arkisto* XII:1. Helsinki.

Thesleff, Rolf (1915): Spannmålstullen och statsinkomsterna

[Corn Duties and State Income]. *Ekonomiska Samfundets Tidskrift* 3, 227–309.

Tjeder, Michaël (1826): *Tankar om Frihet i Handel [Thoughts upon the Freedom of Trade]*. Åbo.

Tugan-Baranowsky, Mikhail (1913): *Soziale Theorie der Verteilung*. Berlin.

Valtiopäivät (1914): *Pöytäkirjat [Parliamentary Records]* I. Helsinki.

Vennola, Juho Heikki (1900): *Pohjois-Suomen maalaisvarallisuus 16:lla ja 17:llä vuosisadalla [Agrarian Wealth in Northern Finland in the 16th and 17th Centuries], I. 1559–1641*. Tutkimuksia Suomen Taloudellisesta Historiasta 2. Helsinki.

Vennola, Juho Heikki (1904): *Viljan ja leivän hintasuhteista Suomen kaupungeissa silmälläpitäen hintatilaa 1890-luvun alkupuolella [On Relative Prices in Finnish Towns Compared to the Level of Prices at the Beginning of the 1890s]. Taloustieteellisiä Tutkimuksia* 1. Helsinki.

Vennola, Juho Heikki (1908): *Luontais- ja rahataloudellinen astetaistelu kansantaloudessa ja valtion finanssit [The Rivalry between Barter, Monetary Economy and State Finances]. Taloustieteellisiä Tutkimuksia* 8. Helsinki.

Vennola, Juho Heikki (1913): *Venäjän asema Suomen viljantuonnissa [Russia and Finnish Corn Imports]. Yhteiskuntataloudellisia kirjoituksia* VII. Helsinki.

Warén, Axel (1898): *Torppariolosta Suomessa [On Crofters' Conditions in Finland]. SKS:n toimituksia* 89. Helsinki.

Westergaard, Harald (1909): *Kansantaloustieteen pääpiirteet [Outlines of Economics; transl. Väinö Juusela]*. Porvoo.

Wicksell, Knut (1893): *Über Wert, Kapital und Rente nach den neueren nationalökonomischen Theorien*. Jena.

Wicksell, Knut (1898): *Geldzins und Güterpreise*. Jena.

Wicksell, Knut (1901): *Föreläsningar i Nationalekonomi. Första delen: Teoretisk nationalekonomi [Lectures on Political Economy. First Part: Theoretical Political Economy]*. Lund.

Willgren, Karl (1891): Om införandet af normalarbetsdag i Finland [On the Introduction of the Normal Working Day in Finland]. *Finsk Tidskrift* 30, 186–204, 262–279 & 420–431.

Willgren, Karl (1892): Työväki osallisena liikevoittoihin [Labour Participation in Business Profits]. *Valvoja* 12, 91–100.

Willgren, Karl (1893): En ny nationalekonomisk skola [A New School in Economics]. *Finsk Tidskrift* 35, 325–341.

Willgren, Karl (1895): Ekonomisk teori och praxis [Economic Theory and Practice]. *Finsk Tidskrift* 39, 157–166.

Willgren, Karl (1897): Nyare finansteorier [Newer Financial Theories]. *Finsk Tidskrift* 42, 354–369.
Willgren, Karl (1899): *Das Staatsbudget, dessen Aufbau und Verhältnis zur Staatsrechnung*. Helsingfors.
Willgren, Karl (1903): A Review of Knut Wicksell: Föreläsningar i nationalekonomi. Första delen: teoretisk nationalekonomi, häft. 1. *Finsk Tidskrift* 48, 280–284.
Willgren, Karl (1905–1907): *Statistikens grunder [The Foundations of Statistics]* I–II. Helsingfors.
Willgren, Karl (1906): *Finlands finansrätt [Finnish Financial Law]*. Helsingfors, Helios.
Willgren, Karl (1909): Arbetarklassens ekonomiska framåtskridande [The Economic Progress of the Labour Class]. *Ekonomiska Samfundets i Finland Föredrag och förhandlingar* (5:III), 33–114.
Willgren, Karl (1910): Uppkomsten af en finansvetenskaplig forskning i Sverige och Finland [The Rise of the Study of Public Finances in Sweden and Finland]. *Tidskrift utgifven af Juridiska Föreningen i Finland* 46, 155–221.
Willgren, Karl (1914): Eugen von Böhm-Bawerk. *Ekonomiska Samfundets Tidskrift* 2, 193–215.
Willgren, Karl (1915a): Den ekonomiska utvecklingen och kriserna [Economic Development and Crises]. *Finsk Tidskrift* 78, 341–355.
Willgren, Karl (1915b): De finansiella institutionernas ursprung [The Origin of Financial Institutions]. *Ekonomiska Samfundets Tidskrift* (3. årg), 133–178.
Willgren, Karl (1916a): Den nationalekonomiska fördelningens grundprinciper [The Principles of the Distribution of the National Income]. *Ekonomiska Samfundets Tidskrift* 4, 145–190.
Willgren, Karl (1916b): Till frågan om nationalinkomstens fördelning [On the Issue of the Distribution of the National Income]. *Ekonomiska Samfundets Tidskrift* 4, 349–379.
Willgren, Karl (1917): Åtta timmars arbetsdagen i Finland [The Eight-hour Working Day in Finland]. *Ekonomiska Samfundets Tidskrift*, (5. årg.), 103–107.
Wright, Tor von (1916): Handelsrelationerna mellan Finland och Ryssland under perioden 1897–1913 [Trade Relations between Finland and Russia, 1897–1913]. *Ekonomiska Samfundets Tidskrift* 4, 191–305.

LITERATURE BY LATER SCHOLARS AND COMMENTATORS

Aerschot, Paul van (1996), *Köyhät ja laki. Toimeentulotukilainsäädännön kehitys oikeudellistumisprosessien valossa [The Poor and the Law. The Evolution of Social Assistance Legislation with Special Reference to Juridification Processes].* Suomalaisen Lakimiesyhdistyksen Julkaisuja A-sarja N:o 210. Helsinki.

Airas, Pentti (1956): *Yksilö ja hänen suhteensa yhteisöön J. V. Snellmanin historianfilosofiassa [The Individual and his Relationship to Community in J. V. Snellman's Philosophy of History].* Jyväskylä.

Alapuro, Risto (1988): *State and Revolution in Finland.* Berkeley, University of California Press.

Alapuro, Risto & Stenius, Henrik (1987): Kansanliikkeet loivat kansakunnan [Social Movements created the Nation]. In *Kansa liikkeessä (eds. Alapuro, Liikanen et al.),* 8–49. Vaasa, Kirjayhtymä.

Alapuro, Risto, Liikanen, Ilkka, Smeds, Kerstin & Stenius, Henrik, eds. (1987): *Kansa liikkeessä [The People in Motion].* Vaasa, Kirjayhtymä.

Alapuro, Risto & Matti Alestalo (1973): Konkreettinen sosiaalitutkimus [Concrete Social Research]. In *Suomalaisen sosiologian juuret (eds. Alapuro et al.),* 84–147. Porvoo, WSOY.

Alapuro, Risto & Matti Alestalo (1992): Konkreettinen sosiaalitutkimus [Concrete Social Research]. In *Suomalaisen sosiologian historia (eds. Alapuro et al.),* 77–148. Juva, WSOY.

Alapuro, Risto, Matti Alestalo & Elina Haavio-Mannila, eds. (1973): *Suomalaisen sosiologian juuret [The Roots of Finnish Sociology].* Porvoo, WSOY.

Alapuro, Risto, Matti Alestalo & Elina Haavio-Mannila, eds. (1992): *Suomalaisen sosiologian historia [A History of Finnish Sociology]*. Juva, WSOY.

Alf-Halonen, E. (1954): *Taistelu ammattikuntalaitoksesta Suomessa 1800-luvun puolivälissä. Kappale J. V. Snellmanin julkista toimintaa [The Debate on the Guild Institution in Finland in the mid-19th Century. A Chapter of J. V. Snellman's public Life]*. Historiallisia tutkimuksia [Historical Studies] 61. Helsinki.

Allardt, Erik (1997), *The History of the Social Sciences in Finland 1828–1918*. The History of Learning and Science in Finland 1828–1918 17b. Ekenäs, The Finnish Society of Sciences.

Barucci, Piero (1972): The Spread of Marginalism in Italy, 1871–1890. *History of Political Economy* 4, 512–532.

Bergholm, Jorma (1987): *'Uuden taloustieteen' vastaanotto Suomessa ennen toista maailmansotaa: talouspolitiikan suomalaisen mallin juurilla [The Reception of the 'New Economics' in Finland before World War II. The Roots of the Finnish Economic Policy Model]*. Unpublished Pro gradu thesis. University of Helsinki, Department of Economics.

Bergholm, Jorma (1988): Talouspolitiikan suomalaisen mallin juurilla [The Roots of the Finnish Economic Policy Model]. *Kansantaloudellinen aikakauskirja [The Finnish Economic Journal]* 1988:2, 153–165.

Björkqvist, Heimer (1986): *Den nationalekonomiska vetenskapens utveckling i Finland intill år 1918 [The Development of Finnish Economics up to 1918]. Meddelanden från stiftelsens för Åbo Akademi forskningsinstitut [Publications of the Foundation of Åbo Akademi Research Institute]*, nr. 109. Åbo, Åbo Akademi.

Blaug, Mark (1972): Was There a Marginal Revolution? *History of Political Economy* 1972: 4, 269–280.

Blaug, Mark (1983): *Economic Theory in Retrospect*. Cambridge, Cambridge University Press.

Boese, Franz (1939): *Geschichte des Vereins für Sozialpolitik 1872–1932. (Im Auftrage des Liquidationsausschusses verfasst vom Schriftführer Dr. Franz Boese). Schriften des Vereins für Sozialpolitik*, Band 188. Berlin.

Braun, Hans-Joachim (1975): Economic Theory and Policy in Germany, 1750–1800. *The Journal of European Economic History* 4:2, 301–322.

Carlson, Benny (1995): *De institutionalistiska ideernas spridning:*

Tyska historiska skolan, amerkansk institutionalism och svenska ekonomers utlandstudier. SNS Förlag.

Clarke, Simon (1982): *Marx, Marginalism and Modern Sociology – From Adam Smith to Max Weber.* Guildford and King's Lynn, Allen & Unwin.

Coats, A. W. (1972): The Economic and Social Context of the Marginal Revolution of the 1870's. *History of Political Economy* 4, 303–324.

Eriksson, Ralf (1978): *Den historisk-etiska nationalekonomin i Finland [Historico-Ethical Economics in Finland].* Unpublished Pro gradu thesis. Åbo Akademi, Department of Economics.

Eräsaari, Risto (1976): *Historiallinen taloustiede – katederisosialismi – Verein für Sozialpolitik. Sosiaalipolitiikan synnyn ongelma Saksassa [Historical Economics – Kathedersozialismus – Verein für Sozialpolitik. The Problem of the Birth of Social Policy in Germany]. Research Reports of the Institute of Social Policy* 5/1976, University of Helsinki.

Eskola, Antti, Seppo Toiviainen, Matti Alestalo & Risto Alapuro (1973): Marxilainen tutkimus [Marxian Studies]. In *Suomalaisen sosiologian juuret (eds. Alapuro, Risto et al.),* 194–225.Porvoo, WSOY.

Eskola, Seikko (1962): Sosiaalipolitiikka suomalaisen puolueen ohjelmassa vuonna 1906 [Social Policy in the Party Program of the Finnish Party in 1906]. *Studia historica Jyväskyläensia* 1, 391–450. Jyväskylä.

Fisher, Robert (1986): *The Logic of Economic Discovery.* Worcester, Wheatsheaf Books Ltd.

Foucault, Michel (1966): *Les mots et les choses. Une archéologie des sciences humaines.* Gallimard.

Foucault, Michel (1969): *L'Archéologie du savoir.* Gallimard.

Gide, Charles & Charles Rist (1953): *A History of Economic Doctrines – From the Time of the Physiocrats to the Present Day.* Bristol, George Harrop & Co. Ltd.

Goodwin, Craufurd (1972): Marginalism Movesto the New World. *History of Political Economy* 4, 551–570.

Grampp, William (1960): *The Manchester School of Economics.* Stanford, Stanford University Press.

Gronow, Jukka (1987): Länsimainen rationalisoitumisprosessi ja modernin länsimaisen kulttuurin irrationaalisuus [The Western Rationalisation Process and the Irrationality of Modern Western Culture]. In *Aiheita Weberistä [Themes on Weber] (ed. Tapani Hietaniemi),* 9–35. Jyväskylä, Tutkijaliitto.

Haapala, Pertti (1990): *Talous, valta ja valtio – tutkimuksia 1800-luvun Suomesta [Economy, Power and the State – Studies concerning 19th-Century Finland].* Helsinki, Vastapaino.

Haapala, Pertti (1992): Suomalainen yhteiskunta [The Finnish Society]. In *Itsenäistymisen vuodet* 2, 10–131. Helsinki, Painatuskeskus,

Haatanen, Pekka (1968): *Suomen maalaisköyhälistö. Tutkimusten ja kaunokirjallisuuden valossa [The Finnish Rural Proletariat – in the Light of Inquiries and Fiction].* Porvoo.

Hagemann, Harald (1996): *German Economic Journals and Economic Debates in the Nineteenth Century. History of Economic Ideas* IV:3, 77–102.

Harmaja, Leo (1922): Miten Suomen maanviljelys menetti tullisuojeluksensa [How Finnish Agriculture lost the Protection of Customs Duties]. *Yhteiskuntataloudellinen Aikakauskirja* 18, 274–287.

Harmaja, Leo (1924): Maatalousmiesten lausuntoja epätasaisesta tullisuojeluksesta vuodelta 1856 [Peasants' Statements concerning uneven Customs Protection in 1856]. *Yhteiskuntataloudellinen Aikakauskirja* 20, 175–84.

Harmaja, Leo (1925): *Tullikysymykset Suomen kansantaloudellisessa kirjallisuudessa [Customs Issues in Finnish Economic Literature].* Kansantaloudellisen yhdistyksen julkaisusarja [Publications of the Finnish Economic Association] n:o 32. Helsinki, Otava.

Harmaja, Leo (1933): *Tullipolitiikan vaikutus suomen kansantalouden teollistumissuuntaan ennen maailmansotaa [The Effect of Tariff Policy on the Industrialisation of Finland before the World War].* Kansantaloudellisia tutkimuksia 11. Helsinki, Otava.

Harmaja, Leo (1934): *Kansantaloudellinen Yhdistys 1884–1934 [The Finnish Economic Association 1884–1934].* Liite *Kansantaloudellisen aikakauskirjan* niteeseen 1934:1. Helsinki, Otava.

Heikkinen, Sakari (1994): *Suomeen ja maailmalle.Tullilaitoksen historia [The History of Finnish Customs Administration].* Helsinki, Tullihallitus.

Heikkinen, Sakari (1997): *Labour and the Market. Workers, Wages and Living Standards in Finland, 1850–1913.* Helsinki, The Finnish Society of Sciences and Letters and The Finnish Academy of Science and Letters.

Heinonen, Visa (1987): *Snellmanista viljatulliin: Keskustelu tullipolitiikasta Suomessa autonomian ajan lopulla [From Snell-*

man to the Corn Duty. The Discourse on Customs Policy in Finland in the late Autonomy Period]. Pro gradu thesis in economics, University of Helsinki.

Heinonen, Visa (1989): Keskustelu vuoden 1914 viljatullista [The Discussion concerning Corn Duties in the Year 1914]. *Kansantaloudellinen aikakauskirja [The Finnish Economic Journal]* 1989:2, 160–169.

Heinonen, Visa (1993): Economics as the Physics of Society – an Interview with Philip Mirowski. *Review of Political Economy* 5, 508–531.

Heinonen, Visa (1996a): Austrian Flavor in the Periphery. First Reactions to the Marginalist Neoclassical Economics in Finland. In *Research in the History of Economic Thought and Methodology (ed. Samuels, Warren J. & Jeff E. Biddle)* vol. 14, 173–194. Greenwich, Connecticut, JAI Press Inc.

Heinonen, Visa (1996b): Zwischen Nationalismus und Liberalismus: J. V. Snellman – ein finnischer Anhänger der nationalökonomischen Ideen von Friedrich List. In *"Die Vereinigung des europäischen Kontinents". Friedrich List – Gesamteuropäische Wirkungsgeschichte seines ökonomischen Denkens (Hrsg. Eugen Wendler)*, 143–165. Ulm, Schäffer-Poeschel Verlag Stuttgart.

Herbst, Jürgen (1965): *The German Historical School in American Scholarship. A Study in the Transfer of Culture*. New York & London.

Hietala, Marjatta (1987): *Services and Urbanization at the Turn of the Century. The Diffusion of Innovations*. Studia historica 23. Helsinki, Suomen historiallinen seura.

Hietaniemi, Tapani, ed. (1987): *Aiheita Weberistä [Themes concerning Weber]*. Jyväskylä, Tutkijaliitto.

Hjerppe, Riitta (1989): The Finnish Economy 1860–1985. Growth and Structural Change. Helsinki, The Bank of Finland.

Honkapohja, Seppo & Antti Suvanto, eds. (1988): *Raha, inflaatio ja talouspolitiikka [Money, Inflation and Economic Policy]*. Helsinki, Valtion painatuskeskus & Helsingin yliopiston kansantaloustieteen laitos.

Howey, Richard (1960): *The Rise of the Marginal Utility School, 1870–1889*. Lawrence, University of Kansas Press.

Howey, Richard (1972): The Origins of Marginalism. *History of Political Economy* 4, 281–302.

Huovinmaa, Kai, ed. (1981): *J. V. Snellman ja nykyaika – Kirjoituksia ja esitelmiä J. V. Snellmanin ajallemme jättämästä henkisestä perinnöstä [J. V. Snellman and the Present –*

Writings and Lectures on the intellectual Heritage of J. V. Snellman]. Helsinki.

Häkkinen, Antti, Vappu Ikonen, Kari Pitkänen & Hannu Soikkanen (1991): *Kun halla nälän toi. Miten suomalaiset kokivat 1860-luvun nälkävuodet [When Hunger came with the Frost. How the Finns experienced the Famine of the 1860s].* Darmstadt, WSOY.

Jussila, Osmo (1987): *Maakunnasta valtioksi. Suomen valtion synty [The Birth of the Finnish State].* Porvoo, WSOY.

Jutikkala, Eino (1958): *Suomen talonpojan historia [A History of the Finnish Peasant]. Suomalaisen Kirjallisuuden Seuran toimituksia* 257. Turku.

Kanerva, Jukka, ed. (1984): *Politiikan teorian klassikoita [Classics of Political Theory].* Hämeenlinna, Gaudeamus.

Kauder, Emil (1965): *A History of Marginal Utility Theory.* Princeton, Princeton University Press.

Kærgård, Niels (1996): Denmark and the Marginal Revolution. In *Research in the History of Economic Thought and Methodology 14 (eds. Warren J. Samuels & Jeff E. Biddle),* 247–258.

Kekkonen, Jukka (1987): *Merkantilismista liberalismiin. Oikeushistoriallinen tutkimus elinkeinovapauden syntytaustasta Suomessa vuosina 1855–1879 [From Mercantilism to Liberalism. A study in the History of Law on the Adoption of Freedom of Trade in Finland 1855–1879].* Suomen Lakimiesyhdistyksen julkaisuja, A-sarja, nr. 172. Vammala.

Kindleberger, Charles P. (1986): *Keynesianism vs Monetarism and other Essays in Financial History.*

Kindleberger, Charles P. (1993): A Financial History of Western Europe. Second edition, Oxford University Press.

Klami, Hannu (1977): *Suomen oikeustaistelijat. Suomen oikeustiede Venäjän vallan aikana [The Finnish legal Strugglers. Finnish Jurisprundence under Russian Rule].* Juva, WSOY.

Klami, Hannu (1981): *The Legalists. Finnish Legal Science in the Period of Autonomy 1809–1917.* The History of Learning and Science in Finland 1828–1918 2. Helsinki, The Finnish Society of Sciences.

Klinge, Matti (1975): *Bernadotten ja Leninin välissä [Between Bernadotte and Lenin].* Juva, WSOY.

Klinge, Matti (1982): *Kaksi suomea [Two Finlands].* Keuruu, Otava.

Klinge, Matti (1988): *Helsingfors universitet 1640–1990 1. Kungliga akademien i Åbo 1640–1808 [The Royal Academy of Åbo 1640–1808].* Helsingfors, Otava.

Klinge, Matti (1989): *Helsingfors universitet 1640–1990 2. Kejserliga Alexanders universitetet 1808–1917 [The Univeristy of Helsinki 1808–1917].* Helsingfors, Otava.

Konttinen, Esa (1991): *Perinteisesti moderniin – professioiden yhteiskunnallinen synty Suomessa [The Traditional Road to Modernity – The Social Origin of Professions in Finland].* Jyväskylä, Vastapaino.

Korkman, Sixten & Jukka Pekkarinen (1988): Kiinteän valuuttakurssin ongelma Suomen markan historiassa [The Problem of the Fixed Exchange Rate in the History of the Finnish Markka]. In *Raha, inflaatio ja talouspolitiikka (eds. Seppo Honkapohja & Antti Suvanto),* 267–290. Helsinki, Valtion painatuskeskus & Helsingin yliopiston kansantaloustieteen laitos.

Koskenkylä, Heikki, Jukka Pekkarinen, Antti Räikkönen & Pentti Vartia, eds. (1984): *Sata vuotta suomalaista kansantaloustiedettä – Kansantaloudellinen Yhdistys 1884–1984 [A Hundred Years of Finnish Economics – The Finnish Economic Association 1884–1984].* Vammala, Kansantaloudellinen Yhdistys.

Kuitunen, Tero & Sullström, Risto (1984): *Kansantaloustieteen opetus, tutkintovaatimukset ja väitöskirjatutkimus Helsingin yliopistossa 1906–1982 [Teaching, Curriculum and Dissertations in Economics at the University of Helsinki 1906–1982], In Sata vuotta suomalaista kansantaloustiedettä – Kansantaloudellinen Yhdistys 1884–1984 (eds. Heikki Koskenkylä et al.),* 51–107. Vammala, Kansantaloudellinen Yhdistys.

Kuusi, Eino (1931): *Sosiaalipolitiikka [Social Policy]* I–II. Helsinki.

Kuusterä, Antti (1987): 1860-luvun epäonnistunut talouspolitiikka [The Unsuccessful Economic Policy of the 1860's]. In *Nälkä, talous, kontrolli (ed. Kari Pitkänen),* 43–57. Helsinki.

Kuusterä, Antti (1989a): *Valtion sijoitustoiminta pääomamarkkinoiden murroksessa 1859–1913 [The Financial Investments of the State and their Effects on Rapidly Evolving Capital Markets, 1859–1913].* Historiallisia tutkimuksia 149. Helsinki, Suomen historiallinen seura.

Kuusterä, Antti (1989b): Verotus autonomian ajan Suomessa [Taxation in the Autonomy Period in Finland]. In *Historian päivät 1988 (ed. Rauno Endén), Historiallinen Arkisto* 93, 147–161. Helsinki, Suomen historiallinen seura.

Kuusterä, Antti (1990): Valtio, talous ja valtiontalous [State, Economy and State Finances]. In *Talous, valta ja valtio –*

tutkimuksia 1800-luvun Suomesta (ed. Pertti Haapala), 37–65. Helsinki, Vastapaino.

Lehmusto, Heikki (1923): *J. V. Snellman ja hänen asemansa Hegelin koulukunnassa [J. V. Snellman and his Position in the Hegelian School]*. Helsinki, Otava.

Lenz, Friedrich (1946): *Friedrich List und die deutsche Einheit (1789–1846)*. Stuttgart, Deutsche Verlags-Anstalt.

Liikanen, Ilkka (1987): Kansanvalistajien kansakunta – Kansanvalistusseura fennomanian aatteellisena ja organisatorisena keskuksena [The Nation of People's Educators' – The Society for Popular Education as the Ideological and Organisational Center]. In *Kansa liikkeessä [People in Motion] (eds. Alapuro, Liikanen et al.)*, 126–141. Vaasa, Kirjayhtymä.

Liikanen, Ilkka (1995): *Fennomania ja kansa. Joukkojärjestäytymisen läpimurto ja Suomalaisen puolueen synty [Fennomania and the People. The Breakthrough of Mass Organization and the Birth of the Finnish Party]*. Historiallisia Tutkimuksia 191. Helsinki, Suomen Historiallinen Seura.

Lilja, Johanna (1993): Den ekonomiska historiens utgångspunkter. Drag i historieuppfattningen i Finland under 1800-talet [Starting Points of Economic History. Characteristics of the Conception of History in Nineteenth-century Finland]. *Historisk Tidskrift för Finland* 78:4, 529–548.

Lindenlaub, Dieter (1967): *Richtungskämpfe im Verein für Sozialpolitik. Wissenschaft und Sozialpolitik im Kaiserreich vornemlich vom Beginn des "neuen Kurses" bis zum Ausbruch des ersten Weltkrieges (1890–1914). Vierteljahrschrift für Sozial- und Wirtschaftsgeschichte*, Beihefte nr. 52–53. Aschaffenburg, Franz Steiner Verlag.

Luther, Georg (1993): *Suomen tilastotoimen historia vuoteen 1970 [The History of Finnish Statistical Office and Study until 1970]*. Helsinki, Tilastokeskus.

Lönnroth, Johan (1991): Before Economics. In *The History of Swedish Economic Thought (ed. Bo Sandelin)*, 11–43. Guildford and King's Lynn, Routledge.

Magnusson, Lars (1987): Mercantilism and "reform" mercantilism: the rise of economic discourse in Sweden during the eighteenth century. *History of Political Economy* 19:3, 415–433.

Magnusson, Lars (1991): Gustav Cassel, Popularizer and Enigmatic Walrasian. In *The History of Swedish Economic Thought (ed. Bo Sandelin)*, 122–140. Guildford and King's Lynn, Routledge.

Manninen, Juha (1976): Huomautukset Snellmanin "Kauppapolitiikan kysymyksiä" -artikkeliin [Remarks on Snellman's Article 'Issues of Trade Policy', transl. Juha Manninen]. *Politiikka* 18:3, 280–283.

Manninen, Juha (1984): Sata vuotta J. V. Snellman-kirjallisuutta [A Hundred Years of *J. V. Snellman Literature]. In J. V. Snellmanin filosofia ja sen hegeliläinen tausta (ed. Ilkka Patoluoto), 189-220. Helsingin yliopiston filosofian laitoksen julkaisuja* n:o 1. Helsinki.

Manninen, Juha (1987): *Miten tulkita J. V. Snellmania? Kirjoituksia J. V. Snellmanin ajattelun kehittymisestä ja taustoista [How to interprete Snellman? Writings on the Development and Background of J. V. Snellman's Thought]. Snellman-instituutin julkaisuja [Publications of the Snellman Institute]* 5. Jyväskylä, Kustannuskiila Oy.

Manninen, Juha & Ilkka Patoluoto, eds. (1986): *Hyöty, sivistys ja kansakunta [Utility, Civilization and Nation].* Oulu, Pohjoinen.

Matsuura, Tamotsu (1972): Marginalism in Japan. *History of Political Economy* 4, 533–550.

Meek, Ronald (1977): *Smith, Turgot and after.* London, Chapman & Hall.

Mirowski, Philip (1984): Physics and the 'Marginalist Revolution'. *Cambridge Journal of Economics* 8, 361–379.

Mirowski, Philip (1987): Shall I Compare Thee to a Minkowski-Ricardo-Leontief-Metzler Matrix of the Mosak-Hicks Type? Or, Rhetoric, Mathematics, and the Nature of Neoclassical Economic Theory. *Economics and Philosophy* 3, 67–96.

Mirowski, Philip (1989): *More Heat than Light – Economics as Social Physics: Physics as Nature's Economics.* Cambridge, Cambridge University Press.

Mitchell, B. R. (1975), *European Historical Statistics 1750–1970.* The MacMillan Press Ltd.

Mäki, Uskali (1984): Metodologisen ajattelun juonteita suomalaisessa kansantaloustieteessä [Methodological Features of Finnish Economic Thought]. In *Sata vuotta suomalaista kansantaloustiedettä – Kansantaloudellinen Yhdistys 1884–1894 (eds. Heikki Koskenkylä et al.),* 109–140. Vammala, Kansantaloudellinen Yhdistys.

Mäki, Uskali (1996): Economic Thought on the Outskirts: Towards a historiographical framework for studying Finnish economics. In *Research in the History of Economic Thought and Methodology 14* (eds. Warren J. Samuels & Jeff E. Biddle), 307–323. Greenwich, Conn., JAI Press Inc.

Nordenstreng, S. (1936–1937): *L. Mechelin: hans statsmannagärning och politiska personlighet [The Biography of Leo Mechelin].* 1–2. Skrifter utgivna av Svenska litteratursällskapet i Finland, 252, 259. Helsingfors.

Olofsson, Jonas & Lars Pålsson Syll (1998): Ekonomporträttet: Johan Leffler (1845–1912). *Ekonomisk Debatt* 26:7, 527–532.

Paasikivi, Juho K. ([1957]1986): *Paasikiven muistelmia sortovuosilta II [Paasikivi's Memoirs from the Years of Oppression].* Juva, WSOY.

Patoluoto, Ilkka ed. (1984): *J. V. Snellmanin filosofia ja sen hegeliläinen tausta [J. V. Snellman's Philosophy and its Hegelian Background]. Helsingin yliopiston filosofian laitoksen julkaisuja [Publications of the Department of Philosophy of Helsinki University]* n:o 1. Helsinki.

Patoluoto, Ilkka (1986): Sivistys kansantalouden liikuttajana – J. V. Snellmanin taloudellisten katsomusten tausta ja muotoutuminen [Civilization as a Mover of Nations – The Background and Formation of J. V. Snellman's Economic Views]. In *Hyöty, sivistys ja kansakunta (eds. Juha Manninen & Ilkka Patoluoto)*, 271–319. Oulu, Pohjoinen.

Patoluoto, Ilkka (1990), *Edistyksellisiä piirteitä 1700-luvun suomalaisessa kansantaloustieteessä [Progressive Features in 18th-century Finnish Economic Thought]. Kansantaloudellinen aikakauskirja [The Finnish Economic Journal]* 1990:2, 188–203.

Pekkarinen, Jukka (1984): Kansantaloudellinen Yhdistys ja taloudellinen keskustelu Suomessa [The Finnish Economic Association and Economic Discourse in Finland]. In *Sata vuotta suomalaista kansantaloustiedettä – Kansantaloudellinen Yhdistys 1884–1984 (eds. Heikki Koskenkylä et al.)*, 11–39. Vammala, Kansantaloudellinen Yhdistys.

Peltonen, Matti (1989): A Bourgeois Bureaucracy? The new mentality of the Finnish aristocracy of the period of autonomy. In *State, Culture & the Bourgeoisie. Aspects of the Peculiarity of the Finnish* (ed. Matti Peltonen). Jyväskylän yliopisto – Nykykulttuurin tutkimusyksikkö. Julkaisu 13.

Peltonen, Matti (1992): *Talolliset ja torpparit. Vuosisadan vaihteen maatalouskysymys Suomessa. Historiallisia Tutkimuksia [Landowners and Crofters. The Peasant Question in Finland at the Turn of the Century]* 164. Vammala, Suomen Historiallinen Seura.

Peltonen, Matti (1993): The Peasant Economy and the World Market. Finnish Peasant Farming in the Age of Agrarian Crises, 1880's–1910's. *Fernand Braudel Center Review* vol. 16:3, 357–381.

Pihkala, Erkki (1970): Suomen Venäjän-kaupan puitteet autonomian ajan jälkipuoliskolla [The Setting for Finnish-Russian Trade during the Last Half of the Autonomy Period]. *Historiallinen Arkisto* 65, 5–85. Loviisa.

Pihkala, Erkki (1977), *Valtion tulojen ja menojen rakenne 1800-luvun jälkipuoliskolla [The Structure of State Income and Expenditure during the late-19th Century].* Helsingin kauppakorkeakoulun julkaisuja B-25. Helsinki.

Pihkala, Erkki (1981): J. V. Snellmanin taloudellisesta ajattelusta [On J. V. Snellman's Economic Thought]. In *J. V. Snellman ja nykyaika – Kirjoituksia ja esitelmiä J. V. Snellmanin ajallemme jättämästä henkisestä perinnöstä (ed. Kai Huovinmaa)*, 35–43. Helsinki.

Pihkala, Erkki (1984): J. V. Snellman och den ekonomiska politiken på 1860-talet [J. V. Snellman and the Economic Policy in the 1860's]. In *J. V. Snellman och hans gärning [J. V. Snellman and his Activities]*, 67–76. Göteborg, Almqvist & Wiksell international.

Pihkala, Erkki (1990): J. V. Snellmanin suhtautuminen Venäjään hänen talouspolitiikkansa valossa [J. V. Snellman's Attitude towards Russia from the Point of View of his Economic Policy]. In *Snellman, valtakunta ja keisarikunta (ed. Heikki Viitala), 53–67.* Snellman-instituutin julkaisuja [Publications of the Snellman Institute] 10. Jyväskylä.

Pipping, Hugo E. (1928): *Myntreformen år 1865 [Monetary Reform of 1865].* Helsingfors.

Pipping, Hugo E. (1944): *Ekonomiska Samfundet i Finland 1894–1944 – En Återblick. Ekonomiska Samfundets Tidskrift,* ny serie hft 61–62.

Pipping, Hugo E. (1961): *Paperiruplasta kultamarkkaan – Suomen Pankki 1811–77 [From the Paper Rouble to the Golden Mark – The Bank of Finland, 1811–77].* Helsinki.

Pipping, Hugo E., Kultakannan turvissa. Suomen Pankki 1878–1914 [Under the Protection of the Gold Standard. The Bank of Finland 1878–1914]. Helsinki.

Pitkänen, Kari, ed. (1987): *Nälkä, talous, kontrolli [Hunger, Economy, Control].* Helsinki.

Pulkkinen, Tuija (1982): *J. V. Snellmanin yhteiskuntafilosofian järjestelmä vuosien 1856–1863 luennoissa [J. V. Snellman's System of Social Philosophy in his Lectures of 1856–1863].*

Pro gradu thesis in political history, Social Science library, University of Helsinki.

Pulkkinen, Tuija (1987): Kansalaisyhteiskunta ja valtio – Kaksi perinnettä poliittisen julkisuuden muotoutuessa [Civil Society and the State – Two Traditions in the Formation of Political Publicity]. In *Kansa liikkeessä (eds. Alapuro, Liikanen et al.)*, 54–68. Vaasa, Kirjayhtymä.

Pulkkinen, Tuija (1989): *Valtio ja vapaus [State and Freedom]*. Jyväskylä, Tutkijaliitto.

Puramo, Eino (1952), *Itä-Suomen vesitiekysymykset 1800-luvulla. Erikoisesti Saimaan kanavaa silmällä pitäen vuoteen 1870 [Waterway Questions in Eastern Finland in the 19th Century, with special reference to the Saimaa Canal until 1870]*. Historiallisia tutkimuksia XXXVII. Suomen historiallinen seura.

Pålsson Syll, Lars (1998): *De ekonomiska teoriernas historia [The History of Economic Theory]*. Lund, Studentlitteratur.

Rasila, Viljo (1966): Vuoden 1914 viljatulliasetus [The Corn Duty Act 1914]. *Historiallinen arkisto* 60, 276–402. Turku.

Rauhala, K. W. (1915, 1921), *Keisarillisen Suomen Senaatti 1809–1909 [The Finnish Imperial Senate] 1. Vuodet 1809–1859, 2. Vuodet 1859–1909*. Helsinki.

Ringer, Fritz (1969): *The Decline of the German Mandarins. The German Academic Community, 1890–1933*. Cambridge, Harvard University Press.

Sandelin, Bo, ed. (1991): *The History of Swedish Economic Thought*. Guildford and King's Lynn, Routledge.

Savolainen, Raimo (1989): *J. V. Snellman ja nälkävuodet 1867–1868 [J. V. Snellman and the Great Famine, 1867–1868]. Snellman-instituutin [Publications of the Snellman Institute],* C-sarja 2. Kuopio, Kuopion kaupunginhallitus.

Schauman, Henrik & Koskela, Mirjam, eds. (1992): *Suomen kansantaloudellinen bibliografia [A Finnish Economic Bibliography]*. Helsinki, Eduskunnan kirjasto.

Schumpeter, Joseph ([1955]1986): *History of Economic Analysis*. Winchester, Mass., Allen & Unwin.

Setälä, Päivi, Pekka Suvanto & Matti Viikari, eds. (1983): *Historiankirjoituksen historia [The History of Historiography]*. Tampere, Gaudeamus.

Simmons, Ernst, ed. (1955): *Continuity and Change in Russian and Soviet Thought*. Cambridge, Harvard University Press.

Simonen, Seppo (1949): *Lypsykarjavaltainen maataloudellinen tuotantojärjestelmä Suomessa. Maataloutta ja maatalous-*

politiikkaa vuosisadan vaihteen molemmin puolin [Dairy Cattle Dominated the Agricultural Production System in Finland. Agriculture and Agricultural Policy at the Turn of the Century]. Helsinki.

Sivenius, Hannu (1984): Georg Friedrich Hegel. In *Politiikan teorian klassikoita (ed. Jukka Kanerva)*, 126–148. Hämeenlinna, Gaudeamus.

Soikkanen, Hannu (1961): *Sosialismin tulo Suomeen. Ensimmäisiin yksikamarisen eduskunnan vaaleihin asti [The Arrival of Socialism in Finland].* Porvoo, WSOY.

Soininen, Arvo (1975): *Vanha maataloutemme. Maatalous ja maatalousväestö Suomessa perinnäisen maatalouden loppukaudella 1720-luvulta 1870-luvulle [Our old Agriculture. Agriculture and Peasantry in Finland during the Early Traditional Period: Agriculture from the 1720s until the 1870s]. Historiallisia tutkimuksia* 96. Forssa, Suomen Historiallinen Seura.

Stenius, Henrik (1990): Julkisen keskustelun rajat suuriruhtinaskunnassa [Limits of Public Discussion in the Grand Duchy]. In *Talous, valta ja valtio– tutkimuksia 1800-luvun Suomesta (ed. Pertti Haapala)*, 153–167. Helsinki, Vastapaino.

Stigler, George (1950): The Development of Utility Theory, I & II. *Journal of Political Economy* 58, 307–327 & 373–396.

Streissler, Erich (1972): To What Extent Was the Austrian School Marginalist? *History of Political Economy* 4, 426–441.

Teljo, Jussi (1934): *Valtio ja yhteiskunta Snellmanin valtiofilosofiassa [State and Society in Snellman's Political Philosophy].* Helsinki, WSOY.

Tervonen, Jukka (1981): *J. R. Danielson-Kalmari ja Hannes Gebhard suomalaisen historiatieteen murroksessa [J. R. Danielson-Kalmari and Hannes Gebhard and the Rupture of Finnish Historical Science]. Unpublished Pro gradu thesis. University of Helsinki, Department of History.*

Tribe, Keith (1984): Cameralism and the Science of Government. *Journal of Modern History* 56:2, 263–284.

Tribe, Keith (1988): *Governing Economy. The Reformation of German Economic Discourse 1750–1840.* Cambridge, Cambridge University Press.

Turunen, Ilkka (1987): Ammattiyhdistysutopia – Vuosisadan vaihteen liberalistista yhteiskuntapolitiikkaa [Trade Union Utopia- Liberal Social Policy during the Turn of the Century]. In *Kansa liikkeessä (eds. Alapuro, Liikanen et al.)*, 194–210. Vaasa, Kirjayhtymä.

Uhr, Carl (1991a): Knut Wicksell, neoclassicist and iconoclast. In *The History of Swedish Economic Thought (ed. Bo Sandelin)*, 76–121. Guildford and King's Lynn, Routledge.

Uhr, Carl (1991b): David Davidson: the transition to neoclassical economics. In *The History of Swedish Economic Thought (ed. Bo Sandelin)*, 44–73. Guildford and King's Lynn, Routledge.

Vanamo, K. A. (1936): *Vientitavarain kuljetusmaksut Suomen Valtionrautateillä ennen maailmansotaa [The Carriage of Export Goods on the Finnish Railways before World War I]*. Kansantaloudellisia tutkimuksia VI. Helsinki, Kansantaloudellinen yhdistys.

Viikari, Matti (1983): Saksalainen historiankirjoitus 1800-luvun puolivälistä ensimmäiseen maailmansotaan [German Historical Writing from the Mid-ninteenth Century until World War I]. In *Historian kirjoituksen historia (eds. Päivi Setälä et al.)*, 70–94. Tampere, Gaudeamus.

Viitala, Heikki, ed. (1990): *Snellman, valtakunta ja keisarikunta [Snellman, Country and Empire]*. Snellman-instituutin julkaisuja [Publications of the Snellman Institute] 10. Jyväskylä.

Viner, Jacob (1937): *Studies in the Theory of International Trade*. New York, Harper & Brothers Publishers.

Wendler, Eugen, hrsg. (1996): *"Die Vereinigung des europäischen Kontinents". Friedrich List – Gesamteuropäische Wirkungsgeschichte seines ökonomischen Denkens*. Ulm, Schäffer-Poeschel Verlag Stuttgart.

Wikström, Kauko (1985): *Valtion tuloveron rakenne. Tutkimus tuloveron rakenteesta ja sen peruspiirteiden historiallisesta kehityksestä [The Structure of Income Tax. A Study concerning the Structure of Income Tax and the Historical Development of its General Features]*. Publications of the University of Turku, ser. C:72. Turku, University of Turku.

Wilenius, Reijo (1978): *Snellmanin linja – henkisen kasvun filosofia [Snellman's Line – a Philosophy of Intellectual Growth]*. Jyväskylä, Gummerus.

Ylikangas, Heikki & Pajuoja, Jussi (1987): *Lauri Kivekäs – aikansa ajaton radikaali [The Biography of Lauri Kivekäs]*. Juva, WSOY.

Zetterberg, Seppo (1982): *Yrjö ja Hilma Jahnsson [The Biography of Yrjö and Hilma Jahnsson]*. Hämeenlinna, Yrjö Jahnssonin säätiö.

INDEX OF PERSONS

NOTE ON CONTRIBUTORS

Sakari Heikkinen
Doctor of Social Sciences
Docent of Economic and Social History
University of Helsinki

Visa Heinonen
Doctor of Social Sciences
Professor of Consumer Economics
University of Helsinki

Antti Kuusterä
Doctor of Social Sciences
Docent of Economic and Social History
University of Helsinki

Jukka Pekkarinen
Doctor of Social Sciences
Director
Labour Institute of Economic Research, Helsinki